Photographer's Guide to the Panasonic Lumix DMC-FZ2500/FZ2000

Photographer's Guide to the Panasonic Lumix DMC-FZ2500/FZ2000

Getting the Most from Panasonic's Advanced Digital Camera

Alexander S. White

WHITE KNIGHT PRESS
HENRICO, VIRGINIA

Published by
White Knight Press
9704 Old Club Trace
Henrico, Virginia 23238
www.whiteknightpress.com
contact@whiteknightpress.com

ISBN: 978-1-937986-68-1 (paperback)
        978-1-937986-69-8 (ebook)

Printed in the United States of America

To my wife, Clenise.

Contents

CHAPTER 5: PHYSICAL CONTROLS — 84

Chapter 6: Playback 122

Chapter 7: The Custom Menu and the Setup Menu 138

CHAPTER 8: MOTION PICTURES 174

Chapter 9: Wi-Fi and Other Topics 201

Appendix A: Accessories 212

INTRODUCTION

This book is a guide to the operation, features, and capabilities of the Panasonic Lumix DMC-FZ2500, one of the most capable and versatile digital cameras available today. (The camera is known as the FZ2000 in some areas outside of the United States, but I am located in the United States and my camera is labeled FZ2500, so I will use that designation in this book.)

I chose this camera to write about partly because of my experience with other Panasonic compact models, including the DMC-LX3, LX5, LX7, LX10, ZS100, and ZS70, but also because this camera stands out from other compact cameras for several reasons. To begin with, the FZ2500 uses a "one-inch-type" image sensor, the same size sensor used in several other advanced compact models, such as the Sony DSC-RX100, the Sony RX10, and their several successor models. This sensor is larger than those of many compact cameras, and lets the FZ2500 provide great image quality and blurred backgrounds.

The camera has an excellent lens with a maximum aperture of f/2.8 at its wide-angle focal length, a strong optical zoom range of 24mm to 480mm, and advanced features such as Raw image quality, manual control of exposure and focus, and excellent burst capability for continuous shooting. The FZ2500 also provides superior video features, centered around its capability to capture 4K (ultra-HD) video. It can output a "clean" HDMI video signal to an external recorder, and it has jacks for headphones and an external microphone. Unlike many cameras in its class, it can record video indefinitely, with the duration limited only by memory card capacity.

In addition, the camera has a large, 3-inch (7.5 cm) diagonal and very sharp (1,000,000 pixels) LCD monitor with touch-screen features and the ability to rotate and swivel in multiple directions for self-portraits and shots from various angles. The camera has a strong set of Wi-Fi features, enabling remote control from a smartphone and transfer of images from the camera to other devices over a wireless network.

The FZ2500 has physical switches and dials that can control many functions, so you don't have to navigate through menus to adjust exposure compensation, white balance, drive mode, and other settings. Several of these controls are programmable, and the camera also has five "virtual" function buttons included with its touch screen capabilities.

Also, the FZ2500 includes a self-timer, macro (closeup shooting) mode, a wide range of shutter speeds (1/16000 second to 60 seconds as well as longer time exposures), many different "filter effects" settings (such as miniature effect, soft focus, sepia, and monochrome, among others), and several features for capturing images with broad dynamic range, including a built-in HDR (high dynamic range) option. The camera is equipped with Panasonic's "Depth from Defocus" system, which provides faster autofocus performance than that of many comparable cameras.

The FZ2500 is an outstanding example of an advanced "bridge" camera with a long-zoom capability. My goal is to provide a useful introduction to the FZ2500's controls and operation along with tips and advice as to when and how to use various features. This book does not provide advanced technical information. If you already understand how to use every feature of the camera and when to use it and are looking for new insights, I have included some references in the Appendices that can provide further information. This book is geared to the beginning to intermediate user who is not satisfied with the documentation provided with the camera, and who is looking for a reference guide that offers additional help in mastering the camera's features.

CHAPTER 1: PRELIMINARY SETUP

When you first receive your FZ2500, the box should contain the camera itself, battery, battery charger, USB cable, shoulder strap, lens cap with string for attaching it to the camera, lens hood, and brief instruction pamphlets. There is no software disc in the box, but Panasonic provides links for downloading software for processing your photographs and videos. For PHOTOfunSTUDIO software, which can be used for editing both stills and movies on Windows-based computers, go to http://panasonic.jp/support/global/cs/soft/download/d_pfs99xe.html. You will probably need to enter an alphanumeric code found on the bottom of the camera in order to proceed with the download.

To download SilkyPix software, which lets you process Raw files on Windows-based or Macintosh computers, go to http://www.isl.co.jp/SILKYPIX/english/p/. To download a 30-day free trial of LoiLoScope2 software for editing videos on Windows-based computers, go to http://loilo.tv/product/20.

Charging and Inserting the Battery

The FZ2500 ships with a single rechargeable lithium-ion battery, model number DMW-BLC12PP. To charge the battery, insert it into the included charger, model number DE-A79 (in the U.S.) so the four metal contacts on the battery are lined up with those on the charger, as shown in Figure 1-1. Then plug the charger into a standard electrical outlet. The Charge light on the charger will light up green; it will turn off when charging is complete. A full charge should take about 140 minutes.

When the battery is fully charged, slide the latch on the camera's bottom and open the battery compartment door. You can only insert the battery into the camera one way; look for the set of four metal contact strips on the battery, then look for the corresponding set of

contacts inside the camera, and insert the battery so the two sets of contacts will meet, as shown in Figure 1-2.

Figure 1-1. Battery Lined Up to Go into Charger

Figure 1-2. Battery Going into Camera

Slide the battery all the way in so it is firmly seated in the camera with the latch clicked into place above the battery, and close and latch the battery compartment door.

Inserting the Memory Card

The FZ2500 does not ship with a memory card. If you turn the camera on with no card inserted, you will see the message "No memory card" with a blinking memory card icon in the center of the screen. If you ignore this message and press the shutter button to take a picture, don't be fooled into thinking that the camera is somehow storing it in internal memory. Some camera models have a small amount of built-in memory so you can take and store a few pictures even without a card, but the FZ2500 does not have that safety net.

To avoid the frustration of having a great camera that can't save images, you need to use a memory card. The FZ2500 uses three varieties of card: Secure Digital (SD), Secure Digital High-Capacity (SDHC), and Secure Digital Extended Capacity (SDXC), representative samples of which are shown in Figure 1-3. All 3 types of SD card are the same size, about the size of a postage stamp. The standard card, SD, comes in capacities from 8 MB (megabytes) to 2 GB (gigabytes). The higher-capacity card, SDHC, comes in sizes from 4 GB to 32 GB.

Figure 1-3. Memory Cards of Various Capacities

The newest type, SDXC, at this writing is available in a 48 GB, 64 GB, 128 GB, 256 GB, or 512 GB size, though its maximum capacity theoretically is 2 terabytes, or about 2,000 GB. I have used a SanDisk Extreme Pro 512 GB SDXC card in the FZ2500 with excellent results, but, at a current price of about $300.00, this card is rather expensive for use in a compact camera. A 128 GB or 256 GB card, though, can be a good option, and I have used cards of those capacities successfully in the FZ2500.

When choosing a memory card, there is one important point to bear in mind: If you want to record video using 4K quality or the highest quality of high-definition (HD) video, you have to use a card rated in UHS Speed Class 3, for ultra-high speed class 3. An example of a card with this speed rating is shown in Figure 1-4.

The numeral 3 inside the U shape on the label indicates this speed class. For some other video quality settings, you have to use a card rated in at least Speed Class 10, or Speed Class UHS-1. I will discuss the details of those requirements in Chapter 8.

If there is any chance you will use the camera's highest settings for video quality, you should purchase a card rated in Speed Class UHS-3, so you will not limit your use of the camera's capabilities.

Figure 1-4. SDXC Card Rated in Speed Class UHS-3

If you're not planning to use the camera's 4K or other high-end video features, you still should get a large-sized, high-speed card if possible. If you're planning to record a good deal of high-definition (HD) video or many Raw photos, you need a card with a fairly large capacity. There are several variables to take into account in computing how many images or videos you can store on a particular size of card, such as the aspect ratio you're using (1:1, 3:2, 4:3, or 16:9), picture size, and quality.

I installed a 64 GB SDXC card and formatted it in the camera to see how many images could be stored using various settings. I set the aspect ratio to 3:2 for all options. Table 1-1 shows the results.

Table 1-1. **Number of Still Images That Can be Stored on 64 GB Card at Large Size**

Raw + Fine	1815
Raw	2659
Fine	5727
Standard	9999+

For video, using the same 64 GB card, you can store about 85 minutes of the highest quality 4K video; with the highest quality of AVCHD video, you can store about five hours. With the lowest quality of MP4 video, you can store about 12 hours and 45 minutes. With the FZ2500, unlike many other compact cameras, there is no internal limit on the duration of video recording. (Some cameras will record video in some or all formats for only about 30 minutes in any one sequence.)

I often use a 64 GB SanDisk Extreme Pro card, rated at a transfer level of 95 MB/second. That speed is more than enough to get good results for recording still images and AVCHD video with this camera. You should try to find a card whose speed is rated in Class 10 or higher if you're going to record HD video. The fastest cards are rated with the UHS designation, for ultra-high speed. As noted above, if you are planning to record 4K video or HD video using the highest-quality settings, you need to use a card with a speed designation of UHS Speed Class 3. (If the card has a UHS-I or UHS-II designation, that label has to do with a certain type of transport system the card uses, not the speed. You need to make sure the Speed Class is UHS-3.)

Whatever type of SD card you get, once you have the card, open the door on the right side of the camera that covers the memory card slot and slide the card in until it catches. The card goes in with its label facing the front of the camera, as shown in Figure 1-5.

Figure 1-5. Memory Card Going into Camera

Once the card has been pushed in until it catches, close the compartment door and push the latch back to the locking position. To remove the card, push in on it until it releases and springs out so you can grab it.

When the FZ2500 is recording images or videos to an SD card, a red icon appears on the left side of the screen showing an arrow pointing to the right inside a little box representing the SD card, as shown in Figure 1-6.

Figure 1-6. Icon When Camera Writes Data to Card

When that indicator is visible on the display, it's important not to turn off the camera or otherwise

interrupt its functioning, such as by taking out the battery or disconnecting an AC power adapter. You need to let the card complete the recording process.

Lens Cap and Lens Hood

The lens cap that comes with the camera can easily be misplaced, so it is a good idea to attach it using the string that is provided with the camera. To do that, thread the smaller loop in the string through the strap holder on the left side of the camera, and pull the larger loop through that loop. Then thread the end of the larger loop through the small openings in the side of the lens cap. Finally, pass the lens cap through the loop, so it is fastened to the camera, as shown in Figure 1-7.

Figure 1-7. Lens Cap Attached to Camera

The lens hood included with the camera is useful especially in bright sunlight to protect against lens flare. Just twist it into place as shown in Figure 1-8.

Figure 1-8. Lens Hood on Camera

Introduction to Main Controls

Before I discuss options for setting up the camera using

the menu system and controls, I will introduce the main controls in a series of images that show the major items. You may want to refer back to these images later for a reminder about each control.

TOP OF CAMERA

On top of the camera are some of the more important controls, as shown in Figure 1-9.

Figure 1-9. Controls on Top of Camera

The on/off switch turns the camera on and off. The status lamp lights up solid green when the camera is powered on. It lights up solid blue when a Wi-Fi connection is active, and blinks blue when the camera is transmitting data over Wi-Fi. You press the shutter button all the way down to take a picture; press it halfway to cause the camera to evaluate focus and exposure. The mode dial sets the camera to a shooting mode for still images or movies. The zoom lever, surrounding the shutter button, zooms the lens from the wide-angle (W) setting to the telephoto (T) setting. It also can be used to move quickly through menu screens. In playback mode, it selects index screens and enlarges images. The front dial and rear dial are both used to adjust settings such as aperture, shutter speed, and others. In playback mode, they are used to scroll through images. The Fn4 button is programmed by default to control exposure compensation, but it can be programmed to have a different function.

The flash is stored inside the top of the camera; you pop it up with the flash release switch on the left side of the viewfinder housing. The two microphone openings receive sounds to be recorded with videos. The hot shoe can be used to attach a more powerful flash unit or another accessory, as discussed in Appendix A.

The focus ring is used to adjust focus when manual focus is in use. The zoom ring is used to zoom the lens

between its wide-angle and telephoto settings. The red movie button starts and stops the recording of a movie sequence. On the left side of the camera's top, the drive mode dial is used to set the camera for continuous (burst) shooting, 4K Photo, Post Focus, self-timer, or interval shooting (time lapse or stop motion animation).

BACK OF CAMERA

Figure 1-10 shows the controls on the camera's back.

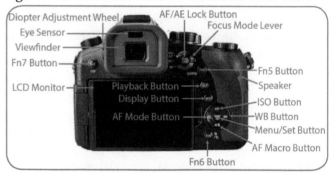

Figure 1-10. Controls on Back of Camera

The Playback button puts the camera into playback mode so you can review your recorded images and videos. The four cursor buttons (sometimes called the Up, Down, Left, and Right buttons in this book) are used to navigate through menu screens, and they also control the settings of ISO, white balance, AF mode, and macro focus. The Menu/Set button, in the center of this group of buttons, is used to get access to the menu system and to select or confirm various menu options.

The focus mode lever is used to switch the focus mode among the autofocus choices (AFS/AFF or AFC) and manual focus (MF). The AF/AE Lock button, located in the middle of the focus mode lever, is used to lock the camera's current autoexposure or autofocus setting, or both, depending on how a menu option is set.

The three function buttons on the back of the camera, Fn5, Fn6, and Fn7, are initially assigned to particular operations, but they can be assigned to other purposes through the menu system. The Fn5 button is initially assigned as the Q.Menu button, which activates the Quick Menu system that gives instant access to various menu settings. It also has some additional functions, such as saving autofocus frame configurations for AF Mode and adding markers to 4K Photo bursts.

The Fn6 button is initially assigned to the Preview function, which lets you see how the current aperture and shutter speed settings will affect the recorded image. That function can be changed for recording mode, but the button will still also act as the Cancel button in that mode. You can press the button to cancel out of menu screens and other operations. In playback mode, the Fn6 button is permanently assigned as the Delete/Cancel button, which lets you delete recorded images and videos, as well as backing out of menu screens and other operations. In Intelligent Auto Plus and Creative Control modes, the Fn6 button is used to activate the defocus control feature, which enables you to achieve a blurred background by opening the aperture wider. When 4K Live Cropping is in use, the button can be used to adjust the positions and sizes of the cropping frames. The button also can be used to end multiple exposure operations.

The Fn7 button is initially set as the LVF Monitor Switch button, which lets you select the viewfinder or the LCD screen for viewing the scene and displaying information.

The Display button is used to switch among the various displays of information on the LCD screen in both shooting and playback modes, and to move through the menus a full screen at a time. The LCD monitor displays the live view, control settings, and other information. It displays recorded images and videos when the camera is in playback mode. It can be tilted and swiveled in several directions, including the ability to rotate forward for taking self-portraits. I will discuss those capabilities in Chapter 5.

The LCD screen also has extensive touch capabilities, letting you control many of the camera's features by touching icons or other areas on the screen.

The viewfinder, which displays the same information as the LCD monitor, is available for use when the sun is bright or when you otherwise would prefer to hold the camera up to your face to view the scene and shooting information, or to review recorded images and videos. The eye sensor, at the top of the viewfinder eyepiece, detects the presence of your face and can switch the view from the LCD to the viewfinder, if automatic switching is turned on.

The small group of holes at the upper right corner of the camera's back marks the location of the speaker, where the camera emits sounds from videos as well as the operational beeps and other sounds produced by the camera.

FRONT OF CAMERA

There are only a few items to point out on the camera's front, shown in Figure 1-11.

Figure 1-11. Items on Front of Camera

The AF Assist/Self-timer lamp lights up to indicate the operation of the self-timer and also turns on in dim light to assist the camera's autofocus system, unless you disable it for that purpose through the menu system. The lens is a high-quality zoom lens with a maximum aperture of f/2.8 at the wide-angle setting, changing to a maximum of f/4.5 at the telephoto end of its range. It has a minimum aperture of f/11.0 at either end of the telephoto range.

The focal length of the lens varies from 8.8mm at the wide-angle range to 176mm at the telephoto setting. Ordinarily, these focal lengths are stated using "35mm-equivalent" figures, meaning the values that these figures would correspond to for a camera using a full-frame, 35mm image sensor. Therefore, the focal length range of the lens is ordinarily stated as from 24mm to 480mm, when the aspect ratio is set to 3:2. (The focal length range varies somewhat with different aspect ratios and when using 4K video settings).

RIGHT SIDE OF CAMERA

Inside the larger door on the right side of the camera is the memory card slot, as seen in Figure 1-12. You insert the card into that slot with the card's label pointing toward the front of the camera. The smaller door above the memory card door covers a small port where you can plug in an optional remote-control device. I discuss that device in Appendix A.

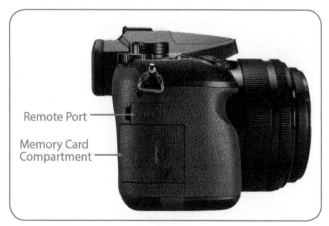

Figure 1-12. Items on Right Side of Camera

LEFT SIDE OF CAMERA

There are several important items on the left side of the camera, shown in Figure 1-13. First, the larger door or flap at the bottom covers the HDMI port and the USB port. You can plug a micro-HDMI cable into the HDMI port to send the camera's video signal to an external TV set, monitor, or recorder. The camera can output this signal in recording mode as well as in playback mode. I will discuss the use of HDMI output in the context of video recording in Chapter 8.

Figure 1-13. Items on Left Side of Camera

The USB port is where you can plug in the USB cable that comes with the camera to connect the camera to a computer to upload images and videos or to send images directly to a printer.

The smaller door above the HDMI/USB door covers the headphones port, where you can plug in a set of stereo headphones with a 3.5mm jack, to monitor the sound being recorded for a video recording.

On the side of the lens barrel, the camera has four other physical controls. First, three function buttons, Fn1, Fn2, and Fn3, are located within reach of your left hand. Each of these buttons can be programmed to

carry out a function in recording mode and in playback mode. By default, the Fn1 button is assigned to the Slow Zoom (T) function, by which the lens is zoomed slowly in toward the telephoto setting, and Fn2 is assigned to the Slow Zoom (W) function, zooming the lens slowly back out. Both of those buttons also are used for the Slow/Quick and Dolly Zoom features for movie recording, discussed in Chapter 8. The Fn3 button is initially assigned to the Dial Operation Switch function, which temporarily assigns the front and rear dials to carry out new operations, such as adjusting white balance, ISO, and other values. I will discuss the use of that feature in Chapters 5 and 7.

The ND Filter switch can be used to operate the camera's built-in ND (neutral density) filter, which reduces the amount of light that reaches the camera's image sensor, so you can use a wider aperture or slower shutter speed than would otherwise be possible. The available settings range from off to reducing the light to 1/64 of its full value, which amounts to a decrease of six stops of exposure value. I will discuss the use of the ND filter in Chapter 5.

BOTTOM OF CAMERA

Finally, as shown in Figure 1-14, on the bottom of the camera are the tripod socket, the door for the battery compartment, and the small flap that is used to accommodate the cord for the AC adapter when it is connected to the camera, as discussed in Appendix A.

Figure 1-14. Items on Bottom of Camera

Setting the Date, Time, and Language

It's important to set the date and time correctly before you start taking pictures, because the camera records that information invisibly with each image, and displays it later if you want. Someday you may be very glad to have the date (and even the time of day) correctly recorded with your archives of digital images.

To get these basic items set, move the on/off switch, on top of the camera, to the On position. Then press the Menu/Set button (in the center of the cursor buttons on the camera's back). Push the Left button to move the selection into the column for choosing the menu type (Intelligent Auto, Recording, Motion Picture, Custom, Setup, or Playback in this illustration, with the camera set to Intelligent Auto mode). The line at the left side of the display will turn yellow to indicate that the column of menu icons is now active, as shown in Figure 1-15.

Press the Down button to highlight the wrench icon that represents the Setup menu, then press the Right button to place the yellow selection rectangle in the list of Setup menu items.

By turning the rear dial or pressing the Up and Down buttons, move the yellow rectangle until Clock Set is highlighted on the first Setup menu screen. Then press the Right button to get access to the time and date settings, as shown in Figure 1-16.

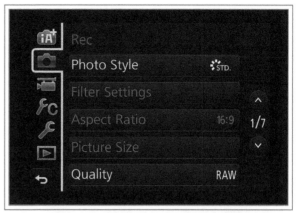

Figure 1-15. Highlight in Line of Menu Icons

Figure 1-16. Date and Time Settings Screen

Navigate by pressing the Left and Right buttons or by turning the front or rear dial, and select values with the Up and Down buttons. When you're done, press the Right button enough times to highlight the Set icon in the lower right corner of the screen, and press the Menu/Set button to save the settings. Then, using a similar procedure, navigate to the Language option on the fourth screen of the Setup menu, if necessary, and change the language the camera uses for menus and messages.

If you prefer to use the camera's touch-screen capabilities, you can navigate through the menu system and make selections by touching the menu selections and icons on the camera's LCD display. I will discuss the use of the touch screen in Chapter 5.

CHAPTER 2: BASIC OPERATIONS

Taking Pictures

Once the camera has the correct time and date set and has a fully charged battery inserted along with a memory card, it is ready for picture-taking. For now, I won't discuss all of the various options and why you might choose one over another. I'll just describe a set of actions for recording a good image on your memory card.

FULLY AUTOMATIC: INTELLIGENT AUTO MODE

Here is a list of steps to follow to set the camera to its most automatic mode and let it make most of the decisions for you. This is a useful approach if you need to grab a quick shot that yields good results without fiddling with numerous menus, controls, or settings.

1. Move the power switch on the camera's top to the On position. The camera makes a whirring sound, the lens extends outward to its open position, and the LCD screen lights up.

2. Turn the mode dial on top of the camera to the iA position, which selects the Intelligent Auto mode of shooting. You should see a red icon with iA and possibly a plus sign in white letters in the upper left corner of the display, as shown in Figure 2-1. (If you don't see this icon, press the Display button to the right of the LCD screen one or more times until the icon appears.)

3. Find the focus mode lever at the top of the camera's back, below the mode dial, and make sure it is turned to the top position, AFS/AFF, as shown in Figure 2-2.

4. Check the ND Filter switch on the left side of the camera and make sure it is set to the Auto position at the top of the list of settings, as shown in Figure 2-3.

Figure 2-1. iA Icon on Display for Intelligent Auto Mode

Figure 2-2. Focus Mode Lever at AFS/AFF Position

Figure 2-3. ND Filter Switch at Auto Position

Figure 2-4. Drive Mode Dial at Single-shooting Position

5. Check the drive mode dial at the left of the camera's top and make sure it is set to the first setting, which looks like a single rectangle, as shown in Figure 2-4.

6. Press the Menu/Set button in the center of the cursor buttons on the back of the camera to call up the menu system. Press the Left button if necessary to highlight the line of icons at the far left of the screen; when they are highlighted, you will see a yellow line, as in Figure 2-5.

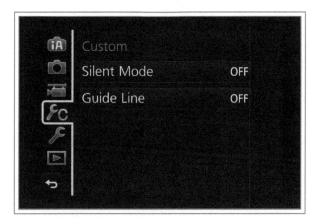

Figure 2-5. Highlight in Line of Menu Icons at Left

7. Use the Up and Down buttons as necessary to highlight the iA icon at the top of the line of icons, as shown in Figure 2-6. Then press the Right button to move to the two icons on the menu, iA and iA+. Use the buttons as necessary to make sure the iA icon is highlighted in yellow. (You can press menu items and icons on the touch screen to make selections if you prefer.)

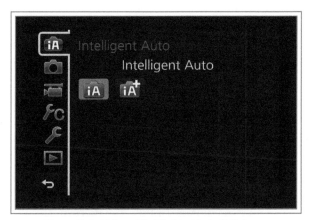

Figure 2-6. iA Icon Highlighted in Left Column

8. Navigate to the red camera icon for the Recording menu, then press the Right button to move the highlight into the menu screen. Using the procedure discussed above, make the settings in Table 2-1 for the other items on the Recording

menu. (If you prefer to use the touch screen to make these settings, just touch the appropriate menu options and icons to select them.)

Table 2-1. **Recommended Settings for General Shooting in Intelligent Auto Mode**

Menu Option	Setting
Aspect Ratio	3:2
Picture Size	L
AFS/AFF	AFS
Burst Rate	H
4K Photo	4K
Self Timer	Any setting
Time Lapse Animation	No setting needed
iHandheld Night Shot	Off
iHDR	Off
Face Recognition	Off

9. If you're taking a picture indoors, or if it's dark enough that you think you might need the camera's flash, find the flash release button on the left side of the viewfinder eyepiece and slide it toward the front of the camera to pop up the built-in flash. If the camera determines that flash is needed, the flash will fire automatically; you cannot change the flash mode setting in this shooting mode. (When you're done with the flash, press it gently back down into the top of the camera.)

10. Aim the camera at the subject and look at the screen to compose the picture as you want it. Locate the zoom lever on the ring that surrounds the shutter button on the top right of the camera. Push that lever to the left, toward the W, to get a wider-angle shot (including more of the scene in the picture), or to the right, toward the T, to get a telephoto, zoomed-in shot.

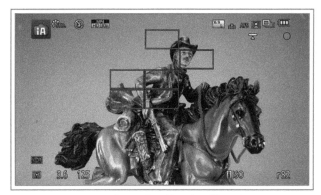

Figure 2-7. Green Dot Meaning Sharp Focus

11. Once the picture looks good on the display, press the shutter button halfway down. You should hear a beep and see a steady (not blinking) green dot in the upper right corner of the screen, indicating that the picture will be in focus, as shown in Figure 2-7.

12. You also may see some green focus frames. (If you hear a series of four quick beeps and see a blinking green dot, that means the picture is not in focus. Try moving to a slightly different angle and then test the focus again by pressing the shutter button halfway down.) Then press the shutter button all the way down to take the picture.

Variations from Fully Automatic

Although the FZ2500 takes care of several settings for you when it's set to Intelligent Auto mode, the camera still lets you make a few adjustments to fine-tune the shooting process. I will discuss some of these options next. For this discussion I am assuming the default settings are in effect. If some options, such as MF Assist and peaking, do not work as described below, go to the Setup menu and select the Reset option on screen 5 to reset the settings to their factory configuration.

Focus

In Intelligent Auto mode, the FZ2500 has limited options for focus settings. If you want to use some of the more sophisticated autofocus settings, you have to switch to an advanced shooting mode, such as Program or Aperture Priority. In Intelligent Auto mode, though, you can adjust some aspects of how the camera uses autofocus and you can choose manual focus.

First, when the camera is set to Intelligent Auto mode, the AF Mode is automatically set to Face/Eye Detection. With that setting, the camera uses its face detection focusing system. It will display a yellow focus frame if it detects a human face. This system works well for portraits and other shots including people, especially if they are not moving. If you are photographing moving subjects, whether people or objects, you may prefer to use tracking focus.

To change to tracking focus, press the left cursor button, marked with an icon that looks like a rectangular focus frame. The camera will place on the shooting screen a white focus frame with small lines protruding in horizontal and vertical directions, as shown in Figure 2-8.

Aim the white focus-tracking frame at your subject and press the shutter button halfway. If the camera can lock on the subject, the frame will turn yellow and then green as focus is locked. Release the shutter button, and the yellow frame will follow a moving subject to maintain focus as the distance changes.

Figure 2-8. **Tracking Focus Frame**

When you are ready, press the shutter button halfway down to lock focus, and all the way down to take the picture. To release the frame so you can start focusing again, press the Menu/Set button. If you want to change back to Face/Eye Detection focus, just press the left cursor button again.

When the camera is in Intelligent Auto mode, there is also another way to change from Face/Eye Detection focus to Tracking Focus. Just aim the camera at a subject and touch the subject on the touch screen with your finger, and the camera will switch to tracking focus and begin tracking that subject.

Another option you can select in this shooting mode is the AFC setting, for continuous autofocus. With this option, the camera will continuously adjust the focus, even if the subject is not moving. This option uses more battery power than the other two. If you are taking photographs of subjects in motion, such as pets or children at play, using the AFC setting will keep the focus approximately correct as the subjects move, and it should result in more accurate focusing when you press the shutter button to take the picture. If you are photographing stationary subjects, stick with the AFS setting to save battery power.

To turn on the AFC setting, use the focus mode lever to the right of the viewfinder on the camera's back, and turn it to the AFC position.

Another autofocus option you can control in this shooting mode is the AFS/AFF setting. To make this choice, first, set the focus mode lever to the AFS/AFF position. Then navigate to the AFS/AFF setting on the first screen of the Recording menu, and press the Right button or Menu/Set to move to the list of two options for this setting, as shown in Figure 2-9.

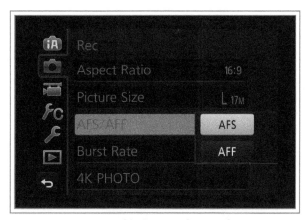

Figure 2-9. AFS/AFF Menu Options Screen

The two available choices control how the camera uses its autofocus process. If you select AFS, for autofocus single, the camera will focus on the subject when you press the shutter button halfway and it will keep the focus locked while you hold it in that position. If you choose AFF, for autofocus flexible, the camera will focus on the subject as with AFS, but, if the subject then moves, the camera will adjust its focus as needed.

Manual Focus

The other major option for focusing is manual focus, which requires you to adjust focus yourself. Many photographers like the control that comes from setting the focus exactly how they want it. In some situations, such as shooting in dark areas or areas behind glass, where there are objects at various distances from the camera, or when you're shooting a small object at a very close distance and only a narrow range of the subject can be in sharp focus, it may be useful to control exactly where the point of sharpest focus lies.

To use manual focus, move the focus mode lever to the MF position, and the letters MF will appear in the upper right corner of the screen. Now, instead of relying on the camera to focus automatically, you need to use the focus ring (the outermost, and thinner, of the two ridged rings around the lens) to adjust focus manually.

When you start turning the ring, the camera will enlarge the display to assist you in deciding when focus is sharp, as shown in Figure 2-10. (In recording modes other than Intelligent Auto, including Intelligent Auto Plus, you need to use the MF Assist option on screen 4 of the Custom menu to activate this enlargement feature. See Chapter 7 for details about the MF Assist menu option.)

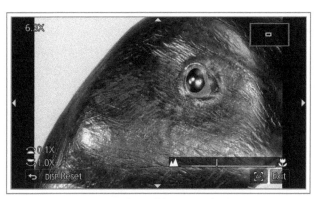

Figure 2-10. Enlarged Screen with MF Assist

You can use the four direction buttons or scroll the touch screen with your finger to select the area that is enlarged, and you can turn the rear dial or the front dial, or pinch and pull the screen with your fingers, to change the enlargement factor. (The rear dial makes large changes; the front dial makes smaller changes.) To reset the enlarged area to the center of the scene, press the Display button. To return to the normal-sized display, press the shutter button halfway. (The display will return to the normal size after ten seconds, if you don't touch the controls.) Continue turning the focus ring until the part of the scene that needs to be in focus looks sharp and clear.

The camera also will add colored pixels to the display to outline areas that are in sharp focus, using a feature known as peaking. When an area of colored pixels appears at its strongest, the image should be in focus at that point. (The peaking feature is activated by default when the camera is in Intelligent Auto mode. In other recording modes, you need to turn it on or off through screen 4 of the Custom menu.)

Drive Mode

In Intelligent Auto mode, you can control several options for burst shooting and the self-timer using the drive mode settings. I will discuss the basics of these features here; further details are in Chapter 5, where I discuss the physical controls. You select any of these options by turning the drive mode dial, located on the top of the camera at the far left.

The first setting, marked by a single-frame icon, shown earlier in Figure 2-4, is the normal setting for taking an individual picture. Leave the dial at this position for normal shooting.

The second position of the dial, marked by an icon for a stack of frames, turns on continuous shooting. With this setting, the camera takes a burst of shots while you hold down the shutter button. You can use this setting to increase your chances of catching the perfect instant of action, or the perfect pose of a subject.

The third dial position, marked by a 4K icon, selects 4K burst shooting, which uses the camera's ultra-high definition video capability to capture a burst of frames. The fourth position, marked by an icon showing a mountain and a flower, selects Post Focus shooting, which captures a burst of shots at different focus points, so you can select the best-focused shots after the fact.

The next icon, which looks like a dial, shown in Figure 2-11, turns on the self-timer. This option causes the camera to delay for a few seconds after you press the shutter button, before it takes a picture. You can set the self-timer delay to either two or ten seconds with a single shot, or ten seconds with three shots. To make this choice, go the second screen of the Recording menu and select the Self-timer menu option. Highlight your choice and press the Menu/Set button to confirm it and return to the shooting screen.

Figure 2-11. Drive Mode Dial at Self-timer Setting

Choose the ten-second delay when you need to leave the camera on a tripod and join a group picture. The two-second setting is useful when the camera is on a tripod and you want to make sure the camera is not moved when you press the shutter button to take a picture. This setting is especially important when you are taking a closeup shot or a shot using a telephoto setting, when any motion of the camera is likely to blur the image. The setting with three shots is good when

taking a group photo, to make it more likely that the camera will capture at least one image with everybody smiling and having their eyes open.

Finally the last icon, which looks like a slightly different sort of dial, selects the camera's intervalometer, which lets you set up time lapse shooting or stop motion animation. With those options, the camera takes a series of shots at intervals over a potentially long period of time. Those shots can be played back at a much faster rate, to speed up a subject such as the sun setting, clouds gathering, or a clay figure moving.

I will discuss the drive mode options in more detail in Chapter 5.

Intelligent Auto Plus Mode

There is another important setting available when the camera's mode dial is set to the Intelligent Auto position. That setting lets you choose between two different varieties of Intelligent Auto mode: basic Intelligent Auto and Intelligent Auto Plus. Until now, I have been discussing the use of basic Intelligent Auto mode, in which the camera controls most settings and leaves few menu options that you can change. If you choose Intelligent Auto Plus instead, the camera opens up numerous other options for adjustment.

To make this setting, with the mode dial at Intelligent Auto, press the Menu/Set button, then press the Left button to highlight the list of menu icons at the far left. Using the front or rear dial, cursor buttons, or touch screen, navigate to and highlight the iA icon at the top of the list of icons. Then, using the Right button or the touch screen, highlight the iA+ icon on the right, and press the Menu/Set button to select it and return to the shooting screen. You should now see the iA+ icon in the top left corner of the screen. (You may instead see an icon showing what kind of scene the camera has detected, such as macro or portrait.)

For a quicker way to switch between Intelligent Auto and Intelligent Auto Plus modes, if the touch screen feature is turned on through the Custom menu, just touch the iA or iA+ icon in the upper left corner of the display, and the camera will display a screen for selecting one of those two modes. On that screen, touch the icon for the mode you want and then touch the Set icon in the lower right corner of the display to confirm the setting.

When Intelligent Auto Plus mode is in effect, one of the most important differences from the standard Intelligent Auto mode is that you can adjust exposure compensation. To do that, press the Fn4 button and then make a brightness adjustment on the camera's display, to compensate for a subject that is excessively bright or dark. I will discuss that process in Chapter 5, where I discuss the physical controls. (The Fn4 button can be assigned to a function other than exposure compensation, but that is its assignment by default.)

Another feature that is available in Intelligent Auto Plus mode is defocus control. That option lets you set a wider aperture, which may result in a pleasantly blurred background. As I will discuss in Chapter 3, in Aperture Priority mode you can control the aperture setting more directly. The wider the aperture (the lower the aperture number, such as f/2.8), the more likely it is that the background will be blurred, while the foreground remains sharp.

In Intelligent Auto Plus mode, the camera selects the aperture initially, based on its automatic exposure reading. However, you can activate the defocus control option by pressing the Fn6 button.

After you press the Fn6 button, the camera displays a graphic representation of two lines of values, as shown in Figure 2-12. The top line shows the shutter speed, and the bottom one shows the aperture. Using the front or rear dial, the Left and Right buttons, or the touch screen, you can change the aperture value, if possible under current conditions. The lower the aperture number you can set, the better the chance there will be of having a blurred background.

Figure 2-12. Graphic Display for Defocus Control

When the defocus control option is in effect, the camera sets the autofocus mode to 1-Area, which I will

discuss in Chapter 4. The camera uses a single autofocus frame, which you can move around the screen with your finger. To turn off defocus control, press Fn6 while the two graphic lines are displayed on the screen.

Another setting you can control in Intelligent Auto Plus mode is color tone. To do this, press the Right (WB) button from the shooting screen, and the camera will display a color scale at the bottom of the display, as shown in Figure 2-13. You can adjust the color tone of images by moving the plus sign along that scale using the Left and Right buttons, the front or rear dial, or the touch screen.

Figure 2-13. Color Tone Scale on Display

In addition, with Intelligent Auto Plus selected, the camera lets you choose many more options from the Recording, Motion Picture, and Custom menus than in Intelligent Auto mode. For example, you can select Photo Style, Quality, Shutter Type, Color Space, Stabilizer, and Profile Setup from the Recording menu, as well as Half Press Release, Focus/Release Priority, MF Assist, and others from the Custom menu.

There still are some important options you cannot use in Intelligent Auto Plus mode, such as ISO sensitivity, HDR, Filter Settings, and Multiple Exposure. For those options, you need to select an advanced shooting mode such as Program, Aperture Priority, Shutter Priority, or Manual. However, you may sometimes want to select Intelligent Auto Plus mode so you can make some settings that are unavailable in Intelligent Auto mode while still having the benefits of largely automatic shooting.

Motion Picture Recording

Next, I'll discuss the basic steps for recording a motion picture sequence with the FZ2500. Later, I'll discuss other options for movie recording, but for now I'll stick to the basics.

1. With the camera set to Intelligent Auto mode, press the Menu/Set button to enter the menu system, and then press the Left button followed by the Up or Down button, to highlight the Motion Picture menu, symbolized by the icon of a movie camera, as shown in Figure 2-14.

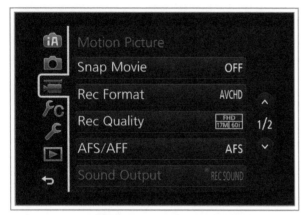

Figure 2-14. Icon for Motion Picture Menu Highlighted at Left

2. Press the Right button to go to the list of menu options. Highlight Rec Format, the second option, and press the Right button, giving the choices of AVCHD, MP4, MP4 (LPCM), and MOV, as shown in Figure 2-15. (AVCHD stands for Advanced Video Coding High Definition; MP4 and MOV are other video formats. I will discuss these options in Chapter 8.)

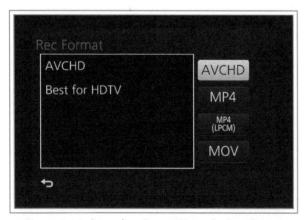

Figure 2-15. Recording Format Menu Options Screen

3. Highlight MP4 and press the Menu/Set button to select it and return to the menu screen. Then highlight the next option down, Rec Quality, and select FHD/20M/30p, the fourth option down, and

press Menu/Set to select it. Then press the Fn6/Cancel button to return to the shooting screen.

4. Be sure the focus mode is set to autofocus. If it is not, turn the focus mode lever at the top center of the camera to the AFS/AFF position.

5. Compose the shot the way you want it, and when you're ready, press the red motion picture button on top of the camera, to the right of the shutter button. Don't hold the button down; just press and release it. The LCD screen will show a blinking red dot as a recording indicator at the right of the screen, and a counter of elapsed time at the left side, as seen in Figure 2-16. The camera will keep recording until it runs out of storage space or until you press the motion picture button again to stop the recording.

Figure 2-16. Display Screen During Movie Recording

6. The FZ2500 will adjust exposure automatically as necessary, and you are free to zoom in and out as the movie is recording. (The sound of the zooming mechanism may be audible on the sound track, though, so you may want to keep zooming to a minimum.) If you want to adjust focus, press the shutter button halfway down to refocus the lens. (If you prefer to have the camera adjust focus automatically while recording a video, set the shooting mode to Intelligent Auto Plus, and, on screen 3 of the Motion Picture menu, set Continuous AF to On.)

There are many other options and considerations for motion picture recording, which I will discuss in Chapter 8.

Basic Playback

Playback of images or videos is activated by pressing the Playback button, located near the top right on the back of the camera with a triangle icon. When you press that button, if there are pictures or videos on the memory card, you will see one of them displayed. It will be whatever image or video was last displayed; the camera remembers which item was most recently on display even after being turned off and back on.

To move to the next picture or video, press the Right button; to move back one item, press the Left button. You can hold either of those buttons down to move quickly through the images and videos. If you prefer, you can move through the items with left or right turns of the front or rear dial or by scrolling the touch screen with your finger. The display on the screen will tell you the number of the picture being displayed. (If it doesn't, press the Display button until it does.) This number will have a three-digit prefix, followed by a dash and then a sequence number, such as 100-0111 or 102-0413.

To see an index view of multiple pictures, use the zoom lever on the top of the camera. Move it to the left, toward the W, one time, and the display changes to show 12 images in three rows of four, as shown in Figure 2-17.

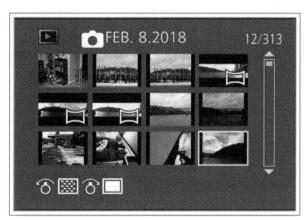

Figure 2-17. Playback Index Screen with 12 Images

Move it to the left one more time, and it shows 30 pictures at a time.

Give it one final leftward push and the screen shows a calendar from which you can select a date to view all images taken on that date, as shown in Figure 2-18.

You can also move the zoom lever to the right to retrace your steps through the options for multi-image viewing and back to viewing single images.

For now, move the zoom lever once to the left to see the 12-picture screen. Note that the Right and Left buttons now move you through the pictures on this screen one at a time, while the Up and Down buttons move you up and down through the rows. If you move to the last row or the last image, the proper button will move you to the next screen of images. Once you've moved the selector to the image you want to view, press the Menu/Set button, and that image is chosen for individual viewing.

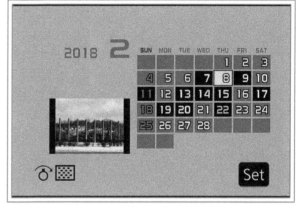

Figure 2-18. Playback Calendar Index Screen

Once you have the single image you want displayed on the screen, you have more options. Press the zoom lever once to the right, toward the T, to zoom the image to twice its normal size, and press it again to enlarge it further, as shown in Figure 2-19.

Figure 2-19. Enlarged Image in Playback Mode

Press the lever repeatedly to zoom up to 16 times normal size. Press the zoom lever back to the left to shrink the image down in the same increments. Or, you can press the Menu/Set button to return the image immediately to normal size. You can pinch and pull on the touch screen with your fingers to change the enlargement of the image, also.

While the zoomed picture is displayed, you can scroll it in any direction with the direction buttons or by scrolling the touch screen with your finger. Also, you can review other images at the same zoom level by turning the front or rear dial to navigate to the next or prior image, while the image is still zoomed.

PLAYING MOVIES

To play back movies, navigate through the images by the methods described above until you find an image that has a movie-camera icon with a yellow upward-pointing triangle at the upper left and a playback triangle icon in the center, as shown in Figure 2-20. (If you don't see the movie-camera icon for a movie file, press the Display button until the screen that shows the icon appears.)

Figure 2-20. Movie Ready for Playback in Camera

The yellow icon indicates that you press the Up button to start the movie playing. With the first frame of the motion picture displayed on the screen, press the Up button to start playback.

After the movie starts to play, you can use the four direction buttons as a set of DVR controls; the camera will briefly display icons that show the arrangement of those controls, as seen in Figure 2-21. The Up button is play/pause; the Right button is fast forward; the Down button is stop; the Left button is rewind. If you press the Up button again to pause the movie, the icons change, as shown in Figure 2-22. They now represent, from left to right, frame reverse, stop, play/pause, and frame advance. The Menu/Set button represents saving a still frame from the movie.

You can raise or lower the volume of the audio by turning the rear dial to the right or left. You will see a volume display change when you activate this control, as shown in Figure 2-22. (This volume control will not appear when the camera is connected to a TV set, because the volume is adjusted by the TV's controls in that situation.)

Figure 2-21. Initial Movie Playback Controls

Figure 2-22. Movie Playback Controls When Paused

To save a frame from a movie as a single image, play the movie to the approximate location of the image you want, then press the Up button, which acts as the play/pause button in this context. Then press the Left and Right buttons to maneuver to the exact frame you want to save. While you are viewing this frame, press the Menu/Set button to select it, then, when prompted, on the screen shown in Figure 2-23, highlight Yes and press Menu/Set to confirm, and you will have a new still image at the end of the current group of recorded images.

Figure 2-23. Confirmation Screen to Save Frame from Movie

Press the Down button (stop) to exit motion picture playback mode. Any still images saved from Full HD or HD video will not be of the highest quality; each one will be of Standard quality and no larger than 2 MP in size. If you need to save higher-quality still images from movie files, save them from 4K or C4K videos or use the 4K Photo option, discussed in Chapter 5.

Chapter 3: The Recording Modes

Until now I have discussed basic settings for quick shots, relying heavily on Intelligent Auto mode, in which settings are controlled mostly by the camera's automation. Like other sophisticated cameras, though, the FZ2500 has many options for setting up the camera to record pictures and videos. One goal of this book is to explain those options clearly. To do this, I need to cover several areas, including recording modes, menu items, and physical controls. In this chapter, I will discuss the camera's recording modes and how the selection of one of these modes affects your images.

Choosing a Recording Mode

Whenever you set out to capture still images or videos, an important first step is to select a recording mode, sometimes called a shooting mode. This "mode" controls the camera's behavior for adjusting exposure and other options. As with most advanced cameras, the FZ2500 provides a standard set of modes: Intelligent Auto, Program AE (also known as Program), Aperture Priority, Shutter Priority, and Manual exposure. These last four are often known as the PASM modes, for the first letter of each mode. This camera also offers some more specialized modes: Creative Video, Custom, Panorama, Scene, and Creative Control.

Each of the FZ2500's ten shooting modes is assigned a slot on the mode dial; you select the mode by turning the dial so the mode's icon is next to the white selector mark. For example, Figure 3-1 shows the dial when Creative Control mode is selected.

Figure 3-1. Mode Dial at Creative Control

With that introduction to the recording modes, I will provide more detailed explanations of the modes for shooting still images in this chapter. (I will discuss Creative Video mode in Chapter 8.)

Intelligent Auto Mode

This is the mode to choose if you need to have the camera ready for a quick shot in an environment with fast-paced events when you won't have time to fuss with settings. It's also handy if you need to hand the camera to a stranger to take a picture of your group. In Figure 3-2, I used this setting for a shot of a mild waterfall in the river in the late afternoon.

Figure 3-2. Intelligent Auto Sample Image

To make this setting, turn the mode dial on top of the camera so the iA icon is next to the white indicator mark on the left, as shown in Figure 3-3. You then should see a red camera icon with white characters for iA in the upper left corner of the screen, as shown in Figure 3-4.

Figure 3-3. Mode Dial at Intelligent Auto

Figure 3-4. iA Icon on Shooting Screen

If the icon has a white plus sign at the right, as shown in Figure 3-5, the camera is set to Intelligent Auto Plus mode.

Figure 3-5. iA+ Icon on Shooting Screen

To change it back to the standard Intelligent Auto mode, press the Menu/Set button to enter the menu system, navigate to the iA icon on the far left of the screen, and then, on the right side of the menu screen, select the icon for iA instead of iA Plus. (I will discuss the differences between the two iA modes later in this section; for now, it will be simpler to leave the camera in iA mode.) Or, you can just touch the iA+ icon to bring up a screen for changing to iA mode.

In iA mode, the camera limits the settings you can make, in order to simplify things. For example, you cannot adjust items such as exposure compensation, white balance, ISO, Photo Style, Metering Mode, Filter Settings, most settings for Autofocus Mode (setting the area for autofocus) and several others. You can select manual focus, though.

The camera turns on several settings, including Auto White Balance, scene detection, image stabilization, and backlight compensation, all of which are useful settings that will not unduly limit your options in most cases.

I'll discuss all of those items in Chapter 4 in connection with Recording menu settings, except scene detection and backlight compensation, which I will discuss here, because they are not menu options; the camera uses them automatically in Intelligent Auto mode.

With scene detection, the camera attempts to figure out if a particular scene type should be used for the current situation. The camera uses its programming to detect certain subjects or environments. For example, it looks for babies (if you have registered them using the Face Recognition menu option); night scenes; close-ups; sunsets; food; landscapes; and portraits. It will identify scenes calling for the iHandheld Night Shot setting if that option is turned on through the menu system. That feature is discussed in Chapter 4. If the camera detects one of these factors, it displays an icon for that type of scene and adjusts its settings accordingly. Otherwise, it displays the standard iA icon.

For example, in Figure 3-6 the camera detected the mannequin's face and displayed the icon for portrait scene detection.

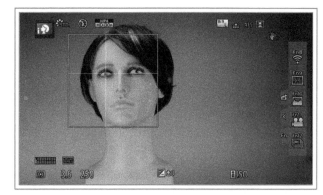

Figure 3-6. Scene Detection: Portrait

In Figure 3-7 the camera detected a closeup situation when I aimed the camera at a small model soldier, and it displayed the flower icon that indicates a macro shot.

Figure 3-7. Scene Detection: Macro

When shooting motion pictures or using the 4K Photo or Post Focus features, the camera detects fewer scene types—only portraits, scenery, low light, and macro shots.

With backlight compensation, the camera will try to detect situations in which the subject of the photograph is lighted from behind. This sort of lighting can "fool" the camera's metering system into making the exposure too dark, because of the light shining toward the lens. The result would be a subject that is too dark, without backlight compensation. With this setting, the camera automatically adjusts its exposure to be brighter, to overcome the effects of the backlighting.

Even though the FZ2500 makes several automatic settings in Intelligent Auto mode, there are still some options you can adjust using the menu system and, to some extent, the physical control buttons.

First, you can use the Recording menu to select certain settings, although the choices are sharply limited compared to the many options that are available in other still-shooting modes. In those other modes (including Intelligent Auto Plus), there are seven screens of options available on the Recording menu; in basic Intelligent Auto mode, there are only two screens of options. I will discuss those options in Chapter 4. I included a table of recommended settings for general picture-taking in this mode in Chapter 2.

Second, you can use the focus mode lever to the right of the viewfinder to select either AFS/AFF or AFC for autofocus, or MF for manual focus. I discussed the general use of those settings in Chapter 2 and I will provide more details in Chapter 5.

Third, you can use the drive mode dial to select one of the drive mode options, which I mentioned briefly in Chapter 2. In Intelligent Auto mode, you can select any option on the drive mode dial, including burst shooting, 4K Photo, Post Focus, the self-timer, and interval shooting. I will provide further information in Chapter 5.

You also can use other controls for their intended purposes in this mode, such as the Q.Menu button to get access to the Quick Menu. You can pop up the flash with the flash release switch, but the camera will decide whether to use it. I will discuss those options, among others, in Chapter 5.

In summary, although the Intelligent Auto shooting mode lets the camera make most of the technical decisions, you still can have a fair amount of involvement in making settings for photographs (and movies). Especially when you're just beginning to use the FZ2500, the basic Intelligent Auto mode provides a good start for exploring the camera's features. The automation in this mode is sophisticated and will often produce excellent results; the drawback is that you don't have as much creative control as you might like. But for ordinary picture-taking opportunities, vacation photos, and quick shots when you don't have much time to decide on particular settings, Intelligent Auto is a wonderful tool to have at your fingertips.

Intelligent Auto Plus Mode

If you want the camera to make its own decisions for several options but you want to be able to make more settings from the menus and physical controls, you can select Intelligent Auto Plus mode. As I discussed earlier, to set this mode, navigate to the iA icon at the top of the line of menu icons at the far left of the menu system, then move the highlight back to the main menu screen on the right and select the iA icon with a plus sign, as shown in Figure 3-8. (Or, you can touch the icon on the touch screen and then select the other mode.)

Figure 3-8. IA+ Icon Highlighted on Menu

In this mode, the camera displays six of the seven screens of the Recording menu, instead of only two screens, as in the basic Intelligent Auto mode. (The camera skips over screen 6.) However, some of the menu items, such as Filter Settings, Metering Mode, Highlight Shadow, and others, are dimmed and unavailable for selection because the camera chooses those settings automatically in this mode.

The FZ2500 also gives you access to many more options on the Custom menu than are available in basic Intelligent Auto mode, including items such as Half Press Release, Focus/Release Priority, MF Assist, and others. Those features are discussed in Chapter 7.

In addition, you can adjust values such as exposure compensation, defocus control, and color tone using physical controls. To use exposure compensation, from the shooting screen, press the Fn4 button to display the adjustment scale shown in Figure 3-9.

Figure 3-9. Exposure Compensation Adjustment Scale

With that scale on the display, use the front or rear dial, the Left and Right buttons, or the touch screen to select a value for positive or negative exposure compensation, up to 5 EV (exposure value) units in either direction. The screen will grow brighter or darker to indicate the effect of the setting.

Press the Menu/Set button to confirm the setting and return to the normal shooting screen. A scale at the bottom center of the screen will show the degree of exposure compensation that is in effect, as seen in Figure 3-10, which shows +2/3 EV (exposure value). I will provide an example of the use of exposure compensation in Chapter 5.

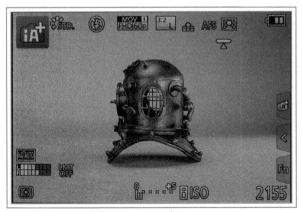

Figure 3-10. Exposure Compensation Icon on Shooting Screen

You also can adjust the settings for exposure bracketing when the exposure compensation scale is displayed. To do that, press the Up (ISO) button repeatedly to cycle through the various options for number of bracketed shots and the interval between exposures. I will discuss bracketing in more detail in Chapter 5.

To use defocus control, from the shooting screen, press the Fn6 button to display the aperture and shutter speed scales at the bottom of the screen, as shown in Figure 3-11. When those dials are displayed, turn the front dial or rear dial to set the aperture value as you want it. With a lower number, such as f/2.8, the background is likely to be more defocused; with a higher number, such as f/8.0, more of the image is likely to be in sharp focus.

Figure 3-11. Defocus Control Adjustment Screen

When the camera is in Intelligent Auto Plus mode, if you press the Right (WB) button, the camera will display a screen for adjusting color tone, as shown in Figure 3-12.

Figure 3-12. Color Tone Adjustment Screen

If you move the center marker to the right using the rear dial, Right button, or touch screen, colors will be adjusted to the bluish, or "cooler" side; if you move it to the left, they will be adjusted to the reddish, or "warmer" side. If any such adjustment is made, a small color block will appear in the lower right corner of the shooting screen, as shown in Figure 3-13, where the icon indicates an adjustment to the blue side.

Figure 3-13. Color Tone Adjustment Icon on Shooting Screen

In Intelligent Auto Plus mode, as in basic Intelligent Auto mode, you can pop up the camera's built-in flash unit, but you have no control over whether the camera will cause it to fire; that process is handled automatically by the camera. If you don't want the flash to fire, leave it retracted inside the camera.

Program Mode

Program mode, also known as Program AE (for autoexposure), with the mode dial set as shown in Figure 3-14, is the most automatic of the advanced (PASM) recording modes.

Figure 3-14. Mode Dial at Program

In this mode, the camera displays a P icon in the upper left corner of the display, as shown in Figure 3-15.

When you aim the camera at your subject, the exposure metering system will evaluate the light and choose both the shutter speed and aperture, which will be displayed in the lower left corner of the display when you press the shutter button halfway.

If those two values flash in red, that means the camera is unable to find settings that will yield a proper exposure. In that case, you may need to adjust the ISO

setting or change the lighting conditions by using flash or taking other steps. In this mode, the camera can use its full range of aperture settings, from f/2.8 to f/11.0, and shutter speeds from 1/4000 second to 60 seconds if the mechanical shutter is in use, or from 1/16000 second to one second if the electronic shutter is in use.

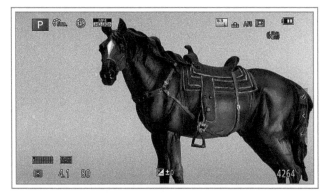

Figure 3-15. P Icon on Shooting Screen

If you want to alter the camera's settings by selecting a different shutter speed or aperture while keeping the same overall exposure, you can do that (if conditions permit) by using a feature called Program Shift. After you press the shutter button halfway to evaluate exposure, you can turn the front dial or the rear dial within the next 10 seconds, and the camera will try to select another combination of shutter speed and aperture settings that will result in a normal exposure.

For example, if the camera initially selects settings of f/4.5 and 1/125 second, when you turn the rear dial, the camera may change the settings to f/5.0 and 1/100 second, or f/5.6 and 1/80 second. If you turn the dial in the other direction, the camera may change the settings to f/4.0 and 1/160 second, or f/3.5 and 1/200 second.

However, if ISO is set to Auto ISO instead of a specific numerical value, the camera may shift the aperture value and ISO value, but not the shutter speed. If ISO is set to Intelligent ISO, Program Shift is not available. (ISO settings are discussed in Chapter 4.)

Program Shift can be useful if you want to have the camera make the initial choice of settings, but you want to tweak them to use a slightly higher shutter speed to stop action, or a wider aperture to blur the background, for example. When Program Shift is in effect, the camera displays the P icon with a double-ended arrow in the lower left corner of the screen, as shown in Figure 3-16.

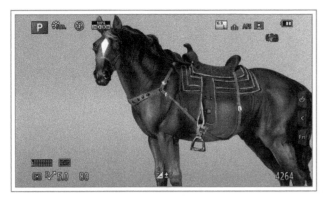

Figure 3-16. Program Shift Icon on Shooting Screen

In addition, if the Exposure Meter option is turned on through screen 6 of the Custom menu, the camera will show the shutter speed and aperture settings in two moving strips, as seen in Figure 3-17. Program Shift is not available when recording motion pictures or 4K photos, or when using the Post Focus feature.

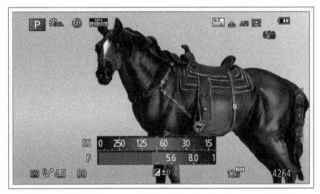

Figure 3-17. Exposure Meter Display for Program Shift

With Program mode, as with Intelligent Auto mode, the camera selects both the shutter speed and the aperture. However, unlike Intelligent Auto mode, with Program mode you can control many settings besides shutter speed and aperture. You don't have to make a lot of decisions if you don't want to, however, because the camera will make reasonable choices for you as defaults.

Program mode greatly expands the choices available through the Recording menu. You will be able to make choices involving white balance, image stabilization, ISO sensitivity, filter effects, metering method, autofocus area, and others. I won't discuss all of those choices here; if you want to explore that topic, see the discussion of the Recording menu in Chapter 4.

Besides unlocking many options in the Recording menu, choosing Program mode provides you with access to settings in the Custom menu that are not

available in Intelligent Auto Mode, such as various focus-related settings and options for setting how the camera's controls operate, including the function buttons. I will discuss those options in Chapter 7.

The one drawback to using Program mode is that you don't have complete control over the camera's settings. You can set many options, such as Photo Style, Quality, Picture Size, and ISO, but you can't directly control the aperture or shutter speed, which are set according to the camera's programming. You can exercise a good deal of control through exposure compensation and exposure bracketing (discussed in Chapter 5) and Program Shift (discussed above), but that's not the same as selecting a particular aperture or shutter speed at the outset. If you want that degree of control, you'll need to select Aperture Priority, Shutter Priority, or Manual exposure for your recording mode.

Aperture Priority Mode

This mode is similar to Program mode in the functions available for you to control, but, as the name implies, it gives you more control over the camera's aperture.

Figure 3-18. Mode Dial at Aperture Priority

In this mode, set by turning the mode dial to A, as shown in Figure 3-18, you select the aperture setting using the front dial or the rear dial, and the camera will select a shutter speed that will result in normal exposure, if possible. The camera will choose a shutter speed anywhere from 60 seconds to 1/4000 second. However, this range is limited to 60 seconds to 1/2000 second if the aperture is set to f/4.0 or wider (lower numbers). The aperture has to be set to f/4.5 or narrower (higher numbers) for the camera to use a mechanical shutter speed of 1/3200 or 1/4000 second. (The range is one second to 1/16000 second when the electronic shutter is in use; that feature is discussed in Chapter 4. The aperture value limits are different if the ND Filter switch is set to Auto.) If none of these values results in a normal exposure, both the shutter speed and aperture values will turn red and flash. In that case, you may need to adjust the aperture or the ISO setting, or change the lighting conditions.

The main reason to choose this mode is so you can select an aperture to achieve a broad depth of field, with objects in focus at different distances from the lens, or a shallow depth of field, with only one area in sharp focus and other parts of the image blurred to reduce distractions. With a narrow aperture (higher f-stop number) such as f/11.0, the depth of field will be relatively broad; with a wider aperture such as f/2.8, it will be more shallow, resulting in the possibility of a blurred background.

Because the range between the widest and narrowest aperture settings available on the FZ2500 is not very great, this camera does not readily produce dramatically blurred backgrounds just from changing the aperture. However, there can be a noticeable difference from this setting, depending on the situation. For example, in Figures 3-19 and 3-20, I made the same shot with two very different aperture settings. I focused on the model knight and horse in the foreground in each case.

Figure 3-19. Image Shot at f/2.8

Figure 3-20. Image Shot at f/11.0

For Figure 3-19, I set the aperture of the FZ2500 to f/2.8, the widest possible. With this setting, because the depth of field at this aperture was relatively shallow, the trees and bushes in the background are blurry. I took Figure 3-20 with the camera's aperture set to f/11.0, the narrowest possible setting, resulting in a broader depth of field, and bringing the background into sharper focus.

These two photos show the effects of varying the aperture by setting it wide (low numbers) to blur the background or narrow (high numbers) to achieve a broad depth of field and keep subjects at varying distances in sharp focus. There are two other ways to achieve a blurred background. First, you can zoom the lens in to a telephoto setting, which reduces the depth of field and renders the background blurry, if the foreground subject is not too distant from the lens. Second, if you focus on a subject at a very close distance, the depth of field will be minimal, and the background will be blurry.

Of course, with either of those techniques, you have to accept the other effects of the setting—either a telephoto shot or a closeup shot, which may not be practical for the image you are making. For example, with a portrait, you may find that the best option for blurring the background is to choose the widest possible aperture.

To set the aperture, turn either the front dial or the rear dial. The number of the f-stop will appear in the lower left corner of the display, as shown in Figure 3-21, where the value is f/6.3.

Figure 3-21. Aperture Value on Shooting Screen

The shutter speed will be displayed also, but not until you have pressed the shutter button halfway down to let the camera evaluate the exposure.

If you turn on the Exposure Meter option on screen 6 of the Custom menu, the camera will display two gray linear scales showing the shutter speed and the aperture, as seen in Figure 3-22.

Figure 3-22. Exposure Meter Display for Aperture Value

It is important to note that not all apertures are available at all times. In particular, the widest-open aperture, f/2.8, is available only when the lens is zoomed out to its wide-angle setting (moved toward the W indicator). At higher zoom levels, the widest aperture available changes quickly so that, when the lens is zoomed in to the 250mm level or beyond, the widest aperture available is f/4.5.

To illustrate this point, zoom the lens all the way out by moving the zoom lever toward the W. Then set the aperture to f/2.8. Now zoom the lens in by moving the zoom lever to the right, toward the T. After the zoom is complete, you will see that the aperture has changed to f/4.5, because that is the widest the aperture can be at the maximum zoom level. (The aperture will change back to f/2.8 if you move the zoom back to the wide-angle setting; so you need to check your aperture after zooming out as well as after zooming in, to make sure you will not be surprised by an unexpected aperture setting.)

Shutter Priority Mode

The next shooting mode is a complement to Aperture Priority mode. In Shutter Priority mode, with the mode dial at the S position as shown in Figure 3-23, you choose the shutter speed and the camera will set the corresponding aperture to achieve a proper exposure of the image.

Figure 3-23. Mode Dial at Shutter Priority

In this mode, you can set the shutter for a variety of intervals ranging from 60 full seconds to 1/4000 of a second when using the mechanical shutter. With the electronic shutter, the range is from one second to 1/16000 second. (I will discuss the Shutter Type menu option in Chapter 4.) However, as with Aperture Priority mode, the shutter speed range places limits on the aperture setting.

If the mechanical shutter speed is set to 1/4000 second, the camera cannot use an aperture wider than f/4.5 (lower numbers). If the mechanical shutter speed is set to 1/2000 second or slower, the camera can select from its full range of aperture settings. (The available shutter speed settings are different for motion pictures.) The camera will select an aperture from its full range of f/2.8 to f/11.0, unless the lens is zoomed in. In that case, as discussed in connection with Aperture Priority mode, the widest aperture available is f/4.5.

If the camera cannot set an aperture to result in a normal exposure, the shutter speed and aperture values will flash red. If you are photographing fast action, such as a baseball swing or a hurdles event at a track meet, and you want to stop the action with a minimum of blur, you should select a fast shutter speed, such as 1/500 of a second. You can use a slow shutter speed, such as 1/8 second or slower, to cause motion blur for effect, such as to smooth out the appearance of flowing water.

In Figures 3-24 and 3-25 I photographed the same action using different shutter speeds to illustrate the different effects. In both cases, I took a picture as I was pouring a group of colored beads from a pitcher into a bowl.

In Figure 3-24, using a shutter speed of 1/2000 second, the camera froze the beads in mid-air, letting you see the beads individually. In Figure 3-25, using a much slower shutter speed of 1/60 second, the beads were blurred together into a stream of colors, because that shutter speed was not fast enough to freeze the motion of the beads.

Figure 3-24. Image Shot at 1/2000 Second

Figure 3-25. Image Shot at 1/60 Second

You select the shutter speed by turning the front dial or the rear dial. For example, to set a value of 1/500 second, turn the dial so the 500 indication appears. Values faster than 1/4000 second are available only if the Shutter Type option on screen 5 of the Recording menu is set to Auto or Electronic, shown as ESHTR on the menu.

On the shutter speed display, be sure to distinguish between the fractions of a second and the times that are one second or longer. The longer times are displayed with what looks like double quotation marks to the right, as in Figure 3-26, which shows a shutter speed setting of four seconds.

One aspect of the camera's display that can be confusing is that some times are a combination of fractions and decimals, such as 1/2.5 and 1/3.2. I find these numbers hard to translate mentally into a time I can understand. Here is a table that translates these numbers into a more understandable form:

Table 3-1. **Shutter Speed Equivalents**

3.2	1/3.2 = 0.31 = 5/16 second
2.5	1/2.5 = 0.4 = 2/5 second
1.6	1/1.6 = 0.625 = 5/8 second
1.3	1/1.3 = 0.77 = 10/13 second (0.8 sec)

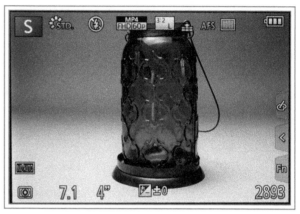

Figure 3-26. Shutter Speed of 4 Seconds on Shooting Screen

When Shutter Priority mode is in effect, you cannot use the Intelligent ISO setting. If it was set previously, the camera will reset it to Auto ISO.

Manual Exposure Mode

Manual exposure mode, set by turning the mode dial to M, as shown in Figure 3-27, helps you take full control over exposure decisions. For example, you may want to underexpose or overexpose an image to convey a feeling or to produce an effect, such as a silhouette. Or, if your subject is deeply shadowed, you may prefer to use manual settings of aperture and shutter speed rather than relying on exposure compensation or settings such as i.Dynamic to expose the subject properly.

Figure 3-27. Mode Dial at Manual

Manual exposure mode is useful when taking shots to be combined in software to create HDR (high dynamic range) composite images. The HDR technique, which I will discuss further in Chapter 4, often is used when the scene is partly in darkness and partly in bright light. To even out the contrast, you can take a series of shots, some considerably underexposed and others overexposed. You then combine these shots in special software that blends differently exposed portions from several shots, resulting in a composite image that is well exposed through a wide range of lighting values.

Figure 3-28 is a composite image that I created using Photomatix Pro software after I took several shots of a vase partly in bright sun and partly in shade, with the FZ2500 set to Manual exposure mode.

Figure 3-29. Aperture Value and Shutter Speed in Manual Mode

Figure 3-28. Composite HDR Image from Manual Exposure Shots

The technique for using Manual exposure mode is not far removed from that for the Aperture Priority and Shutter Priority modes. To control exposure manually, set the shutter speed by turning the rear dial and set the aperture by turning the front dial. As with Aperture Priority and Shutter Priority modes, with the mechanical shutter, when the aperture is set to f/4.0 or wider (lower numbers), the shutter speed can be set from 60 seconds to 1/2000 second. When the aperture is set to f/4.5 or narrower (higher numbers), the shutter speed can be set from 60 seconds to 1/4000 second. (There also is the additional BULB setting in this shooting mode, discussed later in this section.) With the electronic shutter, the shutter speed can be set from one second to 1/16000 second, regardless of the aperture setting.

The camera will display aperture and shutter speed in the lower left corner of the screen, as seen in Figure 3-29. You also will see at the bottom center of the display either an exposure compensation icon, as shown in Figure 3-29, or an exposure scale that can range from -3EV to +3EV, as shown in Figure 3-30. As you change exposure settings, the camera will display tick marks along the scale if the exposure as metered is too bright or too dark. For example, in Figure 3-30, there are tick marks to the right, indicating that the exposure is too bright.

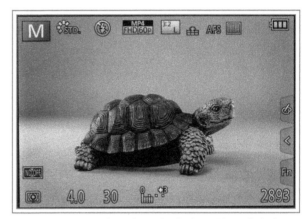

Figure 3-30. Tick Marks at the Right in Manual Mode

If no tick marks appear, as in Figure 3-29, the exposure compensation icon is displayed with the plus-or-minus zero symbol, meaning that the exposure is normal according to the camera's metering system. Of course, you do not have to be concerned with the indication on this on-screen scale, because you can make any settings you want; you may want a darker-than-normal image to create a silhouette, for example. But the EV scale is useful to help you decide what settings to make.

You also should note that the camera's display will not show the effects of your settings unless you set it to do so. That is, with normal menu options, even if you set the aperture and shutter speed to values that would produce a very dark image, the image on the display will appear basically normal, provided there is sufficient ambient light to produce a normal view. If you want to see the effects of your exposure settings, go to screen 6 of the Custom menu and turn on the Constant Preview option. Then the display will become darker or brighter as the settings change. (This feature works only with Manual exposure mode, not with Aperture Priority, Shutter Priority, or Program.)

An important feature of Manual exposure mode is that you can set ISO to Auto ISO. If you do that, then, even though the camera cannot change the aperture or the shutter speed you have set, it can vary the ISO setting within the range permitted by the ISO Limit Set menu option (discussed in Chapter 4). Therefore, the camera may be able to achieve a normal exposure by setting the ISO to an appropriate level. This is a powerful feature, which amounts in effect to giving you a new recording mode, which might be called "Aperture and Shutter Priority" mode.

For example, you might use Manual exposure mode with Auto ISO when you are taking pictures of a person working with tools in a dimly lighted workshop. You might need to use a narrow aperture such as f/8.0 in order to keep the work in focus, and a fairly fast shutter speed such as 1/250 second to avoid motion blur. You can make both of those settings and be assured that they will not vary. The camera will automatically adjust the ISO setting to achieve the best exposure possible, given the lighting conditions.

In other situations, such as when you purposely want to underexpose or overexpose an image, just set ISO to a specific numerical value and adjust the shutter speed and aperture to achieve the exposure you need. You cannot use Intelligent ISO in Manual exposure mode. You also cannot use exposure compensation in this shooting mode.

Another distinguishing feature of Manual exposure mode is that it provides you with an additional option for setting the shutter speed. With Shutter Priority mode, you can set the shutter speed anywhere from 60 seconds to 1/4000 second (when using the mechanical shutter). With Manual mode, you have the additional option of setting the shutter speed dial to the B setting, for BULB.

With the B setting, when you press the shutter button the shutter opens up and does not close again to end the exposure until you release it, up to a limit of about 120 seconds. You can use this feature to take extra-long exposures of trails of cars' headlights, fireworks, or star trails, or to turn night scenes into unusual daylight vistas. You should use a solid tripod and trigger the camera from a remote control device (as discussed in Appendix A) or a smartphone (as discussed in Chapter 9) when taking an exposure of this length. The BULB feature is not available if you are using the electronic

shutter, bracketing, flash with Flash Synchro set to 2nd, 4K Photo, Post Focus, HDR, Time Lapse Shot, or Stop Motion Animation with Auto Shooting turned on.

Panorama Mode

This mode is designed for the shooting of panoramic images. If you follow the fairly simple steps involved, the camera will stitch together a series of images internally and produce a wide (or tall) view of a landscape scene or other subject that lends itself to panoramic depiction.

Figure 3-31. Mode Dial at Panorama

Once you turn the mode dial to the Panorama position, as seen in Figure 3-31, you will briefly see a display with a message showing the direction that is currently set for taking the panorama and advising you to press the shutter button and move the camera in that direction.

When that screen disappears, you will see a display like that shown in Figure 3-32, which provides a guide line for keeping your panorama level.

Figure 3-32. Shooting Screen in Panorama Mode

When you are ready, press the shutter button all the way down and release it, while moving the camera steadily in the direction selected. You will hear a continuous clicking sound as the camera takes multiple images. You should try to keep the camera steady in a single horizontal (or vertical) plane and move it at a steady rate, so that you would complete a full circle in about eight seconds. You can keep moving the camera until the panorama ends of its own accord, or you can press the shutter button down again to stop the recording at any time.

The direction (left, right, up, or down) in which you move the camera is determined by the Panorama Settings option on screen 4 of the Recording menu. That menu option also includes a Picture Size setting, which lets you choose Standard or Wide for the size of the panorama. With the Standard setting, a horizontal panorama has a width of 8176 pixels and a height of 1920 pixels. A vertical panorama has a width of 2560 and a height of 7680. With the Wide setting, a horizontal panorama has a width of 8176 and a height of 960, but it covers a wider area than a Standard panorama. A vertical panorama has a width of 1280 and a height of 7680. If you want the highest quality, choose Standard; choose Wide if you need to include a very wide view in the image.

Because of the different sizes of panoramas taken with the horizontal and vertical orientations, you can use the direction settings with different orientations of the camera to achieve different results than usual. For example, if you set the direction to down and then hold the camera sideways while you sweep it to the right, you

will create a horizontal panorama that has 2560 pixels in its vertical dimension rather than the standard 1920.

I tend to shoot my panoramas moving the camera from left to right, but you may have a different preference. If you move the camera either too quickly or too slowly, the panorama will not succeed; if that happens, just try again. Generally speaking, panoramas work best when the scene does not contain moving objects such as cars or pedestrians, because, when items are in motion, the multiple shots are likely to pick up the same object more than once, in different positions.

It is advisable to use a tripod if possible, so you can keep the camera steady in a single plane as it moves. Focus, exposure, and white balance are fixed as soon as the first image is taken for the panorama.

When a panoramic shot is ready to be played back in the camera, the camera prompts you to press the Up cursor button (or the on-screen icon) to start it playing back; the panorama then scrolls across the screen so it can be viewed using the full area of the screen, rather than being squeezed to fit its full extent within the screen.

Figure 3-33 is a sample panorama, shot with the camera hand-held and using the Standard setting for panorama size.

Figure 3-33. **Sample Panorama: James River, Richmond, Virginia**

Scene Mode

Scene mode, also called Scene Guide mode, does not have a single defining feature, such as permitting control over one or more aspects of exposure. Instead, when you select Scene mode and choose a particular scene type within that mode, you are telling the camera what sort of environment the picture is being taken in as well as what kind of image you are looking for, and

you're letting the camera decide what settings to use to produce that result.

In this mode, you cannot use several options, including ISO, Filter Settings, Metering Mode, Highlight Shadow, and HDR, but you can use all types of bracketing except aperture bracketing. You also can set exposure compensation, white balance, focus mode, and drive mode using the control buttons or dials assigned to those functions.

Figure 3-34. Mode Dial at Scene

Turning the mode dial to the SCN indicator, as shown in Figure 3-34, places the camera in Scene mode, but unless you want to settle for whatever scene setting is already in place, you need to pick one from the fairly impressive list of possibilities.

To make this further choice, you can use the menu system. When you select Scene mode, the menu system itself changes. When the camera is set to Scene mode, there is a new branch of the menu system, named Scene Guide, as shown in Figure 3-35.

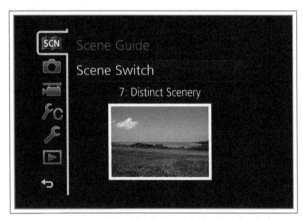

Figure 3-35. Scene Mode Icon Highlighted at Left

The SCN icon takes over as the first choice at the top of the menu system after you press the Menu/Set button. The Scene menu also appears automatically when you select SCN on the mode dial, if the Menu Guide option is turned on through screen 10 of the Custom menu.

To change scene types, press the Menu/Set button and navigate to the SCN icon at the top of the left side of the screen. Next, press the right button, and select the Scene Switch option, as shown in Figure 3-36.

The camera then displays a series of images that will rotate as you touch them with your finger, as shown in Figure 3-37. You also can move through these images using the Left and Right buttons or the front or rear dial. (If you don't see this display, press the Display button repeatedly until it appears.)

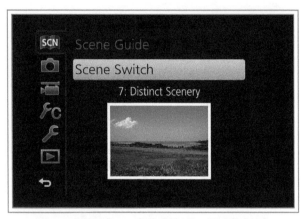

Figure 3-36. Scene Switch Option Highlighted

Figure 3-37. Rotating Display of Scene Selections

If you press the Display button when the rotating images are shown, the display changes to an arrangement that includes a text description of each setting, as shown in Figure 3-38.

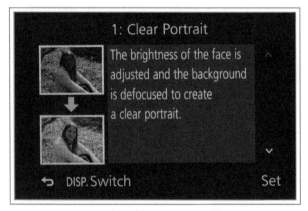

Figure 3-38. Display of Scene Types with Descriptions

You can move through those screens using the touch screen or Left and Right buttons, and scroll through the text of hints for each setting with the front or rear dial or the Up and Down buttons. If you press the Display button again, you will see an array of 12 images on the screen, as shown in Figure 3-39.

Figure 3-39. Display of Scene Types as Thumbnail Images

You can scroll through those images using the touch screen, the cursor buttons, or the front or rear dial. Using any of the three systems of display, scroll through the 24 options and select the scene type you want.

Another way to select one of the 24 scene types is to touch the Scene mode icon on the shooting screen, as shown in Figure 3-40.

Figure 3-40. Scene Type Icon on Shooting Screen

When you touch that icon, the camera immediately displays the Scene settings menu, so you can make a selection of a scene type. Unfortunately, the icon displayed on the shooting screen uses the SCN designation with a small number as the only identification of the scene type, so you either have to memorize 24 scene types or press on the icon for a reminder of what scene type is currently selected.

Each scene type carries with it a variety of settings, including things like focus mode, flash status, range of shutter speeds, sensitivity to various colors, and others.

There are limitations on settings you can make in Scene mode. No matter what scene type you select, you cannot use the Filter Settings, Metering Mode, Highlight

Shadow, HDR, or Multiple Exposure options on the Recording menu. For Photo Style, you cannot select a main setting, such as Portrait, Vivid, or Natural, but you can adjust contrast, sharpness, noise reduction, saturation, and hue (including color tone or filter effect for monochrome options) for the setting that is selected by the camera. For some settings, the camera uses Auto White Balance, but you can fine-tune white balance with color axes as discussed in Chapter 5, and you can use white balance bracketing, as discussed in Chapter 4.

Except for Handheld Night Shot, with all scene settings you can set Quality to Raw. However, special effects that use the Filter Settings or Creative Control settings will not show up in the Raw images on a computer. Therefore, you should shoot using Fine, or Raw & Fine, for Quality if you use a setting of that sort. (For example, with the Glistening Water setting, the Star Filter rays will not show up in a Raw file when it is opened on a computer. You may be able to view the preview JPEG file saved with the Raw file using the Irfanview program, as discussed later in this chapter, but the Raw file will not show the effect.)

With most of the settings you can use burst shooting, and with several you can use flash. (And with some the camera asks you to use flash.) I will provide details about each of the settings, so you can make an informed choice. I will include sample images for some of the settings. Several of the settings are self-explanatory from their names, and I will not discuss them all in detail. I will include the numbers used by Panasonic for the settings, so you can identify them based on the small icons with numbers on the shooting screen.

1. Clear Portrait: This setting is designed to produce rich skin tones. You should get good results if you shoot close to the subject and zoom the lens in to fill the frame with the subject's head, so as to blur the background if possible. The camera sets itself to a wide aperture if it can and initially sets the autofocus mode to Face/Eye Detection. The flash mode is initially set to Forced On/Red-Eye Reduction, but you can change it to Forced On.

2. Silky Skin: This setting is similar to Portrait; it detects skin tones in faces and adds a "soft effect" to those areas, as shown in Figure 3-41. The softening increases as the image is zoomed in further. Flash mode is initially set to Forced On/Red-Eye Reduction.

Figure 3-41. Silky Skin Example

3. Backlit Softness: The camera uses positive exposure compensation and disables the flash. This setting is designed for use with the light source behind the subject.

4. Clear in Backlight: The camera sets the flash mode to Forced On and displays a message asking you to pop up the flash, if it is not popped up. However, you can still take the picture without flash if you don't pop it up. This setting is for use when the subject is lighted from behind and you need to use flash to make the subject show up clearly.

5. Relaxing Tone: The flash is disabled and the camera uses warmer, yellowish tones to add a somewhat subdued, old-time appearance to the image.

6. Sweet Child's Face: With this setting, the flash mode is initially set to Forced On/Red-eye Reduction, but you can change it to Forced On. When you touch a face on the screen, the camera takes a picture with focus and exposure set for that face, using its setting for touch shutter. As the lens is zoomed in, a softening effect is applied increasingly.

7. Distinct Scenery: This style is intended for photographs of landscapes and subjects other than individual people. It is useful for general shots of buildings, gardens, and colorful scenery, as shown in Figure 3-42. The flash is disabled. You cannot select a white balance setting, presumably because you will be shooting outdoor vistas in daylight conditions. However, you can tweak the white balance using the color axes and you can use white balance bracketing.

8. Bright Blue Sky: The camera uses a small amount of positive exposure compensation to allow for shadows or backlighting that might be caused by the sky's

brightness. You can alter that setting as you like. The flash is disabled, and white balance can be tweaked, but the basic setting cannot be changed. An example is shown in Figure 3-43.

Figure 3-42. Distinct Scenery Example

Figure 3-43. Bright Blue Sky Example

9. Romantic Sunset Glow: The camera disables the flash and adds a reddish or purplish hue to the scene to emphasize the colors of a sunrise or sunset. You can tweak white balance but you cannot change the major setting. In Figure 3-44, I used this setting for a typical sky scene at the time of sunset.

10. Vivid Sunset Glow: This setting is similar to the previous one, except that the camera emphasizes yellow and orange hues to enhance the sunset effect. In Figure 3-45, I shot the same scene as in the previous image but used this setting, to show the considerable difference in the way these two options process colors.

11. Glistening Water: The flash is disabled and the camera uses the Star Filter setting, also available with the Filter Settings option and Creative Control mode. That setting adds star-like rays to bright areas, such as the sun's reflections on water. White balance can be tweaked, but not changed to a different setting.

Figure 3-44. Romantic Sunset Glow Example

Figure 3-45. Vivid Sunset Glow Example

12. Clear Nightscape: With this setting, the flash is disabled and white balance can be tweaked but not otherwise changed. The camera is likely to use a long shutter speed to capture a natural-looking scene, such as the city skyline scene shown in Figure 3-46. It is advisable to use a tripod and to set the self-timer, so the camera will not be jiggled when you press the shutter button.

Figure 3-46. Clear Nightscape Example

13. Cool Night Sky: This setting is similar to the previous one, except that the camera adds a bluish tone to the image, to make it look "cooler."

14. Warm Glowing Nightscape: This setting is similar to the previous two, but with this one the camera uses "warmer" reddish/yellowish tones.

15. Artistic Nightscape: This setting is also designed for night scenes, but in this case the camera initially sets a shutter speed of 30 seconds to capture moving trails of cars' headlights and taillights, and similar items, to create an impressionistic view of the night scene. For good results, you need to have the camera firmly anchored on a tripod and trigger it with the self-timer or a remote control. You can change the shutter speed by turning the rear dial. It may take some experimenting to find the right setting to capture an interesting mixture of lights. For Figure 3-47, I left the shutter speed set to 30 seconds for a shot of a downtown highway taken from an overpass.

Figure 3-47. Artistic Nightscape Example

16. Glittering Illuminations: This setting is designed for capturing scenes with some bright lights. The camera uses the Star Filter effect, which adds radiant beams to the brightest areas. Here, again, it is advisable to use a tripod, though the camera is not likely to use a very long shutter speed as with the previous setting. In Figure 3-48, I used this setting for a shot of a building with some bright lights shining.

Figure 3-48. Glittering Illuminations Example

17. Handheld Night Shot: With this setting, the FZ2500 uses a special process to take high-quality images in low light. The camera takes a rapid burst of several shots and combines them internally into a composite image. Because of this processing, the camera can use a high ISO setting, and therefore can use a fast shutter speed to minimize the blur caused by camera motion during a long exposure. Although shots with high ISO settings often have unpleasant visual noise or graininess, by combining the multiple images, the camera can reduce the noise in the final result.

This setting is useful when you cannot use a tripod or flash, and need to take pictures in low light. Of course, because multiple images are being taken, this setting works best for subjects that are not moving, or at least are not moving rapidly. In Figure 3-49, I used this setting for a shot of a couple walking near the river just after sunset.

Figure 3-49. Handheld Night Shot Example

The flash is disabled with this option. This setting is the same as the iHandheld Night Shot option, which is available only in Intelligent Auto mode and can be selected from the Recording menu, as discussed in Chapter 4.

18. Clear Night Portrait: With this setting, the camera expects you to use flash. If you pop up the flash, it will be set to Slow Sync with Red-eye Reduction. You cannot change that setting, but you can use the Flash Adjustment option under the Flash item on screen 5 of the Recording menu to make the flash output brighter or darker. If possible, the subject should be asked not to move for about a second while the image is being exposed. The purpose of the Slow Sync flash mode is to expose the main subject with the flash, and to keep the shutter open long enough to also expose the background with the ambient light.

19. Soft Image of a Flower: This setting is designed for a closeup (macro) shot of a subject such as a flower. The flash mode is set to Forced On if the flash is popped up, but you should avoid using the flash if the camera is very close to the subject, because the flash may overwhelm it or wash it out. It is advisable to use a tripod and the camera's self-timer. The FZ2500 also applies a softening effect to the scene. In Figure 3-50, I used this setting for a shot of a flower on display indoors at the local botanical garden.

Figure 3-50. Soft Image of a Flower Example

20. Appetizing Food: This scene type is for those occasions when you want to take a closeup picture of a plate of food without flash, though the flash will be available if you want to use it. In addition, the camera allows you to control the aperture for this setting by turning the front or rear dial, which usually can be done only with Aperture Priority mode and Manual exposure mode. You might want to do this if you want to select a wide aperture to blur the background, or a narrow aperture to achieve a broad depth of field and keep the entire scene in focus. For Figure 3-51, I used this setting to photograph a plate of artificial fruit.

Figure 3-51. Appetizing Food Example

21. **Cute Dessert:** This setting is very similar to the previous one, though it appears to apply somewhat more saturation and vividness to the image. You cannot adjust the aperture with this setting.

22. **Freeze Animal Motion:** This setting is intended for photos of moving pets, often taken indoors. The camera uses tracking focus and turns off the AF assist lamp to avoid startling the animal, though you can turn it back on through screen 3 of the Custom menu if you want to. The camera turns on Intelligent ISO so it can use a fast shutter speed as needed. (I'll discuss ISO, or sensitivity to light, in Chapter 5. Briefly, with a higher-numbered ISO setting, the camera is more sensitive to light, and therefore can use a faster shutter speed. The tradeoff is the possibility of added "noise" or fuzziness of the image.) You can use the flash, but only with the Forced On setting. You can turn on burst shooting through the drive mode settings, as discussed in Chapter 5.

Figure 3-52. **Freeze Animal Motion Example**

In Figure 3-52, I used this setting to catch a shot of my family's dog as she was deciding on her next activity.

23. **Clear Sports Shot:** This style is similar to the previous one, but it is meant to stop the action of sports in daylight using fast shutter speeds if necessary. The AF assist lamp is not disabled by default. In Figure 3-53, I used this setting to capture an image of a man as he jogged toward me on a pedestrian bridge across the river.

24. **Monochrome:** This final setting for Scene mode sets the camera to take black-and-white images. You can use any flash setting you want.

Figure 3-53. **Clear Sports Shot Example**

Creative Control Mode

Creative Control mode occupies its own place on the mode dial, so I will discuss it here in the context of the other shooting modes, even though it is a bit of a hybrid creature. It has some attributes of the Photo Style setting on the Recording menu, and some attributes of the Scene mode settings.

For example, one of the Creative Control settings, Monochrome, is similar to the Monochrome setting of the Photo Style menu option and to the Monochrome setting of Scene mode. The Expressive setting of Creative Control mode is similar to the Vivid setting of the Photo Style option. However, there are significant differences among these various options, and the Creative Control settings offer adjustments that make these options useful for dramatic alteration of the colors and other attributes of your images. Also, all of the Creative Control settings are available separately through the Filter Settings option on screen 1 of the Recording menu, so you can use any of these settings with the other shooting modes through that option.

Figure 3-54. **Mode Dial at Creative Control**

When you turn the mode dial to the artist's palette position, as shown in Figure 3-54, if the Menu Guide option on screen 10 of the Custom menu is turned on, you will immediately see a screen that lets you browse through the icons for the 22 effects. You can choose from three possible arrangements of the icons by pressing the Display button repeatedly.

With the Normal display, as shown in Figure 3-55, the camera displays a vertical line of icons at the right.

Figure 3-55. Normal Display for Creative Control Settings

As you scroll up and down through that line using the Up and Down buttons or the front or rear dial (or the touch screen), the camera highlights the selected icon and displays a large view at the left of the screen that applies that effect to the live view of the current scene that the camera is aimed at.

With the Guide display, as shown in Figure 3-56, the setup is the same, except that, at the left of the screen, instead of displaying the appearance of the effect, the camera displays a brief description of the effect.

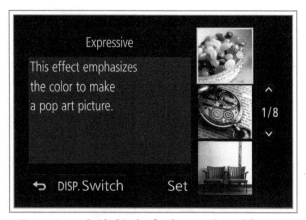

Figure 3-56. Guide Display for Creative Control Settings

With the List display, as shown in Figure 3-57, the camera displays more icons on each screen, in rows and columns. As you scroll through them, the camera displays the name of the effect at the top of the display.

Figure 3-57. List Display for Creative Control Settings

When you have scrolled through the Creative Control effect icons and highlighted the one you want to use, press the Menu/Set button (or touch the Set icon on the screen) to select it and return to the shooting screen. The camera's display will show the name of the effect briefly at the upper left, and the appearance of the scene on the display will reflect the chosen effect, as shown in Figure 3-58, where the Sepia effect is selected.

Figure 3-58. Shooting Screen with Sepia Setting Selected

You also can select a new Creative Control effect quickly by touching the effect icon in the upper left corner of the screen, which calls up the standard menu screen for selecting an effect.

The Creative Control choices provide different "looks" for your images, in some cases producing striking alterations of the normal color, texture, and brightness. It's important to note that, because the Creative Control setting occupies its own slot on the mode dial, whatever setting you make for Creative Control is only in effect when the mode dial is set to that position. So, for example, if you switch the mode dial to Program or Aperture Priority mode, the Creative Control setting will no longer be in effect. If you later switch the dial back to Creative Control, though, whatever setting you previously made in that mode will once more take effect.

You also should note that, when you record a motion picture with the FZ2500, you don't need to move the mode dial; you only need to press the red motion picture button on top of the camera. So, when you record a movie, you need to be sure the mode dial is set where you want it. For example, if you have just taken some still photos using an exotic Creative Control setting, that setting will still be in effect if you press the red button to record a movie. If you want a more ordinary look for your movie, be sure to set the mode dial back to Intelligent Auto, Program, Creative Video, or some other standard mode, to avoid having the movie recorded using the Creative Control setting. On the other hand, being able to use Creative Control settings when shooting a movie can be an advantage when you want to add an atmospheric look to your motion pictures. I'll discuss movie settings in Chapter 8.

Once you have selected a Creative Control setting, you can make some additional settings from the Recording menu and with the camera's physical controls. For example, you can use options such as Picture Size, AFS/AFF, Metering Mode, exposure compensation, exposure or focus bracketing, and AF Mode. However, several other settings are unavailable with the Creative Control shooting mode, including white balance, ISO, Intelligent Dynamic, and Photo Style. With some of the Creative Control options you can use burst shooting or flash; I will indicate those cases as I discuss the settings individually below.

You also can use Raw for the Quality setting with the Creative Control settings. However, as with the Filter Settings menu option, discussed in Chapter 4, there is a pitfall with that capability. If you set Quality to Raw, the Creative Control effect will likely not show up in the image that opens in common Raw-processing software, such as Adobe Photoshop or Silkypix. With those programs, the effect may appear when you view a thumbnail in the software, but it will not be included in the image when it is opened on a computer.

Therefore, if you are using such programs to process Raw files, there is no point in using Raw for Quality with the Creative Control mode. Instead, you should use Raw & Fine or Raw & Standard. In that way, you will have an image that includes the special effect

you selected, as well as a Raw image for flexibility in processing. However, I have found one software package that can preserve the effects of Creative Control and Filter Settings effects. That program is Irfanview, a versatile, free program available from irfanview.com. That program is able to extract the 1920 x 1280-pixel preview JPEG file that is embedded in the Raw file. The extracted JPEG file includes the effects of special settings such as those of Creative Control mode.

In addition to the settings from the Recording menu and physical controls discussed above, with the Creative Control mode you can make several other adjustments, depending on which Creative Control setting is in effect. These adjustments can be made in two ways. First, you can press the Right button, which will take you to the adjustment screen for the effect that is currently selected. For example, when the Expressive effect is active, pressing the Right button takes you to the screen shown in Figure 3-59, with a sliding scale at the bottom.

Figure 3-59. Adjustment Scale for Expressive Setting

Using the front or rear dial, the Left and Right buttons, or the touch screen, you can adjust the slider along that scale to increase or decrease the vividness of the effect. With other effects you can adjust other values, such as coloring, contrast, or graininess.

In this recording mode, you can also use the defocus control option in the same way as with Intelligent Auto Plus mode. To use that feature, press the Fn6 button and then adjust the aperture using the front or rear dial, the Left and Right buttons, or the touch screen.

You also can adjust all of the Creative Control mode settings using the touch screen icons. To do that, touch the small icon that looks like a painter's palette at the right edge of the screen. You will then see a vertical line of three icons at the right edge of the screen, as shown in Figure 3-60.

Figure 3-60. Touch Screen Icons for Creative Control Adjustments

Press the top icon to bring up the adjustment scale for the Creative Control effect. Press the middle icon to bring up the defocus control. Press the bottom icon to call up the brightness adjustment scale (exposure compensation). Press the artist's palette icon again to dismiss the adjustment icons.

Following are details about each of the 22 Creative Control choices. Along with descriptions, I will include a sample photograph taken using the setting being discussed. I will also mention what items can be controlled for each effect, if those adjustments are different from the standard ones (brightness, background defocus, and intensity of the selected effect).

Expressive. I would call this mode something like "super-vivid"; some people call it "pop art." If you like your colors with strong saturation, this style is useful. However, the Vivid setting of the Photo Style menu option can produce a similar result. The Photo Style setting is available in the more advanced shooting modes such as Program, Aperture Priority, and the like; therefore, you can use more menu and other settings in conjunction with that setting than you can with the more limiting Creative Control Expressive setting. Figure 3-61 provides an illustration, with a shot of a walkway and its railings shortly after sunset. I thought this setting helped to emphasize the dark lines of the image.

Figure 3-61. Expressive Example

Retro. This style appears to me to be the opposite of Expressive; it paints the scene with subdued, somewhat yellowish tones, de-emphasizing the glaring qualities of Expressive. It evokes a feeling of past times. For this effect, adjusting the setting to the left on the scale increases yellowish tones, and adjusting it to the right increases reddish tones. In Figure 3-62, I used the Retro setting for an image of the conservatory at the local botanical garden.

Figure 3-62. Retro Example

Old Days. This effect is intended to give a "nostalgic" look by lowering the saturation of colors and reducing contrast for an old-fashioned appearance. With the adjustment slider, you can vary the contrast. In Figure 3-63, I used this setting to give an aged appearance to an old house in an urban area.

Figure 3-63. **Old Days Example**

High Key. "High key" is a technique in which a studio photographer uses high-intensity lighting throughout the scene, striving for a bright look with light colors and few shadows. This technique often is used in advertising photography. With the FZ2500, this single setting cannot necessarily remake your image to look like a traditional high key shot, but the camera does boost the exposure to produce a brighter-than-normal image. Moving the slider for the effect to the left produces more pinkish tones, while setting it to the right yields bluer hues. Figure 3-64 provides an example, in which I used this setting to brighten a scene of a somewhat dilapidated building.

Figure 3-64. **High Key Example**

Low Key. "Low key" lighting, of course, is the opposite of "high key." With this approach, the photographer emphasizes shadows and dark areas in the photograph. Here again, the FZ2500 cannot produce a true "low key" image all by itself; what it can do is reduce the exposure and otherwise process the photograph to look more dark and shadowy than normal. As with the High Key setting, the effect's adjustment slider can be

moved to the left for a redder look, or to the right for a bluer appearance. In Figure 3-65, I used this setting to photograph a bed of colorful flowers in the botanical garden. I thought the dark atmosphere added contrast and interest to the scene.

Figure 3-65. **Low Key Example**

Sepia. With the Sepia setting, the FZ2500 produces a monochrome image with a sepia (brownish) tone and softens the contrast somewhat to give the look of an antique photograph. In this case, adjusting the setting of the adjustment slider decreases the overall contrast of the image, while moving it to the right increases the contrast, producing a somewhat harsher, darker appearance. For Figure 3-66, I used this setting for a view of the city skyline by the river.

Figure 3-66. **Sepia Example**

Monochrome. This setting gives you another way, apart from the Photo Style menu option and the Scene mode option, to capture an image in traditional black and white. The adjustment slider lets you add a color tone, ranging from yellowish to bluish. For Figure 3-67, I used this setting for a view of a Century Plant in the botanical garden, to emphasize the structure and symmetry of the plant rather than its color.

Figure 3-67. Monochrome Example

Dynamic Monochrome. This setting converts the image to black and white, but with heightened contrast to produce a more dramatic effect. As with Sepia, you can use the left or right adjustments to decrease or increase contrast. For Figure 3-68, I used this setting for a scene of utility wires and poles on a wintry evening.

Figure 3-68. Dynamic Monochrome Example

Rough Monochrome. With this setting, the camera also records a monochrome image, but with the appearance altered to add grain by inducing visual noise, like the noise that results from using a high ISO setting. This option can be good for street photography or for other situations in which you want the somewhat primitive look of a grainy image. The adjustment slider lets you reduce or increase the amount of graininess. For Figure 3-69, I used this setting for a shot of a bridge from underneath its structure.

Figure 3-69. Rough Monochrome Example

Silky Monochrome. This option gives you another way to take a monochrome image. In this case, the camera puts the image slightly out of focus to add a soft or dreamlike look. With the adjustment slider, you can alter the amount of defocusing that is used. The left side of the scale provides a sharper, less defocused image. For Figure 3-70, I used this setting for a scene of trees in front of a building, to add some interest to the pattern formed by the branches.

Figure 3-70. Silky Monochrome Example

Impressive Art. This setting has some similarities to the Expressive, Dynamic Monochrome, and High Dynamic settings. It produces images with high contrast and dramatic variations in color intensity. Using the adjustment slider, you can alter the intensity all the way to the left to produce a monochrome image, or all the way to the right to produce an oversaturated image with exploding, vibrant colors. You can achieve some fairly dramatic effects with this setting, as seen in Figure 3-71, which shows the effects of this option on a scene of the sky above the river at sunset.

Figure 3-71. Impressive Art Example

High Dynamic. This setting is oriented less to altering the colors of the image than to leveling out the shadows and highlights. As you can see from the name, it is akin to the "high dynamic range" or HDR processing that is often done with software, and sometimes, as here, through in-camera processing. For Figure 3-72, I used this setting for a shot of the river around sunset, as seen through a gap under a railroad bridge.

Figure 3-72. High Dynamic Example

The High Dynamic setting is useful when you're taking a picture that includes areas of both bright light and shadows. Ordinarily, a camera cannot process that sort of image and preserve the details in both areas. This setting alters the processing so more details are visible in the dark areas, and the bright areas are not so washed out and overexposed. As with the Impressive Art setting, above, the adjustment slider lets you adjust the image from monochrome at the left to oversaturated color at the right.

Cross Process. This setting gives you the ability to add a distinctive color tint to your images, in green, blue,

yellow, or red. In this case, after pressing the Right button you use the front or rear dial, the Left and Right buttons, or the touch screen to select one of those colors, as shown in Figure 3-73.

Figure 3-73. Cross Process Color Selection Screen

Once that selection has been made, your images will be tinted with the selected color. Figure 3-74 is an example of using this setting for a composite image of a model diving helmet. This composite image shows all four settings. Clockwise from upper left, the settings are green, blue, red, and yellow.

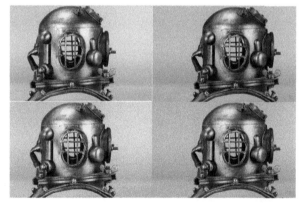

Figure 3-74. Cross Process Composite Image

Toy Effect. As with some of the other Creative Control selections, this one is not strictly an example of color processing. Rather, this setting tries to reproduce the effects that are achieved with a primitive "toy" camera. There has been a popular movement for this sort of photography in recent years, using cameras like the Holga and Diana, which are purposely constructed to lack sharpness and to suffer from vignetting at the corners. The photographs from such cameras can be quite appealing in their own way, and the Toy Effect setting lets you experiment with a good simulation of this sort of image.

Figure 3-75. **Toy Effect Example**

Figure 3-77. Bleach Bypass Example

It can be a pleasing way to highlight a subject in the middle of the frame, as shown in Figure 3-75. With this setting, the adjustment slider produces more reddish tones to the left, and more bluish ones to the right.

Toy Pop. With this setting, the camera combines the vivid, bright appearance of the Expressive setting with the vignetting of Toy Effect, discussed above. In this case, the adjustment slider controls the amount of vignetting. At the left of the scale, the vignetting is reduced so more of the image is bright; at the right, the vignetting increases to darken more of the corners. For Figure 3-76, I used this setting to place a vignette around a colorful group of flowers.

Figure 3-76. Toy Pop Example

Bleach Bypass. This option causes images to have increased contrast and lowered color saturation, to produce a bleached, washed-out appearance. You can reduce the contrast by moving the adjustment slider to the left or increase it by moving the slider to the right. For Figure 3-77, I used this option for a view of plants in the botanical garden, to give the image a subdued appearance.

Miniature. The next Creative Control setting is called the Miniature effect. When you apply this option to an image, the camera adds blurring at one or more sides of an image or at the image's top or bottom, to simulate the appearance of a photograph of a tabletop model or miniature. Such images often appear blurred in one area, either because of the narrow depth of field of these close-up photos, or because of the use of a tilt-and-shift lens, which causes blurring at the edges.

Figure 3-78. Miniature Example

For this feature to work well, you need to choose an appropriate subject. This effect looks interesting when applied to something like a street scene or a house, which might be reproduced in a tabletop model. For example, if you are able to get a high vantage point above a road intersection or a parking area, as in Figure 3-78, you may be able to use this effect to make it look as if you had photographed a high-quality mock-up of an area with model cars.

With this setting, three icons appear at the right side of the screen when you touch the artist's-palette icon at the right side of the screen. The bottom icon adjusts brightness and the middle one adjusts the intensity of the colors. In order to adjust the settings for the miniature effect itself, you use the top icon, which looks like a rectangle with arrows pointing up and down.

When the Miniature setting has been selected, touch the artist's palette icon then touch the top (rectangle) icon, and a long yellow frame will appear on the screen, as shown in Figure 3-79.

Figure 3-79. Yellow Frame for Miniature Setup

This frame represents the area of the image that will remain in sharp focus. The areas outside of that frame will be defocused and fuzzy, contributing to the overall effect. So, for example, if you are shooting from an overpass down toward a highway intersection, you may want to line up the yellow frame over the road that you want to remain in focus, leaving the areas on the sides of the road to be out of focus.

To move the yellow frame, use the cursor buttons. When you see triangles on the frame, press the buttons corresponding to the triangles to move the frame in the direction of the triangle. Use the other two cursor buttons to flip the frame to a different orientation (horizontal or vertical). Turn the front or rear dial to resize the frame. When you have the frame oriented and sized as you want it, press the Menu/Set button to return to the shooting screen and take the picture. You also can use your fingers on the touch screen to move the rectangle, to pinch it to make it larger or smaller, or to change its orientation between horizontal and vertical by touching the icon with intersecting squares and an arrow.

You can press the Right button to get to the adjustment slider, which adjusts color saturation. With this setting, you cannot use burst shooting or the flash, although you can use Raw image quality. Also, note that you can use the Miniature setting when shooting movies. If you do so, no audio is recorded, and the action is speeded up

to about ten times normal speed, which helps reinforce the illusion that you are filming a model scene rather than a life-sized one. (The speed-up factor is about eight times if System Frequency is set to 50 or 24 on screen 5 of the Setup menu.)

Soft Focus. With this setting, the camera defocuses the overall image to achieve a soft, hazy look, as seen in Figure 3-80. You can still use the icons at the right of the screen to control brightness, background defocus, and the overall intensity of the general defocusing effect. You cannot use burst shooting or record movies with this setting in effect.

Figure 3-80. Soft Focus Example

Fantasy. With this option, the camera reduces the intensity of colors and adds a bluish color cast to the scene, with the idea of producing a hazy, fantasy-like appearance. With the adjustment slider, you can vary the intensity of the colors. You cannot use flash, but you can use burst shooting or record movies. For Figure 3-81, I felt that this setting was appropriate for a shot of a train crossing a bridge over the river around sunset.

Figure 3-81. Fantasy Example

Star Filter. This setting adds cross-shaped "stars" of light to your images at bright points in the scene, giving a sparkling effect. You cannot use flash, record movies, or use burst shooting. This effect can be pleasing with a subject that lends itself to this look, like the photograph of buildings with some bright lights in Figure 3-82.

Figure 3-82. Star Filter Example

The effect has three adjustment slider controls. The top slider controls the size of the rays of light; adjust to the left for shorter rays, and to the right for longer ones. The second one controls the number of rays, with more rays produced as you move the slider to the right. The bottom slider adjusts the angle of the rays; they rotate to the right as you adjust the slider to the right, and vice-versa. You cannot use this effect with burst shooting or when recording movies.

One Point Color. This is a setting that I enjoy quite a bit. It lets you select any one color in a scene for the camera to retain, while turning the rest of the image black and white. You can achieve a dramatic effect with this setting, by placing a clear emphasis on a small part of the scene that is in color.

When you activate this setting, a line of four touch icons appears at the right edge of the screen, as shown in Figure 3-83.

Figure 3-83. Icons to Adjust One Point Color Setting

Touch the top icon, which looks like a pencil, and a movable set of yellow arrows will appear in the center of the screen, as shown in Figure 3-84. Using the four direction buttons or your finger on the touch screen, place that square over the object whose color you want to retain, and press the Menu/Set button (or touch the Set icon) to confirm the selection.

Figure 3-84. Frame to Select Color for One Point Color Setting

The setting's adjustment icon (which looks like a palette with a plus sign) is used to determine how closely an item must match the selected color in order to show up in color. Move the slider to the left to restrict the color selection to the minimum, and to the right to include a broader range of similar colors.

Then, as shown in Figure 3-85, only objects matching that color will appear in color on the shooting screen and in the final image after you take the picture. You can use burst shooting with this setting and you also can shoot movies with it, but you cannot use flash.

Figure 3-85. One Point Color Example

Sunshine. Finally, the Sunshine option lets you add a solar flare effect to an image. After you select this option, touch the top adjustment icon at the right edge of the screen, which looks like the sun, and you will see a yellow circle on the display, as shown in Figure

3-86. You can move that circle around the screen using the four direction buttons or your finger on the touch screen and resize it using the front or rear dial or by pinching and pulling with your fingers on the screen.

Figure 3-86. Sunshine Effect Adjustment Circle

When you have the solar flare sized and located as you want, press Menu/Set button (or the Set icon) to lock it in. Then, press the Right button or touch the second adjustment icon (under the sun icon) and you can select yellow, red, blue, or white for the color of the flare. Press Menu/Set, and the effect will be locked in with your selections. You can move the flare outside the edges of the image to avoid having the large, bright ball in the scene. With this setting, you cannot use flash, record movies, or use burst shooting.

For Figure 3-87, I used this option to add a solar flare to an image of a model camera, to simulate the firing of its flash bulb.

Figure 3-87. Sunshine Example

Custom Mode: C Position on Mode Dial

Finally, I will briefly discuss the C position on the mode dial, seen in Figure 3-88.

Figure 3-88. Mode Dial at Custom

(I will discuss the Creative Video mode in Chapter 8.) The C position does not represent an independent shooting mode. Instead, it is used in conjunction with the powerful Custom Set Memory menu item, which I will discuss in Chapter 7. Essentially, you can use this slot on the mode dial to recall three sets of custom values for your important menu settings and some other settings. Once you have stored the settings, just turn the mode dial to the C position to recall one of your three saved groups of settings—C1, C2, or C3. See Chapter 7 for further details.

CHAPTER 4: THE RECORDING MENU AND THE QUICK MENU

Much of the power of the FZ2500 lies in the options provided in the Recording menu, which gives you control over the appearance of images and how they are captured. This menu is not the only source of creative tools for this camera; there are several important settings that can be controlled with physical buttons and dials, as I will discuss in Chapter 5, and there also is the convenient Quick Menu, which gives you ready access to several often-used options. I will discuss both the Recording menu and the Quick Menu in this chapter.

The Recording Menu

As I have discussed earlier, the main menu system of the FZ2500 incudes five separate menus: Recording, Motion Picture, Custom, Setup, and Playback. I'll discuss the Playback menu in Chapter 6, the Custom and Setup menus in Chapter 7, and the Motion Picture menu in Chapter 8.

Figure 4-1. Screen 5 of Custom Menu

When you press the Menu/Set button, you will initially see the main menu screen, as shown in Figure 4-1. The actual screen that is displayed depends on the setting of the Menu Resume item on screen 3 of the Setup menu.

If that option is set to On, then the menu screen you last used will appear first; if it is set to Off, the camera will display the first screen of the Recording menu. In Figure 4-1, screen 5 of the Custom menu is active, with the camera set to Program mode.

If, as in this example, the Recording menu screen is not displayed, press the Left button.

Figure 4-2. Menu Icons highlighted at Left

That action will move the highlight into the left column of the menu screen, as shown in Figure 4-2, where you can navigate up and down with the direction buttons or the rear dial (or the touch screen) to highlight the icons for the various menu systems.

Another way to navigate from one menu system to another is to turn the front dial. When you turn that dial, the camera moves directly from one menu system to another, highlighting the menu icon in the left column of the menu screen, even when the yellow highlight is located on an individual item within the current menu system. For example, if you start from the screen shown above in Figure 4-1, you can turn the front dial to the left to move directly to the Recording menu, with the yellow highlight already in place on a screen of that menu system.

For now, use the buttons to highlight the red camera icon at the top of the line of icons, indicating the Recording menu, as shown in Figure 4-3.

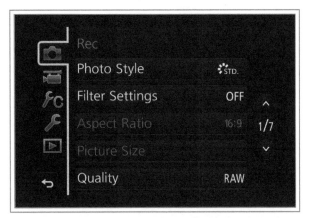

Figure 4-3. Recording Menu Icon Highlighted at Left

Then press the Right button to move back over to the main part of the screen, with the Recording menu items. The yellow selection rectangle will highlight a menu item, as shown in Figure 4-4. You can then navigate through the Recording menu to find the items you want to adjust.

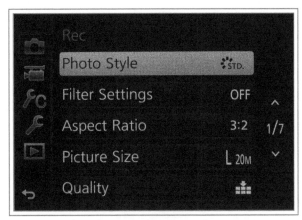

Figure 4-4. Screen 1 of Recording Menu

As I discussed earlier, the menu options will change depending on the recording mode in effect. If you're using the basic Intelligent Auto mode, the Recording menu is limited to two screens, because that mode is for a user who wants the camera to make most of the decisions without input. For the following discussion, I'm assuming you have the camera set to one of the advanced (PASM) modes, because in those modes all seven screens of the menu are available.

On each menu screen you will see a list of options, each occupying one line, with its name on the left and its current setting on the right. (In some cases, the current setting is not shown because it involves multiple options.) You have to scroll through seven screens to see all of the items.

You can scroll through the items on any screen using the Up and Down buttons or the rear dial. You can use the zoom lever on top of the camera to speed through the menus one full screen at a time, in either direction. You also can press the Display button to move through the menu screens, but only in the forward direction. And, you can use the touch screen capability, by touching a desired menu option, or by touching the up and down arrows at the far right of the menu screen. You can tell which numbered screen you are on by checking the numbers at the right of the screen, which show the screen numbers as 1/7, 2/7, and so on, through 7/7.

Depending on the location of a particular menu option, you may be able to reach that option more quickly by reversing direction with the direction buttons and wrapping around to reach the option you want. For example, if you're on the top line of screen 1 of the menu, at Photo Style, you can scroll up to reach the bottom option on screen 7 of the menu, Profile Setup.

Some menu lines may have a dimmed, "grayed-out" appearance at times, meaning they cannot be selected under the present settings. For example, in Figure 4-5, two items are dimmed on screen 6 of the Recording menu.

Figure 4-5. Screen 6 of Recording Menu

In this case, Quality is set to Raw and the recording mode is Program. With Quality set to Raw, you cannot make several other settings, including Intelligent Zoom and Digital Zoom. If you want to follow along with the discussion of the options on the Recording menu, go to screen 1 of the Recording menu and set Quality to

Fine, which is the setting represented by the icon of an arrow pointing down onto two rows of bricks, as shown in Figure 4-6.

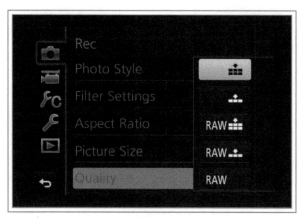

Figure 4-6. Fine Icon Highlighted for Quality Menu Option

To do so, scroll down using the Down button until the Quality line is highlighted, then press the Right button to pop up the sub-menu. Scroll up, if necessary, to highlight the top icon with the six bricks, and then press the Menu/Set button to select that option.

With that setting, you will have access to most of the options on the Recording menu. I'll start at the top and discuss each option on the list. The first screen of options was shown earlier in Figure 4-4.

PHOTO STYLE

This first item on the Recording menu gives you several options for choosing a setting that determines the overall appearance of your images. These settings yield differing results in terms of warmth, color cast, and other attributes.

To select a Photo Style setting, highlight the Photo Style line on the Recording menu and press the Right button or Menu/Set to move to the screen that displays the current setting in the upper right corner, as shown in Figure 4-7. (For all menu settings, you also can use the touch screen to make selections. I will mention that possibility from time to time, but I won't keep repeating it for every menu option.)

Then use the Left and Right buttons or the front or rear dial to scroll through the available settings: Standard, Vivid, Natural, Monochrome, Scenery, Portrait, Custom, Cinelike D, Cinelike V, and V-Log L. (The last three settings are available only when the mode dial is set to Creative Video mode. In addition, the V-Log

L setting is available only if you have purchased that option from Panasonic or a dealer, as discussed in Appendix A. These three settings are discussed in Chapter 8, where I cover movie recording.)

Figure 4-7. Photo Style Menu Options Screen

When your chosen setting is highlighted at the top right of the screen, as shown in Figure 4-7, where the Vivid setting has been highlighted, press the Menu/Set button to select it, then press the Fn6 button to exit to the shooting screen. Or, if you prefer, after highlighting the new setting, just press the shutter button halfway to select the setting and return to the shooting screen.

If you want to fine-tune the setting, the FZ2500's menu system lets you adjust five parameters that are associated with the Photo Style settings: contrast, sharpness, noise reduction, saturation, and hue. (The hue adjustment varies the colors from yellowish green on the negative side to violet-magenta on the positive side.)

Figure 4-8. Sharpness Adjustment Highlighted for Photo Style

To make adjustments to those parameters, press the Down button when the main setting (such as Vivid or Natural) is highlighted in yellow, as in Figure 4-7. A new highlight will then appear in the block that contains the value for one of the four adjustable parameters, as shown in Figure 4-8.

In this case, the second line is highlighted, which means you can adjust the sharpness setting; the word Sharpness appears for a few seconds at the top left of the screen, indicating that that value can now be adjusted.

Once you have placed the highlight block on one of the five parameters, press the Left and Right buttons or turn the front or rear dial to change the value of that parameter up to five levels, either positive or negative. A yellow scale in the center of the screen will reflect those changes, as shown in Figure 4-9. Press Menu/Set or press the shutter button halfway to save the changes. The camera will remember those settings even when it is turned off.

Figure 4-9. Sharpness Adjustment Made for Photo Style

There is one additional point to make about the Monochrome setting for Photo Style. Monochrome means there is no color in the image, only shades of black, white, and gray. Therefore, the saturation and hue adjustments are not available to alter the colors for the Monochrome setting. Instead of the saturation and hue adjustments, the camera provides two additional parameters at the bottom of the list: color tone and filter effect, as shown in Figure 4-10.

With color tone, a positive adjustment makes the monochrome effect increasingly bluish or "cooler," while a negative adjustment makes it increasingly yellowish or "warmer."

The filter effect adjustment lets you add a virtual filter, simulating the effect of a glass filter, which can be used on a camera's lens for black-and-white photography to enhance contrast and for other purposes. You can

choose from a yellow, orange, red, or green filter, or choose the last setting, which turns the filter effect off.

Figure 4-10. Adjustment Scales for Monochrome Setting

For example, Figure 4-11 shows the screen when the yellow filter effect is selected. The yellow, orange, and red effects provide increasing amounts of contrast for blue subjects, and can be used to enhance the appearance of a blue sky. The green effect can be used to reduce the brightness of human skin and lips or to brighten the appearance of green foliage.

Figure 4-11. Filter Effect Set to Yellow for Monochrome Setting

When you set Photo Style to Monochrome with Quality set to Raw, the picture you take will show up as black-and-white on the camera's LCD screen, but, when you import the image file into software that reads Raw files, the image may show up in color, depending on how the software interprets the Raw data from the sensor. With the Silkypix software provided with the camera, Raw images taken with Photo Style settings retain the Photo Style appearance, but you can convert them to other settings in the software.

The Photo Style settings are not available in the basic Intelligent Auto mode or in Creative Control mode, but they are available to some extent in all other shooting modes. In Intelligent Auto Plus mode, you can select only Standard or Monochrome for Photo Style, and you cannot adjust either setting's contrast and other parameters.

In Scene mode, the camera selects a Photo Style setting according to the scene type you select, but also lets you adjust the parameters for that type. For example, if you select Clear Portrait for the scene setting, the camera selects Portrait for the Photo Style setting, but lets you adjust the contrast and other values.

The Photo Style settings also are available for recording a movie with one of the advanced shooting modes. As noted above, when the mode dial is set to Creative Video, you have access to two additional settings: Cinelike D and Cinelike V, as well as a third setting, V-Log L, which is available as an extra-cost option.

The chart in Figure 4-12 shows the same scene photographed with each of the main Photo Style settings. (A chart showing the effects of the three movie-oriented settings is included in Chapter 8.)

Photo Style Chart for FZ2500

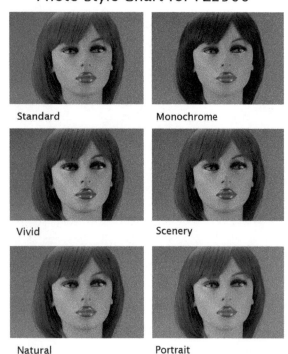

Figure 4-12. Comparison Chart for Main Photo Style Settings

Here are summaries of each of these Photo Style settings:

Standard: No change from the normal setting; good for general photography. The camera uses moderate sharpening and contrast to provide a clear image for everyday purposes.

Vivid: Increased saturation (intensity or vividness) and contrast of the colors in the image to make the colors "pop" out in dramatic fashion.

Natural: Reduced contrast to produce a softer, more subdued appearance.

Monochrome: Standard settings, but monochrome image, with all color removed (that is, saturation reduced to zero), unless you use the color tone adjustment to add a yellow or blue tone. You also can use the filter effect setting to add a yellow, orange, red, or green filter effect.

Scenery: Increased emphasis on the blues and greens of outdoor scenes, with increased saturation of those hues.

Portrait: Emphasis on flesh tones.

Custom: The Custom slot is available to store a setting that you have customized using your own settings for the parameters that can be adjusted (contrast, sharpness, noise reduction, saturation, and hue, as well as color tone and filter effect for the monochrome setting). To use this option, select any one of the Photo Style settings (Standard, Vivid, Natural, Monochrome, Scenery, Portrait, Cinelike D, Cinelike V, or V-Log L), then press the Down button and proceed to adjust any or all of the parameters for that setting as you want them. (For V-Log L, the only available parameters are sharpness and noise reduction.) Next, press the Display button, as prompted by the DISP. Save message on the display, as shown in Figures 4-7 through 4-10.

The camera will display the message shown in Figure 4-13, asking you to confirm that you want to overwrite the current Custom slot with the settings you just made. If you highlight Yes and press Menu/Set, the settings you have made will be stored in the Custom slot of the Photo Style setting.

After you have stored the Custom setting, you can recall it at any time by selecting Custom for your setting from the Photo Style menu. You can alter the Custom setting in the future by choosing a different set of settings and storing it to the Custom slot, overwriting the previous entry.

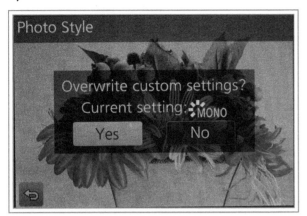

Figure 4-13. Confirmation Screen for Saving Custom Photo Style

FILTER SETTINGS

This second option on the Recording menu lets you apply special picture effects to your images. As I discussed in Chapter 3, the Creative Control shooting mode provides a set of 22 effects, including Expressive, Retro, Old Days, and 19 others. Each of these settings includes adjustments to things such as brightness, sharpness, focus, colors, and other factors, to achieve a special appearance for a given shot. I discussed the details of those settings in Chapter 3.

The Filter Settings menu option lets you apply any of these same effects without using that shooting mode. So, for example, while shooting in Program or Aperture Priority mode, you can select one of the 22 Filter Settings options to alter the look of an image or video. Using this option, you can have the benefit of the special setting while using one of the more advanced shooting modes. If you select one of the Filter Settings options while using Manual exposure mode, you can select the aperture and shutter speed you want, in order to have more complete creative control over the image. If you use the Creative Control shooting mode, you can apply the same effects, but you have to rely on the camera's automation for the exposure.

To use this option, navigate to the Filter Settings menu item and select it. You will see a screen like that in Figure 4-14. Highlight Filter Effect and select it, and you will see a screen like that in Figure 4-15, with the choices On, Off, and Set. Select On or Off to activate or turn off the currently selected effect. Use Set to change to a different effect. When you select Set, you are taken to a screen where you can select one of the 22 available settings.

Figure 4-14. Filter Settings Main Options Screen

Figure 4-15. Filter Effect Menu Options Screen

The settings screen is the same as that discussed in Chapter 3 for Creative Control mode; see that chapter for details about selecting one of the settings.

If you want to protect against accidentally leaving one of the effects activated, you can go to the main options screen for Filter Settings and select Simultaneous Record Without Filter. That option can be selected only when Filter Effect is turned on through the menu.

If you turn this option on, then, when you take a picture using one of the special effects, such as Expressive, Retro, or Soft Focus, the camera also takes an image at the same time that does not use that effect. This feature offers protection against accidentally taking a picture with the Filter Settings feature turned on, resulting in an image that is not usable for ordinary purposes because of the special coloration or other effects.

You have to have one of the Filter Effects turned on and Quality set to Standard or Fine in order to turn this simultaneous recording option on. If you do that, then, when all filter effects are turned off, this option will be turned off. However, if you have not purposely turned this option off, it will turn itself back on automatically as soon as you activate a filter effect. So, I recommend that you turn on a filter effect, turn on this menu option, and then turn off the filter effect. In that way, this option will be available when needed.

As with the Creative Control settings, the Filter Effects settings do not affect Raw files when those files are opened on a computer. So, if you want to use one of these effects, you should shoot with Quality set to Fine or Raw & Fine. However, as I noted in Chapter 3, the Irfanview program can recover an effect from a Raw file by extracting the preview JPEG image from the Raw file.

ASPECT RATIO

This menu option has four settings, as shown in Figure 4-16: 4:3, 3:2, 16:9, and 1:1, representing the ratio of the width of an image to its vertical height.

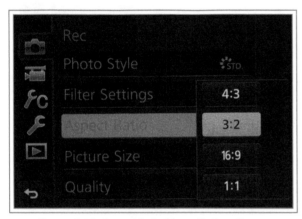

Figure 4-16. Aspect Ratio Menu Options Screen

This setting does not affect just the shape of the image; it also helps determine how many megapixels (MP or M) an image contains. When the aspect ratio is set to 3:2, the maximum resolution of 20 MP is available. When the aspect ratio is set to 4:3, the greatest possible resolution is 17.5 MP. At 16:9, the greatest possible resolution is 17 MP. At the 1:1 ratio, the largest resolution available is 13.5 MP. If you want to view the scene using the entire area of the LCD screen, choose 3:2, which is the aspect ratio of the screen. With 4:3, there will be black bars at the sides of the screen as you compose your shot; with 16:9, there will be black bars at the top and bottom of the screen; with 1:1, there will be black bars at the sides.

Figures 4-17 through 4-20 show the shapes of images taken with the FZ2500's various aspect ratio settings.

Figure 4-17. Aspect Ratio Set to 4:3

Figure 4-18. Aspect Ratio Set to 3:2

Figure 4-19. Aspect Ratio Set to 16:9

Figure 4-20. Aspect Ratio Set to 1:1

In Figure 4-17, the aspect ratio is set to 4:3. This aspect ratio crops the image slightly in the horizontal direction. Figure 4-18 is an image taken with the 3:2 setting, which uses the maximum number of available horizontal and vertical pixels. For Figure 4-19, the aspect ratio was set to the 16:9 position, which uses the maximum number of horizontal pixels, and crops the vertical pixels. Finally, the 1:1 setting was used for Figure 4-20. This setting uses the maximum number of vertical pixels, but crops the pixels in the horizontal direction.

PICTURE SIZE

This next item on the Recording menu controls the number of megapixels in the images you record with the camera, up to and including its maximum of 20 MP. The maximum available MP setting when using the L (for Large) setting for Picture Size is affected by the aspect ratio that you have set using the Aspect Ratio menu item, discussed above. If you set the aspect ratio to 3:2, the maximum Picture Size setting is the full 20 MP, as shown in Figure 4-21, using the full horizontal and vertical extent of the available pixels on the sensor.

Figure 4-21. Picture Size Highlighted on Recording Menu

As noted above in connection with the Aspect Ratio setting, the number of megapixels decreases with other aspect ratio settings.

The higher the Picture Size setting, the better the quality of the image, all other factors being equal. However, you can create a fuzzy and low-quality image with a high Picture Size setting; this setting does not guarantee a great image. But if other factors are equal, a higher megapixel count should yield higher image quality. Also, when you have a large megapixel count in your image, you have some leeway for cropping; you can

select a portion of the image to enlarge to the full size of the print, with good image quality.

On the other hand, images with high megapixel counts eat up storage space more quickly than those with low megapixel counts. If you are running low on space on your SD card and still have a lot of images to capture, you may need to reduce the Picture Size setting so you can fit more images on the card.

As noted earlier, the Picture Size setting is dimmed and unavailable when you have selected Raw for the Quality setting. However, if you select Raw & Fine or Raw & Standard, with which the camera records both a Raw and a JPEG image, the Picture Size option is available for setting the size of the JPEG image.

If 4K Photo is turned on through the drive mode dial, the Picture Size menu options change, because 4K Photo images use fewer pixels than normal images.

Extra Optical Zoom

Another point to consider in setting Picture Size is how much zoom power you need to have available. You might not think that picture size is related to zoom, but with the FZ2500 it is. The camera has a feature called Extra Optical Zoom, designated as EX. When you set the Picture Size to 5 MP (S), for example (with aspect ratio of 3:2), you can zoom in farther than you can with Picture Size set to its maximum. You will see an EX designation appear on the menu screen to the left of the Picture Size setting of S, as shown in Figure 4-22.

Figure 4-22. Picture Size Item with EX Designation

You will not see the EX designation unless Quality is set to Fine or Standard, because Extra Optical Zoom is not available with Quality set to Raw. This feature also is incompatible with some other settings, such as 4K Photo, Post Focus, Handheld Night Shot, Multiple

Exposure, HDR, Macro Zoom, and others. It cannot be used when recording movies.

You will see that the zoom scale goes beyond the normal optical zoom limit of 480mm as you move the zoom lever on top of the camera toward the T setting, for Telephoto, as shown in Figure 4-23.

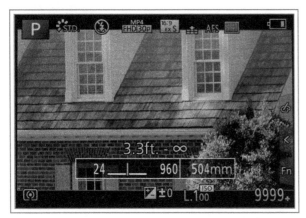

Figure 4-23. Zoom Scale with Extra Optical Zoom in Effect

Depending on the Picture Size setting, the scale will extend to a zoom level of as much as twice normal, or an equivalent of 960mm. (If you turn on Intelligent Zoom or Digital Zoom, discussed later in this chapter, the zoom range will extend even farther; for now, I am assuming that both of those options are turned off.)

To summarize the situation with Extra Optical Zoom, whenever you set Picture Quality to a level below Large, you gain additional zoom power because of the reduced resolution. You could achieve the same result by taking the picture at the normal zoom range with Picture Size set to the full 20M and then cropping the image in your computer to enlarge just the part you want. But with Extra Optical Zoom, you get the benefit of seeing a larger image on the display when you're composing the picture, and the benefit of having the camera perform its focus and exposure operations on the actual zoomed image that you want to capture, so the feature is not useless. You just need to decide whether it's of use to you in a particular situation.

I'll discuss Intelligent Zoom and Digital Zoom later, in the discussion of other Recording Menu options.

QUALITY

The next setting on the Recording menu is Quality. It's important to distinguish the Quality setting from the Picture Size setting. Picture Size concerns the

image's resolution, or the number of megapixels in the image. Quality has to do with how the image's digital information is compressed for storage on the SD card and, later, on the computer's hard drive. There are three levels of quality available in various combinations: Raw, Fine, and Standard, as shown in Figure 4-24. From the top, the five icons stand for Fine, Standard, Raw & Fine, Raw & Standard, and Raw.

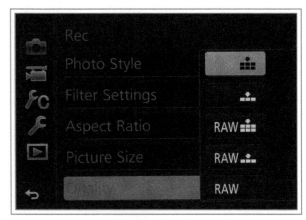

Figure 4-24. Quality Menu Options Screen

Raw is in a category by itself. There are both pros and cons to using Raw in this camera. First, the cons. A Raw file takes up a lot of space on your memory card, and, if you copy it to your computer, a lot of space on your hard drive. In addition, there are various functions of the FZ2500 that don't work when you're using Raw, including panorama shooting, Digital Zoom, Intelligent Zoom, Extra Optical Zoom, Macro Zoom, Resize, Cropping, Title Edit, Text Stamp, Favorite, Print Set (printing directly to a photo printer), and White Balance Bracket. You also cannot get the benefit of using the Filter Settings menu option or Creative Control mode to add picture effects to your images, though you can use those effects when shooting with Raw for Quality. (The resulting image will show the effect when displayed in the camera, but not when opened on a computer unless you can extract the JPEG file embedded in the Raw file.)

You cannot shoot in Raw quality with the Handheld Night Shot, 4K Photo, Post Focus, or HDR options. Burst shooting will be slowed down when shooting in Raw.

Finally, you may have problems working with Raw files on your computer because of incompatibility with editing software, though those problems can be overcome by getting updates for your program.

On the other hand, using Raw files has several advantages. The main benefit is that Raw files give you a large amount of control and flexibility with your images. When you open up a Raw file in a compatible photo-editing program, the software gives you the opportunity to correct problems with exposure, white balance, color tints, sharpness, and other settings. If you had the aperture of the camera too narrow when you took the picture, and it looks badly underexposed, you can make exposure adjustments in the software and recover the image to a proper brightness level. Similarly, you can adjust the white balance after the fact and remove unwanted color casts. In effect, you get a second chance at making the correct settings, rather than being stuck with an unusable image because of unfortunate settings when you pressed the shutter button.

For example, Figure 4-25 is an image I took with Quality set to Raw, but with settings purposely made to result in underexposure and incorrect white balance.

Figure 4-25. Raw Image Taken with Abnormal Settings

Figure 4-26 is the same image after I opened it using Adobe Camera Raw software and made corrections after the fact. The corrected image looks essentially as if it had been shot with proper settings to begin with.

The drawbacks to using Raw files are either not too severe or they are counterbalanced by the flexibility Raw gives you. The large size of the files may be an inconvenience, but the increasing size of hard drives and SD cards, with steadily dropping prices, makes file size much less of a concern than previously. I have had problems with Raw files not loading when I didn't have the latest Camera Raw plug-in for Adobe Photoshop or Photoshop Elements, but with a little effort, you can download an updated plug-in and the software will then process and display your Raw images. Panasonic provides a free download of Silkypix, a program for

processing Raw files, so you don't have to buy any additional software to process Raw files.

Figure 4-26. Raw Image After Adjustments in Software

You don't have to use Raw, but you may be missing some opportunities if you avoid it.

The other two settings for Quality—Fine and Standard—are levels of compression for digital image files that use the JPEG standard. Images saved with Fine quality are subjected to less compression than those saved with Standard quality. In other words, Standard-quality images have their digital data "compressed" or "squeezed" down to a smaller size to allow more of the files to be stored on a memory card or computer drive, with a corresponding loss of image quality. The more compression an image is subjected to, the less clear detail it will contain. So unless you are running out of space on your storage medium, you probably should leave the Quality setting at Fine to ensure the best quality. (Of course, you may prefer to shoot in the Raw format for maximum quality and flexibility in editing.)

With the FZ2500, besides choosing one of the individual Quality settings (Raw, Fine, or Standard), you also have the option of setting the camera to record images in Raw plus either Fine or Standard. If you choose that option, the camera will record each image in two files—one Raw, and the other a JPEG file in either Fine or Standard quality, depending on your selection. If you play the image back in the camera, you will see only one image, but if you copy the files to your computer, you will find two image files—one with a .jpg extension and one with an .rw2 extension. The Raw file will be much larger than the JPEG one. In a few examples I have saved on my computer, the Raw files from the FZ2500 are all about 22 MB and JPEG files with Picture Size set to Large are between about 4 and 10 MB. (Note that MB stands for megabytes, a measure of file size, as distinguished from

MP or M, meaning megapixels, a measure of the number of pixels in an image.)

Why would you choose the option of recording images in Raw and JPEG at the same time? If you're taking pictures of a one-time event such as a wedding or graduation, you may want to preserve them in Raw for highest quality and later processing with software, but also have them available for quick review on a computer that might not have software that reads Raw files. Or, you might want to be able to send the images to friends or post them to social media sites without first converting them from Raw into a JPEG format that is easily viewed on computers or mobile devices. Also, as I discussed earlier, if you are using Creative Control mode or the Filter Settings menu option to add special effects to images, those effects will not show up in Raw files when the files are opened on a computer. In order to have the benefit of the special setting as well as the benefits of a Raw file, you can use the Raw & Fine or Raw & Standard option to record images both ways.

The next menu options to discuss are on screen 2 of the Recording menu, shown in Figure 4-27.

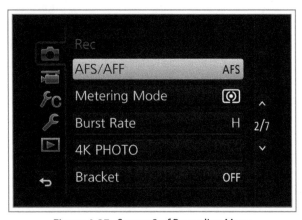

Figure 4-27. Screen 2 of Recording Menu

AFS/AFF

This next menu option lets you choose how the autofocus system operates when the camera is using the AFS/AFF setting of the focus mode lever. As I will discuss in Chapter 5, that lever, located on the camera's back to the right of the viewfinder window, has three positions: AFS/AFF, AFC, and MF. If you choose AFC, the camera uses continuous autofocus; if you choose MF, the camera uses manual focus. If you set the lever to the AFS/AFF position, you can use this menu option to determine whether the camera uses the AFS or AFF setting.

With AFS, for autofocus single, when you press the shutter button halfway, the camera locks focus on the subject and keeps it locked while the button is held there, even if the subject moves. With AFF, for autofocus flexible, the camera locks focus but will adjust focus if the subject (or the camera) moves.

If you are shooting images of a landscape or other stationary subject, AFS will work well. The camera will lock focus and keep it there, and the battery will not be drained by adjusting focus. If you are shooting handheld shots at a fairly close distance, though, you might want to use the AFF setting because the camera will adjust the focus if the camera moves slightly, and the focus could be thrown off by that movement, especially when the focus distance is small or the lens is zoomed in.

If you are shooting pictures of children or pets moving around unpredictably, you may want to use the AFF setting and let the camera continue to adjust focus as needed. With that setting, the camera's battery will be drained faster than with AFS, but it may be worth it to capture an action shot in sharp focus.

This setting is fixed at AFS in Panorama mode. This menu option is not available when 4K Photo or Post Focus is in use.

METERING MODE

The next option on the Recording menu lets you choose the method the camera uses to meter the light and determine the proper exposure. The choices are Multiple, Center-weighted, or Spot. If you choose Multiple, the camera evaluates the brightness at multiple spots in the image shown on the display, and calculates an exposure that takes into account all of the various values. With Center-weighted, the camera gives greater emphasis to the brightness of the subject(s) in the center of the screen, while still taking into account the brightness of other areas in the image. With Spot, the camera evaluates only the brightness of the subject(s) in the small spot-metering area.

The Panasonic user's manual recommends Multiple mode for normal usage, presumably on the theory that it produces a reasonable exposure based on the overall brightness of the scene. However, if you want to make sure that one particular item in the scene is properly exposed, you may want to use the Spot method, and aim the spot metering area at that object or person, then lock in the exposure. The Spot option is useful when you are photographing a performer who is lit by a spotlight on stage. For a shot with a central subject of prime importance, such as a portrait, the Center-weighted option may work best.

To make this selection, scroll to the line for Metering Mode, then press the Right button to activate the sub-menu with the three choices, as shown in Figure 4-28.

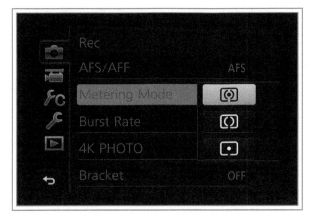

Figure 4-28. Metering Mode Menu Options Screen

The first icon, a rectangle with a circle and a dot inside, represents Multiple mode; the second, a rectangle with a circle inside, represents Center-weighted; and the third, a rectangle with just a dot inside, represents Spot.

With Multiple or Center-weighted, the metering process is simple: Point the camera at the subject(s) you want and let the camera compute the exposure. If you choose Spot as your metering technique, the process can be more involved. Presumably, you will have a fairly small area in mind as the most important area for having the correct exposure; perhaps it is a small object you are photographing for an online auction.

The LCD screen will display a small blue cross in the center of the focusing brackets, as shown in Figure 4-29, and you need to be sure that the cross is over the most important object.

If your subject is not in the center of the screen, you may need to lock the exposure while the Spot-metering cross is on the subject, and then move the camera so the subject is in the proper part of the scene. To do this, press the shutter button halfway while the cross is on the subject, and hold it in that position while you move the camera back to the final position for your composition. (You also can use the AF/AE Lock button for this operation, as discussed in Chapter 5.)

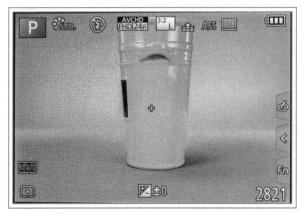

Figure 4-29. Blue Cross for Spot Metering Area

As another option, there is a sparsely-documented feature of the camera that lets you move the little cross around the camera's screen so you can place it directly over the area of the picture that you want properly exposed. This will work only if, in addition to using the Spot metering mode, you are using one of the AF Mode settings that let you move the autofocus area, such as 1-Area or Face/Eye Detection, as discussed in Chapter 5. In that case, whenever you move the focusing target, the Spot-metering target moves along with it, so the target serves two purposes at once. For example, Figure 4-30 shows the display when both Spot metering and 1-Area autofocus are in effect.

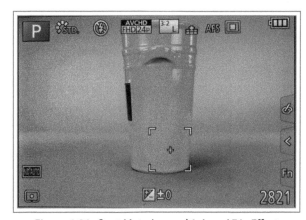

Figure 4-30. Spot Metering and 1-Area AF in Effect

The Metering Mode setting is not available in Intelligent Auto mode, Intelligent Auto Plus mode, or Scene mode. When Multiple metering is selected and AF Mode is set to Face/Eye Detection or Tracking, the camera will attempt to expose a person's face or the tracked subject correctly. The current setting for Metering Mode is indicated by an icon in the lower left of the display, as shown in Figures 4-29 and 4-30.

BURST RATE

This next item on screen 2 of the Recording menu sets the rate for burst shooting. The control for turning on burst shooting is the drive mode dial, located at the left side of the camera's top. That dial selects the drive mode settings, including burst shooting, 4K Photo, Post Focus, the self-timer, and interval shooting, as discussed in Chapter 5. However, in order to choose the rate of speed for burst shooting, you have to use this Burst Rate menu option. The choices for burst rate are H, M, and L, for high, medium, and low. I will discuss those options in Chapter 5, in connection with the drive mode options.

4K PHOTO

The 4K Photo menu option, like the Burst Rate option, works together with the burst-shooting features of the FZ2500. 4K Photo is a special sub-option of drive mode. You activate 4K Photo by turning the drive mode dial to the 4K position. In order to choose a sub-option for the 4K Photo shooting, you have to use the 4K Photo menu option. I will discuss the details of the various 4K Photo settings in Chapter 5, where I discuss the physical controls.

BRACKET

The Bracket menu option gives you access to several ways to take a series of images with one press of the shutter button, using a different value for a particular setting for each of those images. In this way, you will have several images to choose from, increasing your chance of having one that suits your needs for that setting. The settings that can be varied are exposure, aperture, focus, and white balance.

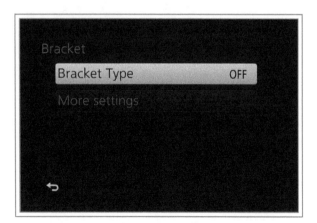

Figure 4-31. Bracket Menu Options Screen

After highlighting the Bracket menu option, select it to move to the next screen, shown in Figure 4-31.

On that screen, select Bracket Type, and the camera will display the menu shown in Figure 4-32, with a vertical line of five icons. From the top, the first four icons represent exposure bracket, aperture bracket, focus bracket, and white balance bracket. I will discuss each of these in turn below.

Figure 4-32. Screen to Select Bracket Type

Exposure Bracket

When you select this first bracket option, the camera varies the exposure within a range you select so you will have several differently exposed images to choose from. This option gives you an added chance of getting a usable image. If you're shooting with Raw quality, exposure is not so much of an issue, because you can adjust it later with your software, but it's always a good idea to start with an exposure that's as accurate as possible.

Also, you can use this feature to take several differently exposed shots that you can merge into a single HDR image, in which the images combine to cover a wider range of lights and darks than any single image could. This merging can be accomplished using software such as Photoshop (use the command File-Automate-Merge to HDR Pro) or a more specialized program such as PhotoAcute or Photomatix Pro. For HDR shooting, I suggest you set the interval between the exposures to the largest amount available, which is 1 EV (exposure value). If possible, you should use a tripod so all of the images will include the same area of the subject and can be easily merged in the software.

Once you have selected this option from the Bracket menu, the More Settings menu option becomes available for selection. Select it, and the camera displays the screen shown in Figure 4-33, with options for Step, Sequence, and Single Shot Setting. First, select Step, which lets you choose the interval for the exposure difference among the multiple shots the camera will take. When you press the Menu/Set button with that option highlighted, the camera displays the screen shown in Figure 4-34, which lets you set the number of exposures and the EV interval.

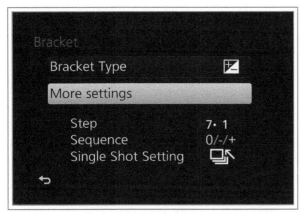

Figure 4-33. Exposure Bracket More Settings Screen

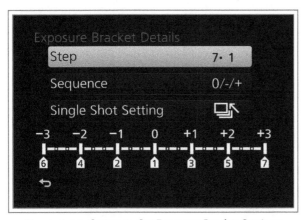

Figure 4-34. Screen to Set Exposure Bracket Settings

Then turn the front or rear dial, press the Up and Down buttons, or touch the screen icons to scroll through the nine possible options. These options let you choose three, five, or seven images, taken at EV intervals of 1/3, 2/3, or one. For example, if you select the 5·2/3 option, the camera will take five images with an interval of 2/3 stop between them.

After selecting the Step option, press the Fn6 button to return to the Exposure Bracket Details screen and select Sequence. The camera will display two options at the right side of the screen: 0/-/+ and -/0/+, as shown in Figure 4-35.

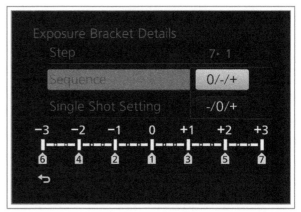

Figure 4-35. Sequence Options for Exposure Bracket

With the first option (the default), the exposures will be in order of normal exposure, followed by lower and then higher. With the second option, the exposures will be in order of lowest to highest. As you can see in Figures 4-34 through 4-36, the camera will display markers at the bottom of the screen indicating the order in which the images will be taken, using your chosen settings.

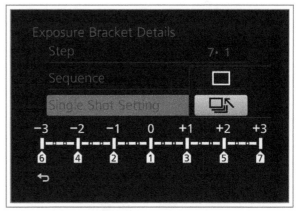

Figure 4-36. Single Shot/Burst Options for Exposure Bracket

Next, proceed to the Single Shot Setting option and select it. The camera will display the two options shown in Figure 4-36. With the top option, the camera will take the multiple (three, five, or seven) shots individually; with the bottom option, the camera will take all of the shots in a continuous burst and you will hear multiple shutter sounds as the exposures are recorded. You may want to use the individual-shots option if you need to pause after each exposure so you can evaluate the scene, adjust costumes or props, and the like. With that setting, you have to press the shutter button to take each shot in the series.

When exposure bracketing (or another type of bracketing) is turned on, the camera displays an icon for that setting in the bottom center of the display, as shown in Figure 4-37.

Figure 4-37. Bracket Icon on Shooting Screen

Aperture Bracket

This option, which is available only in Aperture Priority or Manual exposure mode, sets the camera to take a series of images using different aperture settings, so you can test various approaches in order to vary the depth of field or blur the background. After you select the F icon on the Bracket Type menu that represents the f-stop (aperture), go to the More Settings menu option and you will see the screen shown in Figure 4-38.

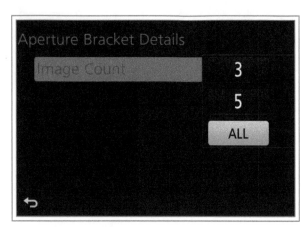

Figure 4-38. Aperture Bracket Details Screen

Select Image Count, and you will see a screen with choices of 3, 5, or All, to select the number of different aperture settings the camera will use in its aperture bracket set.

Press the shutter button halfway or press the Fn6 button multiple times to return to the shooting screen. The camera will display a small BKT icon above the number of the f-stop that is currently selected. You can still change the initial aperture setting for the bracket; just turn the front or rear dial to do so.

When you are ready, press the shutter button and the camera will take the specified series of images in a burst, starting with the aperture that is currently set. The order of the images it takes is determined by the initial aperture and that aperture's position on the aperture scale. For example, if the initial aperture is f/2.8 and three images are selected for Image Count, the resulting images will be at f/2.8, f/4.0, and f/5.6.

If the initial aperture is f/11.0, the three images will be at f/11.0, f/8.0. and f/5.6. If Image Count is set to All and the initial aperture is f/5.6, the order of the images taken will be f/5.6, f/4.0, f/8.0, f/3.0, and f/11.0, because it would not be possible for the images to proceed in ascending or descending order through the whole group of apertures. Of course, if the lens is zoomed in to 250mm or beyond, the widest aperture that can be included in the series will be f/4.5, because that is the widest aperture available at that focal length.

As noted above, the Aperture Bracket option is available only with the two shooting modes in which it is possible for the user to change the aperture: Aperture Priority and Manual exposure. However, with Manual exposure, Aperture Bracket is available only when Auto ISO is in effect.

Focus Bracket

This next option for bracketing sets the camera to take a series of images with different focus settings, so you can decide later which image has the focus point in the best location for your needs. This is a very useful option, because it helps you avoid the frustration of finding out after the fact that the camera focused on the wrong subject, or that the focus was slightly off of the subject you wanted to concentrate on. You can cause the camera to produce a large number of alternative shots and choose the one(s) with the best focus at your leisure.

After you select Focus on the Bracket Type menu, select the More Settings menu item, and the camera will display the screen shown in Figure 4-39, with options for Step, Image Count, and Sequence. You can set Step to any value from 1 to 10, which determines how much the camera will alter focus from one image to the next. Image Count can be set to any number from 1 to 999. If Sequence is set to 0/-/+, the camera varies the focus to points both closer and farther from the lens than the original focus point. If Sequence is set to 0/+, then the camera varies the focus only to points farther from the lens than the original focus point.

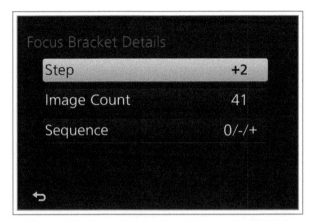

Figure 4-39. Focus Bracket More Settings Highlighted

With the Focus Bracket option, the resulting images are treated by the camera as a burst of shots. That means that, in order to view them in the camera, you need to use the playback controls for bursts. As shown in Figure 4-40, for a burst of Focus Bracket images in playback mode, the camera displays an icon at the lower left of the screen that says Focus, with a down-pointing arrow. This means that, in order to view the images within the burst, you have to press the Down button.

Figure 4-40. Focus Bracket Playback Screen

After you do that, the icons on the screen change, as shown in Figure 4-41, indicating that you can now view the individual images in the Focus Bracket series by scrolling through them with the normal playback controls. You can then use the Right and Left buttons, the front and rear dials, or the touch screen to scroll through the images to find the ones with the best focus.

The numbers in the upper right corner, 3/9 in this example, indicate that the current image is the third in a series of nine images. You will not be able to view any images outside of that set of images unless you

press the Down button again to return to the normal playback mode, in which the Focus Bracket burst is displayed as a single image. You also can press the Up button, which takes you to a screen for uploading the images via Wi-Fi, as discussed in Chapter 9.

Figure 4-41. Focus Bracket Playback Screen After Pressing Down Button

Of course, you also can use the Post Focus option, which uses the camera's 4K video recording capability to record a burst of images from which you can select those with the best focus, but Focus Bracket lets you use more of the advanced Shooting menu options, without the constraints imposed by using 4K video-oriented settings.

White Balance Bracket

Before selecting White Balance Bracket, make sure you have the white balance setting selected as you want it; that setting is made by pressing the Right button and then selecting a setting such as Auto White Balance, Daylight, Cloudy, Shade, and the like. Once that setting has been made, go to the Bracket menu option and select WB for the Bracket Type option, then select the More Settings menu item. The camera will display the white balance color axes adjustment screen, as shown in Figure 4-42. This screen includes a color chart with two axes, labeled G-M for green-magenta and A-B for amber-blue.

Figure 4-42. White Balance Bracket - Color Axes

When this screen is displayed, you need to decide on which axis to set the bracketing: the amber-blue axis, or the magenta-green axis. If you want to use the amber-blue axis, turn the front or rear dial to the right; if you want to use the magenta-green axis, turn either of those dials to the left. As you turn the dial in either direction, you will see small circles appear on the chosen axis. The circles will spread apart as you continue to turn the dial. The final positions of those circles indicate the differences among the three shots that the camera will take. If you have also made an adjustment to the overall white balance setting using the adjustment screen (as discussed in Chapter 5), the white balance bracketing will take the adjustment into account and bracket the exposures with the adjustment factored in.

Figure 4-43. White Balance Bracket Setting in Place

For example, Figure 4-43 shows white balance bracketing set up to take its three shots with the greatest possible differences along the amber-blue axis.

Once the circles are set up as illustrated here, press the Fn6 button until the shooting screen is restored, or press the shutter button halfway to return to that screen.

The display will then show the BKT icon just above the icon for the white balance setting, in the lower right corner of the display. Now, when you press the shutter button, the camera will take three pictures with different white balance adjustments, from more amber to more blue. You will only hear the sound of the shutter once, though; the camera alters the white balance settings electronically. To cancel the bracketing, return to the adjustment screen and press the Display button.

This function does not work with Intelligent Auto mode, Panorama mode, Creative Control mode, Raw images, or with certain other settings, including HDR, 4K Photo, Post Focus, burst shooting, and Time Lapse Shot.

You also can turn on White Balance Bracket without using this menu option. After pressing the Right button to get to the white balance menu, press the Down button to get to the adjustment screen, then turn the front dial or rear dial to set the bracketing as you want it.

None of the bracketing options are available with the basic Intelligent Auto mode, Panorama mode, or when shooting movies, nor with several other settings, including some Scene mode and Creative Control mode options. The flash can be used with White Balance Bracket, but not with the other Bracket settings. Bracket options are not canceled when the camera is turned off, so be sure to cancel any bracket setting when you have finished using the feature.

Screen 3 of the Recording menu is shown in Figure 4-44.

Figure 4-44. Screen 3 of Recording Menu

SELF-TIMER

The first option on this menu screen is another one that lets you adjust settings for a drive mode setting. With this option, you can set the self-timer to a delay of two seconds or ten seconds for a single shot, or to a delay of ten seconds for a series of three shots. In Chapter 5, I will discuss the use of the drive mode dial to turn on the self-timer.

TIME LAPSE/ANIMATION

This menu option, like the previous one, lets you make settings for a feature that is activated using the drive mode dial, in this case the last position on that dial, which provides for time lapse shooting or stop motion animation. In order to determine how the camera will behave when you turn the drive mode dial to that position, you have to use this menu item. I will discuss the use of this option in Chapter 5, where I discuss the drive mode dial and other physical controls.

HIGHLIGHT SHADOW

This menu option gives you a tool for adjusting the highlights and shadows in your images and videos. It is available only with the more advanced shooting modes: Program, Aperture Priority, Shutter Priority, Manual, and Creative Video. When you select this menu option, the camera displays a screen like that shown in Figure 4-45, with seven small icons at the bottom available for selection.

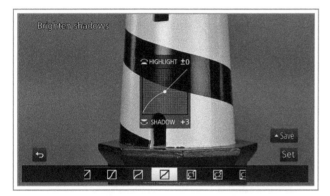

Figure 4-45. Highlight Shadow Menu Options Screen

(For this illustration I have scrolled to the fourth icon, so all seven icons are visible.) Each small icon represents a different curve shape for the larger graph in the center of the screen, which includes a line that represents the adjustments to highlights and shadows for your images. When the line is a straight diagonal, no adjustments are present. When the upper part of the line bulges to the left, highlights are increased. When it bulges to the right, the brightness of highlights is lowered. Similarly, the lower part of the line bulges to the left or right to increase or decrease the brightness of shadow areas.

The first four icons are presets for standard (no adjustments), higher contrast (highlights brighter and shadows darker), lower contrast (highlights darker and shadows brighter), and brighten shadows. The last three icons represent custom settings 1, 2, and 3.

If you want to use one of the four presets, just select it. If you want to make other adjustments, you can select any one of the seven icons and make adjustments to the settings. To make the highlights brighter, turn the front dial to the right; to make them darker, turn it to the left. To make the shadows brighter, turn the rear dial to the right; to make them darker, turn it to

the left. You also can adjust the curves by moving the graph lines with your finger on the touch screen. When you have adjusted the curves as you want, press the Up button to save the settings. You will then see the screen shown in Figure 4-46, prompting you to select Custom 1, 2, or 3 as the slot in which to save your settings.

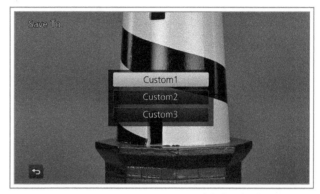

Figure 4-46. Screen to Save Custom Highlight Shadow Setting

Highlight any one of those and press the Menu/Set button to save the settings. Then, whenever you want to recall those settings, go to the Highlight Shadow menu option and select the Custom 1, 2, or 3 icon, depending on which slot you used to save your custom settings.

If you press the Display button, the camera will switch to a display like that in Figure 4-47, with the graph at the right side and the live view in a large area at the left, so you can more easily see what effect the current setting will have on your images. Press the Display button again to switch back to the original view.

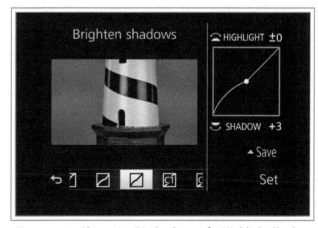

Figure 4-47. Alternative Display Screen for Highlight Shadow

The Highlight Shadow option can be useful if you are often faced with situations with your subject partly in shadow and partly in bright light. It can be particularly helpful because you can see the effects of the adjustments you make on the live view, as you turn the dials to adjust highlights and shadows. Of course, the FZ2500 also has other options to deal with that situation, such as the HDR setting, discussed later in this chapter, and the Intelligent Dynamic setting, discussed next.

INTELLIGENT DYNAMIC

The next option on screen 3 of the Recording menu is shown as i.Dynamic, which I will refer to here as Intelligent Dynamic. This option gives you another way to accomplish what the Highlight Shadow option does—that is, to deal with a situation in which there is considerable contrast between the dark and bright areas of the scene. This option, unlike the previous one, does not let you make precise adjustments to the shadow and highlight curves. Instead, it adjusts contrast and exposure generally; it lets you set the intensity of the camera's adjustments to a level of Low, Standard, or High, as shown in Figure 4-48.

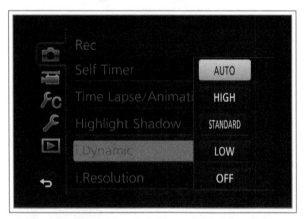

Figure 4-48. i.Dynamic Menu Options Screen

You also can leave the option turned off, or you can set it to Auto and let the camera make the adjustments based on its analysis of the scene. Like the Highlight Shadow option, this setting is available with the advanced shooting modes, but, unlike that option, Intelligent Dynamic also is available with Scene mode. It is not available when HDR is turned on through the Recording menu.

Figures 4-49 and 4-50 are images with two views looking down a wooden staircase, partly in sunlight and partly in deep shade.

As you can see, in Figure 4-49, with Intelligent Dynamic turned off, the contrast is quite stark. In Figure 4-50, with Intelligent Dynamic set to High, the contrast is evened out and the shadowed areas are brightened

noticeably. This is a good setting to use when you are taking photos in an area with both sunlight and shade.

Figure 4-49. i.Dynamic Turned Off

Figure 4-50. iDynamic Set to High

INTELLIGENT RESOLUTION

This last setting on the third screen of the Recording menu is shown as i.Resolution, which I will call Intelligent Resolution. This option can be set to Off, Extended, Low, Standard, or High, as shown in Figure 4-51.

Figure 4-51. i.Resolution Menu Options Screen

It is available with all shooting modes except for Intelligent Auto and Intelligent Auto Plus. However, the Extended setting is automatically reduced to Low when shooting motion pictures or using the 4K Photo or Post Focus features.

This setting increases the apparent resolution in images by providing additional sharpening through in-camera digital manipulation. It does seem to improve image quality somewhat in certain situations. I recommend that you try shooting with it turned on and off to see if it provides actual benefits for your shots. I do not often use it myself, because I prefer to shoot with Raw quality and add sharpening with my editing software.

Screen 4 of the Recording menu is shown in Figure 4-52.

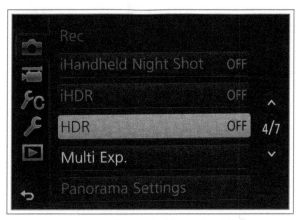

Figure 4-52. Screen 4 of Recording Menu

iHandheld Night Shot

This setting is available for selection only when the camera is set to Intelligent Auto or Intelligent Auto Plus mode. (It appears on the second of two screens when the camera is in the basic Intelligent Auto mode.) This option is designed to minimize the motion blur that can result from taking a handheld shot at the slow shutter speed that is likely to be needed to get a sufficient exposure at night. If the camera detects darkness and senses that it is handheld, the camera will raise its ISO setting in order to permit the use of a faster than normal shutter speed. Also, because using a higher ISO can increase the visual "noise" or grainy look in an image, the camera will take a burst of several shots and combine them internally into a final image. By blending the contents of several images together, the camera can reduce the noise in the final, composite result. This setting is a useful one to activate when shooting in low-light conditions without flash or a tripod.

You cannot decide when to capture an image with this feature yourself—all you can do is turn it on and see if the camera determines that conditions call for it to be used. You cannot use the flash, burst shooting, 4K Photo, Post Focus, bracketing, time lapse shooting, auto stop motion animation, or the Raw setting for Quality with this setting turned on.

If you want to have more control over the use of this setting, you can turn the mode dial to the SCN position and select scene type number 17, Handheld Night Shot.

iHDR

The next menu option, iHDR, is another one that is available only when Intelligent Auto or Intelligent Auto Plus mode is in use, and only when the camera determines that its use is called for. (It is on screen 2 of the Recording menu in Intelligent Auto mode.) In this case, the option is triggered when the camera detects a scene with strong contrast between the dark and light areas. When the camera makes that determination, the FZ2500 will take a burst of shots and combine them internally to create a final result. In this situation, the camera will place on the screen a message saying HDR Shutters 3 to let you know that the shutter will fire three times. You should try to hold the camera steady while it takes the burst of shots.

I will discuss high dynamic range, or HDR photography, further in the next section of this chapter. Essentially, with HDR, the camera combines the most normally exposed parts of multiple images in order to achieve a final result that appears to be properly exposed throughout most or all of its various areas. This setting can be useful when you are taking photographs in highly contrasty conditions. If you want to use HDR in more advanced shooting modes, see the discussion below.

HDR

The option discussed directly above, iHDR, is activated only when the camera determines that it is needed, in Intelligent Auto or Intelligent Auto Plus mode. If you want to use the FZ2500's built-in HDR capability on your own terms, you can set the camera to one of the PASM modes and choose this HDR option on screen 4 of the Recording menu.

HDR photography was developed because cameras, whether using film or digital sensors, cannot record images that retain clear details when the scene includes wide variations in brightness. If part of the scene is in dark shadows and another part is brightly lighted, the scene has a "dynamic range" that may exceed the ability of the camera to expose both the dark and the bright areas in a way that looks good to the human eye.

One way to deal with this issue is to take multiple shots of the scene using different exposure settings, so the photographer has a range of shots, some exposed to favor dark areas, and some to favor bright areas. The photographer merges those images using Photoshop or special HDR software to blend differently exposed portions from all of the shots. The end result is a composite HDR image that can exhibit clear details in all parts of the image.

More recently, camera makers have incorporated HDR processing in their cameras to help the cameras even out areas of excessive brightness and darkness to preserve details, without the need to use software to merge multiple shots. With the FZ2500, Panasonic provides several settings that, to one degree or another, attempt to process shots of scenes with wide dynamic range to produce a pleasing result. I discussed earlier the Highlight Shadow, Intelligent Dynamic, and iHDR options. The HDR option is a more direct approach to using traditional HDR techniques. It lets you set up the camera to take a burst of shots at different exposure levels, and the camera combines the images internally to create a composite image with overall exposure that attempts to even out the areas of heaviest contrast.

When you select the HDR option, the camera displays a sub-menu with choices of On, Off, or Set. To use the HDR option, first select the Set item from this sub-menu. You will then see a menu with choices of Dynamic Range and Auto Align. Highlight Dynamic Range, press the Menu/Set button, and you will see the screen shown in Figure 4-53, letting you choose the exposure interval among the three shots the camera will take.

You can choose Auto, which causes the camera to choose an interval, or you can choose a specific EV interval of one, two or three stops. Use the higher settings for scenes involving relatively large degrees of contrast, such as a view including a shaded area next to an area in bright sunshine.

When you have set the interval, go back to the Auto Align option on the menu and set it either on or off.

If it is turned on, the camera will do its best to align the three shots automatically when it processes them internally. However, in doing so, it will crop them slightly in order to delete the outer edges of areas that are not in alignment. This setting is useful for handheld shots. If you are using a tripod, it is better to leave Auto Align turned off.

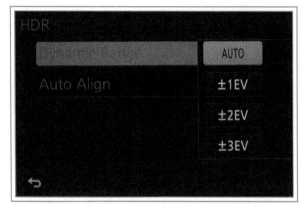

Figure 4-53. HDR Settings Screen

When the settings are all made, go back to the main HDR menu and set HDR to On. Then aim at the subject and press the shutter button. You will hear the shutter fire three times and a composite image will be saved to the memory card.

To test this feature, I took several shots of a watering can in conditions with bright light and shadows. In Figure 4-54, I took a shot with HDR turned off. In Figure 4-55, I used the HDR setting at an interval of EV1, and in Figure 4-56 I used an interval of EV3. Then, for Figure 4-57, I took a series of images using Manual exposure mode at various exposure levels, and combined them using Photomatix Pro HDR software.

Figure 4-54. HDR Turned Off

Figure 4-55. HDR Set to LV1

Figure 4-56. HDR Set to LV3

Figure 4-57. HDR Composite Image from Photomatix Pro

As you can see, the camera's HDR menu option did a fairly good job of reducing the heavy contrast, with more even exposure at the higher HDR setting, though the differences between the effects with LV1 and LV3 are not dramatic. The composite image from the HDR software did a better job, but that is to be expected. The in-camera HDR option is a useful one when you are confronted with a scene with sharp contrast between light and dark areas.

MULTIPLE EXPOSURE

The Multiple Exposure option is more in the category of creative photography than control of normal image-making. It lets you create double, triple, or quadruple exposures in the camera. The steps to take are a bit unusual, because you actually carry out the picture-taking through the Recording menu system.

On the Recording menu, highlight Multiple Exposure, then press the Right button (or touch the menu option on the screen), which takes you to a screen with the word Start highlighted, as shown in Figure 4-58.

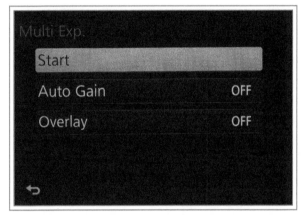

Figure 4-58. Initial Screen for Multiple Exposure Option

Unless you want to overlay new images on an existing Raw image, as discussed below, make sure the Overlay option is set to Off. Then press the Menu/Set button to select Start. The screen will have the notation Fn6 End displayed, meaning you can press the Fn6 button to end the process if you have had second thoughts.

If you are going to proceed, compose and take the first picture. At this point the screen will display the image you just took along with the choices Next, Retake, and Exit. If you're not satisfied with the first image, scroll to Retake and select that option with the Menu/Set button, then retake the first image. If you're ready to proceed to taking a superimposed image, leave Next highlighted and press the shutter button halfway down, or, if you prefer, press the Menu/Set button to select Next. Either action produces the interesting effect of leaving the first image on the screen and making the screen live at the same time to take a new image, as shown in Figure 4-59, where the large bottle was captured in the first shot, and the model lighthouse is being viewed live along with the recorded image of the bottle.

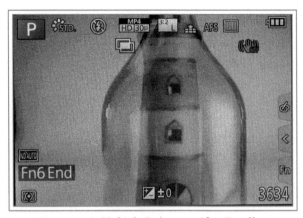

Figure 4-59. Multiple Exposure - After First Shot

Compose the second shot as you want it while viewing the first one, and press the shutter button fully to record that image. You can repeat this process to add a third image, retake the second image, or exit the whole process. You can then add a fourth image if you want. When you are done, you will have a single image that combines the two, three, or four superimposed images you recorded.

Before you take the images using the Multiple Exposure procedure, the menu gives you the option of setting Auto Gain on or off. If you leave it on, the camera adjusts the exposure based on the number of pictures taken; if you turn it off, the camera adjusts the exposure for the final superimposed image. In my experience, the On setting produces results with clearer images of the multiple scenes; Off produces images that may have excessive exposure.

You also have the option of starting with a Raw image that was taken earlier by this camera. It has to be a Raw image, not a JPEG one, and it has to have been taken in a mode in which Multiple Exposure is available, which means one of the PASM modes.

To use this option, set the Overlay option of the Multiple Exposure menu item to On. Then, from the Multiple Exposure screen, highlight Start and press the Menu/Set button. The camera will display your images in playback mode. Scroll through them until you find the Raw image you want to use as the first image in the multiple exposure series. When it is displayed, press the Menu/Set button to select it as the first image of the series. Then line up the next image, with the Raw image displayed on the screen, and press the shutter button to take the next image; it will be overlaid over the existing

Raw image. You can then proceed with the rest of the sequence, as before.

Figure 4-60. Multiple Exposure: Final Image

Figure 4-60 shows the final result of using the Multiple Exposure feature for the image of the lighthouse appearing to be inside the large bottle.

I have found that the Multiple Exposure feature usually works best if you remove the first item from the scene before taking the next shot. For example, in making the image shown here, I first photographed the bottle, then removed it from the scene before photographing the lighthouse. If you leave the first item in place, it is likely to overwhelm the other objects because it will be photographed more than once.

PANORAMA SETTINGS

The next menu option, which is available only when the mode dial is set to Panorama mode, has two sub-options that let you select the direction and image size for panoramic shots.

With the Direction sub-option, you can choose right, left, up, or down as the direction in which you will move the camera when shooting panoramas. The Picture Size sub-option lets you choose Standard or Wide for the size of your panoramic images. With Standard, the camera records the image at a higher pixel density, but in a smaller area. With Wide, the camera records a larger image but with fewer pixels in a given area.

With the Standard setting, a horizontal panorama has a width of 8176 pixels and a height of 1920 pixels. With the Wide setting, a horizontal panorama has a width of 8176 pixels and a height of 960 pixels, but it covers a much wider area than a Standard panorama. So, if you want the highest quality, choose Standard; choose Wide only if you need to include a very wide panorama in the image. (Similar considerations apply for vertically oriented panoramas.)

I discussed the procedure for panorama shooting in Chapter 3.

The options on screen 5 of the Recording menu are shown in Figure 4-61.

Figure 4-61. Screen 5 of Recording Menu

Shutter Type

The FZ2500 is equipped with two different types of shutter—electronic and mechanical. With this menu option, you can set the camera to choose the shutter type automatically, or you can select one or the other shutter type for use. The three options for this setting are Auto, MSHTR, and ESHTR. With Auto, the camera will choose the shutter type based on the current settings and conditions. With MSHTR or ESHTR, it will use only the mechanical or electronic shutter, depending on your selection.

For most purposes, the mechanical shutter is the better option. With that choice, the camera operates a physical iris with leaves that open and close to allow light to pass through to the sensor. With the electronic shutter, the circuitry in the camera starts and stops the exposure, with no mechanical parts involved. Therefore, the electronic shutter can produce faster shutter speeds than the mechanical one. Also, because of the lack of moving parts, the camera can remain silent when the electronic shutter is activated. However, using the electronic shutter can result in a "rolling" effect that distorts images or videos, especially if the camera or subject is moving horizontally.

If you select Auto or ESHTR, the shutter speed can be set as fast as 1/16000 second; with MSHTR, the fastest speed available is 1/4000 second, and that speed is available only when the aperture is set to f/4.5 or narrower (higher numbers). At wider apertures, the fastest shutter speed available is 1/2000 second.

I almost always leave this setting at Auto so the camera will use the electronic shutter when needed, but will use the mechanical shutter in most cases. One reason to turn on the ESHTR option is if you want the camera to remain completely silent for a particular shooting session. Another way to make the camera silent is to select the Silent Mode option on screen 1 of the Custom menu. In that case, the camera will automatically activate the electronic shutter, even if the MSHTR option had been selected on the Recording menu. With the electronic shutter, the slowest shutter speed available is one second; the mechanical shutter can be set to 60 seconds in most modes and to B for Bulb exposure in Manual mode.

Flash

The second item on screen 5 of the Recording menu, simply called Flash, is the gateway to several options for using the built-in flash unit or an external unit that is compatible with the FZ2500. The Flash item does not appear on the menu in Intelligent Auto mode. In Intelligent Auto Plus mode and Creative Control mode, the Flash item is dimmed and cannot be selected. In those modes, the camera makes flash settings with no input from you. In Panorama mode, the flash cannot be used, and this menu option is not available for selection. With some Scene mode settings you can set the flash mode, and with others that menu item is not available.

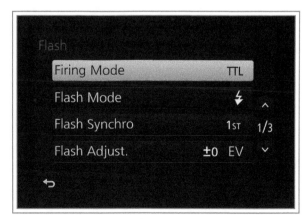

Figure 4-62. Flash Menu Options Screen

When you highlight Flash on the menu and press the Right button or the Menu/Set button (or press the menu item on the touch screen), the camera will display the screen shown in Figure 4-62. That screen has four sub-options: Firing Mode, Flash Mode, Flash Synchro, and Flash Adjustment.

Firing Mode

The first sub-option for the Flash menu is Firing Mode. When you are using the built-in flash unit, the Firing Mode menu option lets you choose whether to have the camera set the flash exposure automatically using its metering system (TTL, for "through the lens") or to set the output of the flash manually (Manual).

This option works only with the built-in flash unit. With other units, even recent Panasonic models that are compatible with the FZ2500, like the DMW-FL200L, this menu option is not available. With such flash units, you can control the flash mode using controls on the flash itself.

If you select TTL for Firing Mode, the camera will do its best to achieve a normal exposure by regulating the flash output based on the camera's metering system. If you choose Manual, the flash will fire at the level it has been set to, regardless of lighting conditions. It will be up to you to adjust the output of the flash to achieve a good exposure, using the Manual Flash Adjustment option on screen 2 of the Flash menu item. The current output setting of the flash will be displayed on the camera's shooting screen, to the right of the flash mode icon. For full output, the indication will be 1/1. Using the Manual Flash Adjustment menu option, discussed later in this section, you can change this setting to a level as low as 1/128 of full power, as shown in Figure 4-63.

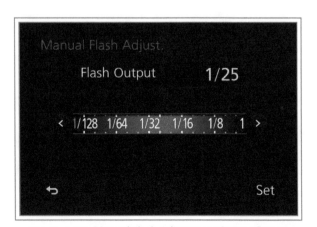

Figure 4-63. Manual Flash Adjustment Setting Screen

For everyday use, you will probably want to select TTL, so the camera will communicate with the flash to calculate the best exposure. But if you are faced with an unusual situation in which you want to adjust the output of the flash for a manual exposure, choose Manual and then use the Manual Flash Adjustment option. If you are using a flash other than the built-in unit, make such adjustments on the flash itself, if possible.

Flash Mode

This second sub-option lets you set the flash mode for your shot. There are four options for this setting when using the built-in flash: Forced On, Forced On with Red Eye, Slow Sync, and Slow Sync with Red Eye. These settings are represented by icons, as shown in Figure 4-64. When you are using an external flash in the hot shoe, if it is compatible with this camera, there will be a fifth option, Forced Off, so you can turn off the flash completely. (This option is not necessary with the built-in flash, because you can just push the flash back into its storage position, so it cannot fire.)

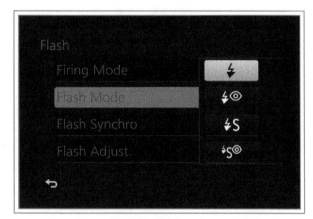

Figure 4-64. Flash Mode Menu Options Screen

If you choose Forced On, sometimes referred to as fill-flash, the flash will fire every time you press the shutter button, if the flash is operating properly and no other settings interfere. This is the mode to choose when you are certain you want the flash to fire, such as when you are taking snapshots in a dimly lighted area.

It also is the mode to choose when you want to use flash to soften the shadows or brighten the scene slightly when you are taking a shot, especially a portrait, outdoors. A bit of fill-flash can offset the harsh shadows and highlights from direct sunlight, and can provide a different look for a shot taken under a cloudy sky. For example, Figures 4-65 and 4-66 are two images I took outdoors on a sunny day.

For Figure 4-65, I left the flash turned off; for Figure 4-66, I used the Forced On setting. Figure 4-66 has more even lighting, because the on-camera flash filled in the shadows that were cast on the subject.

Figure 4-65. Image Taken with No Flash

Figure 4-66. Image Taken with Fill-flash

The next option, Forced On with Red Eye, is for use when you are aiming the camera with flash directly at a person's face. In that situation, the flash can bounce off the person's retinas and light up blood vessels, resulting in the unpleasant "red eye" effect that is common in flash snapshots. With this setting, the camera will fire a pre-flash before the main flash, to narrow the subject's pupils before the image is captured and thereby reduce the risk of the red eye effect.

The next setting, Slow Sync, is for use in dark conditions when you want to give the ambient light time to illuminate the background. With a normal flash shot, the exposure may last only about 1/60 second, enough time for the flash to illuminate the subject in the foreground, but not enough time for natural lighting to reveal the background. So, you may end up with an image in which the subject is brightly lit but the background is black. With Slow Sync, the camera

will use a relatively slow shutter speed so the ambient lighting will have time to register on the image.

For example, Figures 4-67 and 4-68 were taken at the same time and in the same conditions except for the flash mode. I took Figure 4-67 with the shutter speed set at 1/60 second, in normal flash mode (Forced On). The background is quite dark, because the exposure was too short to light up the area beyond the model knight and horse. I took Figure 4-68 using Slow Sync flash mode, which caused the camera to use a shutter speed of 0.3 second, allowing time for the ambient lighting to illuminate the scene so the background showed up more clearly.

Figure 4-67. Image Taken with Normal Flash

Figure 4-68. Image Taken with Slow Sync Flash

The Slow Sync option is not available for selection on the Recording menu when the camera is set to Shutter Priority or Manual exposure mode, because you set the shutter speed in those modes, so the camera cannot select a slow one. In Intelligent Auto mode, the camera may use the Slow Sync option, but you cannot select the setting yourself in that mode.

Slow Sync with Red Eye is the same as Slow Sync, except that the camera fires a pre-flash to try to reduce the red eye effect. In Scene mode, Slow Sync with Red Eye is the only flash mode setting available when the Clear Night Portrait setting is selected. When the Monochrome setting is selected for Scene mode, you can select any one of the four flash mode settings, including either of the two Slow Sync settings, when using the built-in flash.

Flash Synchro

The next sub-option for the Flash menu item, Flash Synchro, is designed for a particular situation that can arise when using slow shutter speeds, especially with a subject that has leading or trailing lights.

The Flash Synchro menu option, as shown in Figure 4-69, has two settings—1st and 2nd. Those terms are references to 1st-curtain sync and 2nd-curtain (also known as rear-curtain) sync. The normal setting is 1st, which causes the flash to fire early in the process when the shutter opens to expose the image. If you set it to 2nd, the flash fires later, just before the shutter closes.

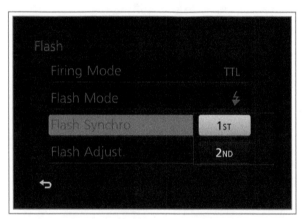

Figure 4-69. Flash Synchro Menu Options Screen

The 2nd-curtain sync setting can help you avoid a strange-looking result in some situations. This issue arises when you are taking a relatively long exposure, such as 1/4 second, of a subject with taillights, such as a car or motorcycle at night, that is moving across your field of view. With 1st-curtain sync, the flash will fire early in the process, freezing the vehicle in a clear image. However, as the shutter remains open while the vehicle continues on, the camera will capture the moving taillights in a stream that seems to extend in front of the vehicle.

If, instead, you use 2nd-curtain sync, the first part of the exposure will capture the lights in a trail that appears behind the vehicle, while the vehicle itself is not frozen by the flash until later in the exposure.

Therefore, with 2nd-curtain sync in this particular situation, the final image is likely to look more natural than with 1st-curtain sync.

Figures 4-70 and 4-71 illustrate this concept with two images showing a flashlight in motion from right to left. Both pictures were shot with the FZ2500's built-in flash, using an exposure of 1/2 second in Shutter Priority mode. In Figure 4-70, the flash fired quickly, and the light beam continued on during the long exposure to make the streak of light appear to move in front of the flashlight's motion.

Figure 4-70. Flash Synchro Set to 1st

Figure 4-71. Flash Synchro Set to 2nd

In Figure 4-71, using the 2nd setting, the flash did not fire until the flashlight had moved to the left, overtaking the place where the light had made its streak visible. If you are trying to convey a sense of natural motion, the 2nd setting for Flash Synchro is likely to give you better results than the default setting.

My general rule is to use the 1st setting unless I have a specific need for the 2nd setting. Using the 2nd setting makes it harder to compose and set up the shot, because you have to anticipate where the main subject will be when the flash finally fires late in the exposure process.

The Flash Synchro setting is available for selection only in the PASM shooting modes. When the 2nd setting is turned on, you cannot use either of the Red Eye Reduction settings for flash mode.

Flash Adjustment

The Flash Adjustment sub-option lets you adjust the intensity of the flash when Firing Mode is set to TTL. If the exposure with flash seems too bright or too dark, you can use this setting to adjust it downward or upward in small increments. The adjustment screen for this item is shown in Figure 4-72.

Figure 4-72. **Flash Adjustment Setting Screen**

Use the front or rear dial or the Left and Right buttons (or the touch screen) to dial in the amount of positive or negative EV adjustment you want.

Of course, you also have the option of using regular exposure compensation, causing the camera to adjust the exposure using settings other than flash. This choice is up to you; it depends on what effect you are looking for. I rarely find a reason to increase the flash output, but I find that it can be useful to decrease the flash output to reduce the harshness of the lighting for a portrait in some cases.

Auto Exposure Compensation

The first item on screen 2 of the Flash sub-options is Auto Exposure Compensation, which you can turn either on or off. This option controls the way the flash setting is affected when the flash is in TTL mode and you use exposure compensation. If you want the exposure compensation adjustment you make to be effective when using flash, turn this menu option on. Then, when the camera takes the shot, it will try to adjust the flash to give effect to the exposure compensation amount you selected.

If you leave this option turned off, then, when you adjust exposure compensation and use TTL flash, the camera will adjust the exposure with aperture and shutter speed, but it also will adjust the flash to counteract that change. The result may be an exposure that does not reflect the adjustment made. In other words, the flash output will be automatically adjusted in the reverse direction from the exposure compensation. Depending on the ambient lighting, the result may be to cancel the effect of the flash.

I recommend leaving this option turned on so your exposure compensation choices will be effective, unless you have a particular reason to turn it off.

Manual Flash Adjustment

As I noted earlier, this option is available only when you have set the Firing Mode option to Manual. In that case, you can use this menu item to increase or decrease the intensity of the flash, assuming the flash is compatible with the camera's circuitry. As I also noted earlier, the only flash unit that allows you to set the Firing Mode option is the built-in flash.

This adjustment works in a similar way to the Flash Adjustment option, discussed earlier. The difference is that, in this case, you are setting the intensity of the flash manually, rather than adjusting the intensity as set by the camera based on its autoexposure metering. This option could be useful if you are faced with an unusual situation in which you are trying to achieve a particular result, such as by using a minimal amount of flash in a dark environment, and you do not want to rely on the camera's metering system.

Wireless

The next few settings on the Flash menu have to do with the FZ2500's system for using wireless off-camera flash. To take advantage of this capability, you need to use one or more off-camera flash units that support the wireless protocol used by this camera. As of this writing, the only models I am aware of that support this protocol are the Panasonic DMW-FL200L, DMW-FL360L, and DMW-FL580L. You can use one or more of these units in each of three groups. Panasonic recommends using no more than three flash units in each of the three groups, for a total of nine off-camera flash units. If you are going to need that many flash units, you might be better off using more powerful flash heads, such as studio monolights, but the option to use multiple units is available.

Once you have one or more off-camera flash units, you will need to trigger them with a flash unit fired by the camera. For this triggering unit, you can use the FZ2500's built-in flash, or you can attach one of the wireless-compatible flash units listed above to the camera's hot shoe.

When you have the compatible on-camera and off-camera units assembled, you have to set up the off-camera units within about 10 feet (3 meters) of the camera in a fairly straight line, or within about 6 feet (2 meters) if they are off to the sides, within a 50-degree angle from a line from the center of the lens. (See the diagram at page 155 of the Panasonic user's guide for more details on this point.) Once the transmitting unit and the receiving unit(s) are set up, it is time to use the menu options on the FZ2500. First, set the Wireless menu option to On. Then, you need to use more menu options, as discussed below.

Wireless Channel

Once the flash units are set up and the Wireless menu option is turned on, use the Wireless Channel option to select channel 1, 2, 3, or 4. Then make sure that each of the off-camera flash units is also set to that channel using the controls on the flash.

Communication Light

This next menu option can be set to High, Standard, or Low. It controls the brightness of the light that is emitted by the on-camera flash as it uses flashes of light to communicate with the off-camera flash units. If you are taking pictures in a relatively dark location, these flashes of light can affect your images. If that happens, you can set the intensity to a lower level to minimize those effects.

Wireless Setup

Finally, the Wireless Setup menu option, shown in Figure 4-73, lets you make settings for the triggering flash and for flash groups A, B, and C. The camera will detect an external flash if you have attached a compatible one to the hot shoe. If you have, the first line on this menu screen will say External Flash. If not, the first line will say Built-in Flash, as shown in Figure 4-73.

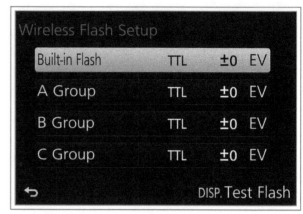

Figure 4-73. Wireless Setup Menu Options Screen

For the external flash or built-in flash and each of the remote flash groups, you can make settings that are similar to those you can make for the single flash, when you are not using the wireless capability: Firing Mode, Flash Adjustment (when using TTL for Firing Mode), and Manual Flash Adjustment (when using Manual for Firing Mode). However, there are some significant differences. First, the Flash Synchro setting is not available, so you cannot turn on 2nd-curtain flash. Second, and more significant, the Firing Mode menu item has two additional options when you are using wireless flash with an external unit in the flash shoe. Instead of having only the options of TTL or Manual, the Firing Mode item, when using wireless flash, lets you choose from TTL, Auto, Manual, or Off. (With the built-in flash, the only options are TTL or Off.)

The effects of these choices are different for the triggering flash and the remote flash units. If you choose TTL, the camera sets the exposure of the flash, either on-camera or off-camera. You can adjust that exposure using the Flash Adjustment menu option, if you want. If you choose Auto for the triggering flash, then the flash unit determines the flash output. (The Auto setting is not available if the DMW-FL200L is used as the triggering flash.)

If you choose Manual for the triggering flash, then you will set the output of that flash yourself, using the Manual Flash Adjustment menu option. Finally, if you choose Off for the triggering flash, that unit will not fire its flash, but will still transmit wireless signals to the off-camera unit(s). You can use this setting if you don't want the on-camera flash to contribute to the exposure. In practice, I have found that the light from the on-camera flash is quite noticeable even if you choose Off for this setting, because of the triggering light this unit emits. If you set the Communication Light option to Low, that helps somewhat to reduce the intensity of that light.

For the off-camera units in Groups A, B, and C, you have the same options as for the triggering, but with some differences in how they work. For Firing Mode, if you select Auto, the remote flash unit will determine the exposure. If you select Manual, you can set the exposure for that group using the Manual Flash Adjustment menu option. If you select Off, then the flash units in that group will not fire at all.

Once you have all the flash units set up and the menu options configured, you can press the Display button to test-fire the units, to make sure everything is working as you intended. You have to press the Display button while the Wireless Setup menu is displayed, as shown in Figure 4-73; otherwise, the button will have a different effect, such as switching display screens.

Figure 4-74. Equipment Setup for Wireless Flash

Figure 4-74 shows an arrangement using the Panasonic DMW-FL200L flash on the camera and a Panasonic DMW-FL360L flash off the camera, to illustrate a typical setup.

I set up the off-camera flash with its sensors and LED light facing the camera, as recommended by Panasonic, but with the flash head facing the subject. In the Wireless Setup menu options, I used TTL for the Firing Mode options for both the on-camera and off-camera flashes. The result was the image shown in Figure 4-75, with the subject lighted by both flash units. (I often use a softbox or other diffuser for the off-camera flash, but I omitted that option in order to make the setup more visible.)

Figure 4-75. Image Taken Using Wireless Flash Setup

If you are using the Panasonic DMW-FL360L as your off-camera flash, the bright LED on the front of the unit fires once every few seconds as a "ready" light to let you know that it is ready to fire wirelessly. Apparently there is no way to turn off this light in this mode, though you can try to cover it with gaffer's tape. You have to be careful not to cover up the two sensors that are located on either side of the LED, though, or this flash will not be triggered by the on-camera flash.

RED-EYE REMOVAL

This next setting on screen 5 of the Recording menu is not to be confused with Red-eye Reduction, which is an aspect of how the flash fires. As I noted earlier, "red eye" is the unpleasant phenomenon that crops up when a flash picture is taken of a person, and the light illuminates his or her retinas, causing an eerie red glow to appear in the eyes. One way the FZ2500 (like many cameras) deals with this problem is with the Red-eye Reduction settings for the flash mode, which cause the flash to fire twice: once to make the person's pupils contract, reducing the chance for the light to bounce off the retinas, and then a second time to take the picture.

The FZ2500 has a second line of defense against red eye, called Red-eye Removal. When you select this option, which can be turned either on or off, then, when the flash is fired, the camera also uses a digital red eye correction method, to actually remove from the image the red areas that appear to be near a person's eyes. This option operates only when the flash mode is set to one of the two options with Red-eye Reduction.

I do not often use this option, because I process my images using Photoshop or other software, and it's easy to fix red eye at that stage. However, when I tested this feature it did a very good job of removing red spots from eyes in a portrait shot in Scene mode. So, this feature may be of use when taking pictures at a party, for example.

ISO LIMIT SET

ISO Limit Set, whose setting screen is shown in Figure 4-76, lets you set an upper limit for the value the camera will choose for ISO, when you have selected either Auto ISO or Intelligent ISO, as discussed earlier in this chapter. The choices for this setting are 200, 400, 800, 1600, 3200, 6400, 12800, or Off. If you choose Off, then the ISO limit is automatically set to 3200, or 1600 if the flash is in use. This option does not have any effect for motion picture recording.

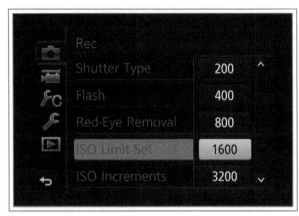

Figure 4-76. ISO Limit Set Menu Options Screen

If you want to make sure the camera will use a relatively low ISO to preserve image quality, you can set this value down to 200, 400 or 800. If you are shooting in dark conditions and your priority is to make sure you can capture the image even if image quality suffers, you might want to set a high limit, such as 12800.

You don't have to use this menu option to set the limit for Auto ISO. When you are setting ISO after pressing the ISO button, you can turn the front dial to adjust the ISO limit setting.

ISO INCREMENTS

Using this option, whose setting screen is shown in Figure 4-77, you can expand the range of values available for the setting of ISO.

Normally, when you set ISO to a numerical value, you can use only 125, 200, 400, 800, 1600, 3200, 6400, or 12800. However, if you select the increment of 1/3 EV instead of the normal 1 EV for this menu option, then

several interpolated values for ISO are added, such as 160, 250, 320, 500, 640, 1000, 8000, and others. You can then set these values using the ISO button on the back of the camera.

Figure 4-77. ISO Increments Menu Options Screen

This menu option applies only to the settings you make yourself. Even if the ISO Increments option is set to 1 EV, the camera can still set intermediate ISO values when Auto ISO or Intelligent ISO is in effect and the camera is choosing the ISO value. I have never found a need to use the 1/3 EV option, so I leave this setting at its default value of 1 EV.

Screen 6 of the Recording menu is shown in Figure 4-78.

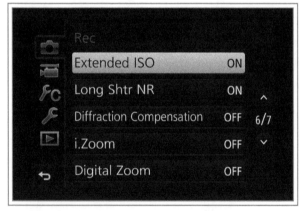

Figure 4-78. Screen 6 of Recording Menu

EXTENDED ISO

This next ISO-related option on the Recording menu, Extended ISO, can be turned either on or off. When it is turned on through this menu item, you get access to the lowest ISO levels of 80 and 100, and to the highest value of 25600, which are not available otherwise. If you have set the ISO Increments option, discussed above, to 1/3 EV, then you will also get access to the ISO settings of 16000 and 20000.

The additional ISO values of 80, 100, and those above 12800 are considered "extended" because they are not values that are native to the sensor. Therefore, using one of them does not increase the dynamic range or improve the image quality; it just acts to change the light sensitivity of the sensor. Using a low value such as 80 ISO reduces the sensitivity so you can use a slower shutter speed or wider aperture than you could otherwise. Using one of the very high settings can be helpful when light is very low, as long as you don't mind the increased noise from using such a high value.

Long Shutter Noise Reduction

When you take a picture using a shutter speed of several seconds, the image sensor may generate an excessive amount of visual noise because of the way its circuitry reacts to long exposures. If you turn on the Long Shutter Noise Reduction menu option, the camera will use noise-reduction processing that lasts as long as the exposure itself to reduce the noise. For example, if your exposure lasts for 12 seconds, the camera will continue processing the image for another 12 seconds after the exposure ends. This action will delay your ability to take another shot, and the processing can reduce the details in your image. If you don't want to experience this delay or if you want to deal with the possibility of noise using post-processing software, turn this option off.

This option is available only in the PASM, Scene, and Creative Control shooting modes. It is not available for motion picture recording, when Post Focus is active, when recording with the 4K Photo feature, or with the electronic shutter.

Diffraction Compensation

When the camera uses a narrow aperture such as f/8.0 or f/11.0, the diffraction effect comes into play and can cause distortion in the image. If you set the Diffraction Compensation option to Auto, the camera uses its processing to counteract that effect, when needed. If you would rather deal with that issue with your post-processing software or leave it untouched, choose Off. This option is available with all shooting modes except Intelligent Auto and Intelligent Auto Plus.

Intelligent Zoom

The Intelligent Zoom, or i.Zoom, option is related to the i.Resolution feature, discussed earlier, although you do not have to turn on i.Resolution in order to take advantage of i.Zoom. When i.Zoom is turned on, the camera automatically takes advantage of i.Resolution processing in the zoom range to improve the appearance of the image, so you can zoom to a higher level of magnification without image deterioration, using either normal optical zoom or Extra Optical Zoom. (As discussed earlier in this chapter, Extra Optical Zoom is available when Picture Size is set to Medium or Small, because extra pixels are available for enlarging the image.)

For example, without the i.Zoom setting, the limit for the optical zoom is 20x; with i.Zoom turned on, the maximum is 40x. The question of image quality in this situation is a matter of judgment; as with i.Resolution, I recommend that you try this setting to see if you are satisfied with the quality of the images. If so, you can then use an effective zoom range up to 960mm, rather than the 480mm of the optical zoom alone. The range can be even greater if combined with Digital Zoom and Extra Optical Zoom, although the quality of the image will suffer with excessive zoom range in effect.

The i.Zoom feature is not available in conjunction with Macro Zoom or with certain types of shooting that involve special processing, including panorama shots, shots with the Raw format, Multiple Exposure, shots using the Handheld Night Shot or HDR options, or shots using the filter effects of Impressive Art, Toy, or Toy Pop.

Digital Zoom

With Digital Zoom, unlike Intelligent Zoom and Extra Optical Zoom, the camera produces what Panasonic calls "deteriorated" picture quality. As with many digital cameras, Digital Zoom is available on the FZ2500 as a way of enlarging the pixels that are displayed so the image appears larger; there is no additional resolution available, so the image can quickly begin to appear blocky and of low quality.

As with Extra Optical Zoom and Intelligent Zoom, this option can help you in viewing a distant subject. Digital Zoom has a maximum power of four times the normal lens's magnification, or 1920mm. When you combine all of the zoom options, including Digital Zoom and using a smaller picture size for Extra Optical Zoom, there is a maximum total zoom power of eight times normal, or 3840mm.

Digital Zoom is not available in Intelligent Auto, Intelligent Auto Plus, or Panorama mode, or with some other settings, including Raw quality, Multiple Exposure, Post Focus, HDR, Handheld Night Shot, or with the filter effects of Impressive Art, Toy, Toy Pop, or Miniature.

Screen 7 of the Recording menu is shown in Figure 4-79.

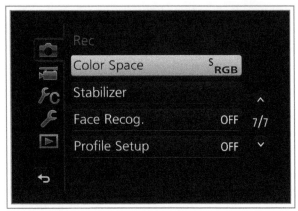

Figure 4-79. Screen 7 of Recording Menu

COLOR SPACE

With this option, you can choose to record your images using the sRGB "color space," the more common choice and the default, or the Adobe RGB color space. The sRGB color space has fewer colors than Adobe RGB; therefore, it is more suitable for producing images for the web and other forms of digital display than for printing. If your images are likely to be printed commercially in a book or magazine or it is critical that you be able to match a great many different color variations, you might want to consider using the Adobe RGB color space. I always leave the color space set to sRGB, and I recommend that you do so as well unless you have a specific need to use Adobe RGB, such as a requirement from a printing company that you are using to print your images.

If you are shooting your images with the Raw format, you don't need to worry so much about color space, because you can set it later using your Raw-processing software. This menu item is available in all shooting modes except the basic Intelligent Auto mode, Creative Video mode, and Creative Control mode.

STABILIZER

The FZ2500 is equipped with both an optical image stabilization system and an electronic stabilization system. These two systems are designed to counteract the effects of camera shake on an image or video. The optical system is controlled by the first sub-option under the Stabilizer menu item, which is Operation Mode. This system has three possible settings, as shown in Figure 4-80, from top to bottom: Normal, Panning, and Off.

Figure 4-80. Stabilizer Operation Mode Menu Options Screen

With the Normal setting, the camera corrects for both horizontal and vertical motion. With the Panning setting, the camera assumes that you are moving the camera from side to side in order to pan over the scene, so it does not attempt to correct for horizontal motion, only vertical. I generally leave this setting at Normal when I am hand-holding the camera. If I have the camera on a tripod, the setting is unnecessary and possibly could cause some distortion as the camera tries to correct for camera movement that does not exist.

The Normal stabilization setting is not available when you are shooting panoramas; Panning will be used instead if you select Normal. The Panning setting is not available when recording movies or using 4K Photo or Post Focus.

The second major option for the Stabilizer menu item is E-Stabilization (Video), which can be turned either on or off. If it is turned on, the camera uses its electronic five-axis stabilization system. You can also activate the optical stabilizer system along with the electronic one. When the electronic system is turned on, the camera uses processing that crops the frame somewhat, reducing the area that is included in the video footage. This setting is not available when recording 4K or C4K video footage, when digital zoom is in use, or when the Variable Frame Rate option has been activated through screen 2 of the Motion Picture menu.

The electronic stabilization system is useful when you are recording video with a hand-held camera from a moving car or in other situations involving rapid and uneven motion.

The Stabilizer menu option is not available for selection in the basic Intelligent Auto mode.

FACE RECOGNITION

With this menu option, you can register the faces of up to six people so the camera will recognize them when Face Recognition is turned on. Here are the essential steps to follow. First, go to the Face Recognition menu item and select the third option, Memory, as shown in Figure 4-81.

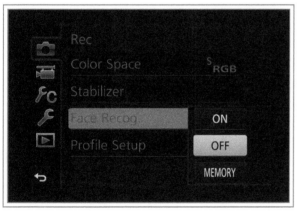

Figure 4-81. Face Recognition Menu Options Screen

Press Menu/Set (or use the touch screen) to go to the screen with six blue blocks, shown in Figure 4-82. Move the yellow highlight to the first available blue block that says New, and press Menu/Set; you will see the screen shown in Figure 4-83, which prompts you to position the face to be registered in the yellow frame.

When you have the face properly positioned, press the shutter button to take a picture. If the registration fails, you will see an error message. If it succeeds, you will see a screen like that in Figure 4-84. You can then proceed to register the person and enter data for him or her, including name and birthdate.

Once you have one or more faces registered, you can turn Face Recognition on through this item on the Recording menu whenever you want the camera to try

to recognize those faces. You also have to set AF Mode to Face/Eye Detection using the Left cursor button.

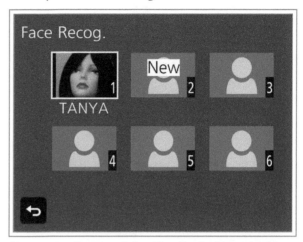

Figure 4-82. Screen to Select New Slot for Recognized Face

Figure 4-83. Screen to Take Picture of New Face

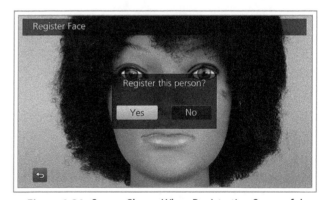

Figure 4-84. Screen Shown When Registration Successful

When the camera recognizes a face, it will place a frame over the face and display the name if one was entered into the camera's memory, as shown in Figure 4-85.

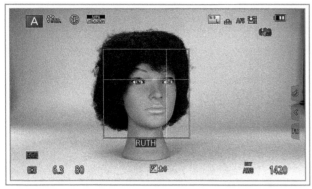

Figure 4-85. Screen When Registered Face is Recognized

The camera will adjust its focus and exposure for the recognized face or faces. It can recognize up to three faces at a time. When the image is played back, the camera will display the name and age of the person briefly, though that information does not become part of the image.

You can add additional images for any person, taken from different angles and in different lighting, to increase the camera's ability to recognize that person. To do that, choose the Memory option and then select the person for whom you want to add images. You also can edit a person's information, including name and birthdate.

I do not often use this feature, but I can appreciate how useful it could be if, for example, you are taking photos at a school event and you want to make sure the camera focuses on your child when you are aiming at a group of children.

If you don't want the camera to use face recognition, turn this menu item off.

PROFILE SETUP

This final option on the Recording menu lets you set up profiles for two babies and one pet, so the camera will display the name and age of the baby or pet when you take a picture of him or her. For example, you can enter a profile for a baby named Rachel, born February 1, 2018. Then, whenever you take a picture of Rachel, you can recall that profile and the camera will display her name and age as of the date the picture is taken. So, if you take her picture on June 1, 2019, the camera will display: Rachel 1 year 4 months. This information will be recorded with the image, and it will display in playback mode with the detailed information screen,

but it will not become a permanent part of the image unless you take further steps.

One way to imprint the information in the image is to use the PHOTOfunSTUDIO software provided with the camera, though it is available only for Windows-based computers. Another way to imprint the information is to use the Text Stamp option on screen 2 of the Playback menu to add the name from Profile Setup, as discussed in Chapter 6.

This menu option does not cause the camera to recognize a pet or baby; it just lets you call up the profile you have entered for Baby 1, Baby 2, or Pet. So, you actually could enter any name and birthdate in any of those three profiles. When you call up the profile and take a picture with the profile activated, the camera will record the name and age, regardless of the actual subject matter of the image.

Quick Menu

The FZ2500 has another menu system with settings for recording images and videos. (I will discuss the menu for movie settings in Chapter 8.) This system is called the Quick Menu. It is not part of the regular menu system; instead, you get access to it by pressing the Q.Menu button. By default, the Fn5 button is assigned as the Q.Menu button, though you can change that function to a different button using the Function Button Set option on screen 7 of the Custom menu. I recommend leaving it as it is, especially because the Q.Menu label is printed on the camera next to the Fn5 button.

When you press the Q.Menu button while the camera is in recording mode, a mini-version of the camera's menu system opens up, with several options in two lines, one at the top of the screen and one at the bottom, as shown in Figure 4-86.

Navigate through these menu options by pressing the Left and Right buttons, by turning the front dial, or by touching icons on the screen until you find the category you want. The name of the setting that is currently active will appear near the top of the screen for items in the bottom row, and near the bottom of the screen for items in the top row. For example, in Figure 4-86 the Photo Style icon is highlighted at the top of the screen, and its name appears near the bottom of the screen. The highlight will wrap around between the bottom and top of the screen, so you can keep turning the front dial or pressing the Left and Right buttons to cycle through all of the items continuously.

Figure 4-86. Quick Menu on Shooting Screen

If the item you highlighted is at the top of the screen, you can then press the Down button to move down to the row or rows of icons with settings for that item. If the highlighted item is at the bottom of the screen, press the Up button to move to the row or rows of icons with settings. For example, Figure 4-87 shows the white balance item highlighted at the bottom of the screen. To move to the icons with settings for white balance, you would press the Up button to move the highlight into the area in the middle of the screen with those icons.

Figure 4-87. White Balance Item Highlighted on Quick Menu

Another way to move the highlight into the area where you can change the settings is to use the rear dial. When a main option, such as Photo Style, White Balance, or Quality, is highlighted, just start turning the rear dial to adjust the setting for that option. You can then turn the front dial to move directly to another main option if you want.

Once you have highlighted the icons with settings, move left and right through the sub-menu with the direction buttons, rear dial, or touch screen. When you have highlighted the setting you want to make, you can then move to another item in the Quick Menu to make another setting. When you have finished making settings, press the Menu/Set button, the Q.Menu button, the Fn6 button, or the Exit icon in the lower right corner of the screen to exit from the Quick Menu to the recording screen. You also can press the shutter button halfway to return to that screen.

The menu options vary according to what mode the camera is in; not surprisingly, the Quick Menu offers the largest variety of choices when the camera is in Program, Aperture Priority, Shutter Priority, or Manual mode. It offers a smaller variety in Intelligent Auto mode, though it still offers several choices.

The Quick Menu is a useful alternative to the Recording menu. This system lets you make certain settings very efficiently that otherwise would require a longer time, in part because you can see all available options at the same time on the screen as soon as you press the Q.Menu button.

For example, I find that the Quick Menu is an excellent way to select Raw or Fine quality for still images. Access to the feature is very fast this way, and, even better, when you later press the Q.Menu button again to go back to change the Quality setting again, the Quality option is still highlighted, and it takes just a couple of button presses, dial turns, or touches of icons on the screen to change from Raw to Fine or vice-versa.

You can customize the settings included on the Quick Menu using the Quick Menu item on screen 9 of the Custom menu. I will discuss that process in Chapter 7.

CHAPTER 5: PHYSICAL CONTROLS

Not all settings that affect the recording of images and videos are on the Recording menu. Several important functions are controlled by physical buttons and switches on the FZ2500. In addition, the camera is equipped with a versatile touch screen, which is helpful for quick and efficient focusing as well as for controlling camera settings.

I have talked about many of these controls in previous chapters. But to make sure all information about physical controls is included in one place, I'll discuss each control, starting with the items on top of the camera, as shown in Figure 5-1.

Figure 5-1. Controls on Top of Camera

Controls on Top of Camera

SHUTTER BUTTON

This control is the most important one on the camera. With the default settings, you press it halfway to check focus and exposure, and press it the rest of the way to record the image. You can press it halfway to wake the camera up from sleep mode, or to return to recording mode from a menu screen or from playback mode. You can press this button to take a still image while recording a video sequence, in most situations. When the camera is set for burst shooting or auto bracketing, you hold this button down to fire a burst of shots. When the shutter speed is set to B, for Bulb exposure, in Manual

exposure mode, you press this button down to open the shutter, and release it after a number of seconds to end the exposure. When you are using the 4K Photo option, pressing the shutter button starts and stops a 4K video recording. When that option is in use, you cannot use the shutter button to take still images. When the mode dial is at the Creative Video position, pressing this button starts or stops a video recording; you cannot take still pictures with the camera in that mode.

You can change the behavior of this button in a couple of ways using options on the Custom menu. With the Shutter AF item on screen 1 of that menu, you can disable the function of focusing when the button is pressed halfway. With the Half Press Release item on screen 2 of that menu, you can set the camera so a half-press of the shutter button will release the shutter. I will discuss those options in Chapter 7.

ZOOM LEVER

The zoom lever is the ring with a small handle that encircles the shutter button. The lever's basic function is to change the lens's focal length to various values ranging between wide-angle, by pushing it to the left, toward the W indicator, and telephoto, by pushing it to the right, toward the T indicator. You can set the lever to zoom in specific increments (step zoom) using the Zoom Lever item on screen 7 of the Custom menu. When you are viewing pictures in playback mode, the lever enlarges the image on the LCD screen when pushed to the right, and selects different arrangements of thumbnail images to view when pushed to the left. Also, you can use this lever to speed through the menu screens a full page at a time, either forward or backward.

ON/OFF SWITCH

The on/off switch is at the rear of the camera's top, next to the mode dial. Push it forward to turn the camera on and pull it back to turn it off. If you leave the camera unattended for a period of time, it automatically powers off, if the Sleep Mode option is turned on through the Economy item on screen 3 of the Setup menu. I'll discuss the Setup menu in Chapter 7, but this option can be set to be off altogether so the camera never turns off just to save power, or to turn the camera off after 1, 2, 5, or 10 minutes of inactivity. You can cancel the Sleep Mode shutdown by pressing the shutter button halfway.

STATUS LAMP

The small status indicator lamp in front of the word On, next to the on/off switch, lights up green when the camera's power is turned on. It lights up solid blue when a Wi-Fi connection is initiated, and it blinks blue when data is being transmitted over a Wi-Fi connection.

MODE DIAL

The mode dial is marked with icons or letters representing each of the camera's shooting modes, including Intelligent Auto, Shutter Priority, Scene, and the others. Just turn this dial to select the mode you want. That mode controls what features are available for shooting and how the camera's controls behave. You can shoot still images by pressing the shutter button with the dial set to any position other than Creative Video (M with movie camera icon). With the mode dial at that position, if you press the shutter button the camera will start (or stop) recording a movie. You can record a movie with the mode dial set to any position except Panorama, by pressing the red motion picture button on top of the camera.

For the most automatic settings, turn the dial to the iA icon, for Intelligent Auto, and make sure the Intelligent Auto item, the top icon on the list of menu icons, is set to the iA selection, rather than iA+.

FRONT DIAL

This dial, whose edge sticks up just behind the zoom lever and shutter button, carries out a variety of functions. In Program mode, it operates the Program Shift function, to select a new pair of exposure settings. In Aperture Priority and Manual exposure mode, it selects the aperture setting. In Shutter Priority mode, it selects the shutter speed. When you are viewing menu screens, you can turn this dial to move directly from one menu system (Recording, Motion Picture, Custom, Setup, and Playback) to another, even if the highlight is inside one of the menu screens and not on the menu

icons in the left column. In various other situations, it carries out navigational duties.

For example, when the Quick Menu is displayed, you can turn this dial to move among the main options on the menu. In many cases, such as when setting white balance, you can turn either this dial or the rear dial to navigate among settings for a menu option. After you press the ISO (Up) button, you can turn this dial to set the upper limit for the Auto ISO setting. In playback mode, you can turn this dial to move through your recorded images and videos. When you are using the Highlight Shadow menu option, this dial is used to adjust the highlight areas of images. After you press the exposure compensation button to adjust exposure compensation, you can turn this dial to adjust flash output.

You can change the operation of this dial (as well as the rear dial) in several ways, using the Dial Settings option on screen 9 of the Custom menu, as discussed in Chapter 7. One of the options available through that menu item is called Dial Operation Switch. With that option, you can assign a function to the front dial (as well as the rear dial) that will be activated temporarily when you press a function button that is assigned to the Dial Operation Switch function. (By default, that function is assigned to the Fn3 button.) I will discuss that feature in Chapter 7.

MOTION PICTURE BUTTON

The red motion picture button is located to the right of the mode dial. Press this button once to start recording a movie, and press it again to stop recording. As noted above, you can use this button to record a movie in any shooting mode except Panorama. In Chapter 8, I will provide details about how the various menu and control settings affect the recording of movies.

FN4 BUTTON

This button, located to the left of the motion picture button, is one of the camera's seven physical function buttons. By default, it is assigned to adjust exposure compensation, as indicated by the exposure compensation icon on the camera next to the button. However, the button can be assigned to carry out a different function using the Function Button Set option on screen 7 of the Custom menu, as discussed in Chapter 7.

Here is an example of how to control exposure to account for an unusual, or non-optimal, lighting situation. Suppose you have the FZ2500 set to Program mode and you are photographing a fairly dark subject, such as a model fire hydrant, in front of a white background, as shown in Figure 5-2.

Figure 5-2. Image Needing Exposure Compensation

The camera will do a good job of averaging the amount of light coming into the lens, and will expose the picture accordingly. The problem is, the very light background will likely "fool" the camera into closing down the aperture, because the overall picture will seem quite bright. But the subject, which is not nearly as light as the background, will seem too dark in the picture. One solution to this problem is to use exposure compensation. (Another is to use spot metering.)

First, compose the image as you want. Then, press the Fn4 button (or other button assigned to exposure compensation) to place the exposure compensation scale on the display, as shown in Figure 5-3.

Figure 5-3. Exposure Compensation Adjustment Scale

Use the rear dial, the Left and Right buttons, or the touch screen to select the desired setting. The values range from –5 to +5 EV, with one-third steps in between. EV stands for exposure value, a standard

measure of brightness. If you move the value down to -5, the picture will be much darker than the automatic exposure would produce. If you move it to +5, the picture will be much brighter.

The camera's screen shows you how the exposure is changing, before you take the picture, as shown in Figure 5-4. In this case, after 1 2/3 EV of positive exposure compensation is added, the image becomes brighter and the model hydrant can be seen more clearly.

Figure 5-4. Adjustment Made to Exposure Compensation

A small EV scale at the bottom center of the display shows the amount of exposure compensation that has been applied after the exposure compensation screen has been dismissed.

Once you've taken the picture, you should reset the EV scale back to zero so you don't unintentionally affect the pictures you take later. (You can set the camera so exposure compensation is reset to zero when the camera is turned off, by turning on the Exposure Compensation Reset option on screen 4 of the Setup menu.)

When the exposure compensation scale is displayed, you can also use the front dial to adjust flash compensation, and the Up and Down buttons to select a setting for exposure bracketing, unless there is a conflicting setting in place that would prevent either of those adjustments.

At any time when the exposure compensation screen is displayed, you can press the Display button to switch the functions of the rear dial and front dial, so the front dial controls exposure compensation and the rear dial controls flash compensation.

Rear Dial

Although this dial is located on top of the camera, Panasonic calls it the rear dial. This name makes sense, because you are likely to move this dial with your thumb at the rear of the dial while holding the camera. However, because it is located on top of the camera, I will discuss it in this section.

The default function of the rear dial varies according to the shooting mode that is currently set. Table 5-1 lists the default assignments of the dial for each shooting mode, on the shooting screen.

Table 5-1.   **Default Assignments for Rear Dial in Various Shooting Modes**

Shooting Mode	Function of Rear Dial
Intelligent Auto	No Function
Program	Program Shift
Aperture Priority	Adjusts Aperture
Shutter Priority	Adjusts Shutter Speed
Manual Exposure	Adjusts Shutter Speed
Panorama	No Function
Scene	No function, with two exceptions below
Scene–Artistic Nightscape	Adjusts Shutter Speed
Scene–Appetizing Food	Adjusts Aperture
Creative Control	No Function
Creative Video	Adjusts Aperture or Shutter Speed if Exposure Mode Permits

The functions outlined above for the rear dial are the default functions programmed at the factory. You can change the function of the rear dial through the Dial Settings option on screen 9 of the Custom menu, which I will discuss in Chapter 7. With that menu option, you can switch this dial's function with that of the front dial; change its rotation direction; set it to control exposure compensation; or assign it a function to be activated temporarily when you press the function button assigned to the Dial Operation Switch function.

Apart from its main functions, this dial has a few other uses. You can turn it to move through menu screens by one item at a time. You can turn it to adjust the size of the focus frame when the focus mode permits that adjustment, or to adjust the size of the frame used for the Miniature filter effect setting. You can also use it to adjust the size of the light source for the Sunshine

effect. This dial is also used to adjust the shadows settings for the Highlight Shadow option on screen 3 of the Recording menu and to set the interval for white balance bracketing. In playback mode, turning this dial moves through your recorded images, and it is used to adjust the audio volume during a slide show or motion picture playback. It also is used to adjust settings such as white balance, exposure compensation, AF mode, and ISO, when those adjustment screens are active.

Built-in Flash Unit and Flash Release Switch

The FZ2500's built-in flash is stored inside the top of the camera. In order to use it, you have to press the flash release switch, on the left side of the viewfinder eyepiece. To retract the flash, press gently on the top of the unit and fold it back in place. In most shooting modes, you can control the operation of the flash using the Flash item on screen 5 of the Recording menu.

Hot Shoe

The shoe on top of the camera, which is protected by the hot shoe cover that comes with the camera, is where you can attach an external flash unit that provides more power than the built-in flash. You also can attach other accessories, such as an external microphone or video recorder, as discussed in Appendix A.

Built-in Microphone

The camera's built-in stereo microphone receives sounds through the two sets of openings directly behind the built-in flash unit. Be sure not to cover up these openings when recording a movie, so as not to block the recording of sounds. This camera also has a jack for an external microphone, as discussed later in this chapter.

Zoom Ring

Although this control is not on top of the camera, it is visible in the view of the camera's top, so I will discuss it here. The zoom ring is the larger of the two ridged rings that surround the lens, and it is the closer to the camera's body of the two rings. You can turn this ring to zoom the lens throughout the range of its wide-angle to telephoto focal lengths. You also can zoom the lens using the zoom lever that is located with the shutter button, or with function buttons that are assigned to the Slow Zoom function. By default, the Fn1 and Fn2 buttons are assigned to that function, but you can change those assignments using the Function Button Set option on screen 7 of the Custom menu.

By default, the zoom ring moves the lens through all focal lengths continuously. You can, instead, turn on the step zoom function through the Zoom Ring option on screen 8 of the Custom menu. If step zoom is activated, the ring zooms the lens only to certain specific positions: 24mm, 28mm, 35mm, 50mm, 70mm, 90mm, 135mm, 160mm, 200mm, 250mm, 300mm, 400mm, and 480mm. (If 4K Photo is in use, the steps are different, because the camera uses a cropped portion of the sensor for its recording: 36mm, 42mm, 52mm, 75mm, 105mm, 135mm, 202mm, 240mm, 300mm, 375mm, 450mm, 600mm, and 720mm.)

FOCUS RING

This ring is the more narrow of the two ridged rings around the lens, and is located farther from the camera's body than the zoom ring, discussed above. You can use the focus ring to adjust the focus when the camera is set to manual focus using the focus mode lever.

DRIVE MODE DIAL

The last control located on top of the camera is the drive mode dial, which sits alone on the far left side. This dial provides access to all of the drive mode settings by turning it to any one of its six positions, as shown in Figure 5-5. Starting with the single-frame icon that is selected in the illustration, the icons represent single shooting (all drive mode settings turned off); burst shooting; 4K Photo; Post Focus; self-timer; and interval timer. I will discuss all of these functions below.

Figure 5-5. Drive Mode Dial

The first position on the dial is used to turn off all burst shooting, including the self-timer. Leave the dial at this position when you want to make sure the camera is not set to use any of the burst shooting or other drive mode options. There are some camera settings, such as

Intelligent Zoom, Digital Zoom, and HDR, that conflict with one or more of the drive mode options. So, if you find a feature is not working, you may want to move this dial to the single-shooting position to disable all drive mode features and see if that removes the conflict.

Burst Shooting

Turning the dial to its second position activates burst shooting. With this option, sometimes called continuous shooting, the camera takes a series of images while you hold down the shutter button. This capability is useful in many contexts, from shooting an action sequence at a sporting event to taking several shots of a portrait subject to capture changing facial expressions. I often use this setting for street photography to increase my chances of catching an interesting image.

The FZ2500 can shoot bursts of images at three different speeds, labeled H, M, and L, for high, medium, and low. You select one of those settings using the Burst Rate option on screen 2 of the Recording menu. With the H setting, the camera can shoot a rate of up to 12 frames per second with AFS in effect, or seven frames per second with AFF or AFC in effect. The camera will not update the live view with the H setting. If the focus mode is set to AFS or MF, the exposure and white balance settings will be fixed with the first shot. If the focus mode is set to AFF or AFC, the exposure and white balance settings will be adjusted as the focus is adjusted.

With the M or L setting, the camera can shoot at a rate of seven or two frames per second, respectively, with any of the AFS/AFF/AFC settings, and with a live view that is updated during shooting. Exposure and white balance will be adjusted with each shot.

With any of the speed settings, the camera can shoot about 30 files using the Raw setting for Quality before stopping, although shooting will slow down partway through the burst. If Raw files are not being shot, the number of continuous shots is limited only by the capacity of the memory card, but the shooting will slow down after a number of shots.

When the camera is set for burst shooting, if you press the shutter button halfway with one of the detailed information screens displayed, the camera displays the letter "r" followed by the number of images the camera can capture in a continuous burst. For example, in Figure

5-6, the display shows that the camera can capture 54 images, with Burst Rate set to H, Quality set to JPEG-Fine, and AFS selected for autofocus. When you press the shutter button down to capture the burst, that number will continuously decrease; it should reach zero at the point when the rate of shooting starts to slow down.

Figure 5-6. Shooting Screen with Remaining Burst Shots Shown

With all burst shooting, the specifications for speed and numbers of images will vary according to conditions. When conditions are dark and the camera has to use a slower shutter speed, that factor alone will slow down the shooting. Other factors that affect shooting capacity and speed include image quality and the speed and capacity of the memory card in the camera. I carried out some indoor experiments with my FZ2500 using a very fast card, the SanDisk Extreme PRO 32 GB SDXC card, rated in UHS Speed Class 3, the highest speed category currently available. I used Shutter Priority mode at 1/100 second or faster in order to have consistent conditions. Table 5-2 gives the results of my tests.

Table 5-2. **Results of Burst Shooting Tests with Panasonic Lumix DMC-FZ2500 Camera**

Burst Rate	Image Quality	Image Size	Focus Mode	No. Images Before Slowdown
H	Raw & JPEG	L	AFS	30
H	Raw	-	AFS	35
H	Raw & JPEG	L	AFC	35
M	Raw & JPEG	L	AFS	33
L	Raw & JPEG	L	AFC	38
H	JPEG-Fine	L	AFS	160

The fastest speed the camera achieved in these tests was about 11 frames per second. The results did not always agree with the expected results according to the specifications, though Panasonic makes it clear that results will be affected by shooting conditions.

My recommendation is to use the slower speeds when you don't need super-fast shooting. For example, if you are taking a portrait and would like to capture changing expressions but don't need to freeze an action as you might at a sporting event, try using the L or M setting to increase your chance of getting usable shots, especially if you are using continuous autofocus.

Your results also can vary according to the setting for the Focus/Release Priority option on screen 3 of the Custom menu, if you are using the AFF or AFC setting for autofocus. With the Focus option, the camera waits until focus is achieved before capturing the image. With Release, the camera uses predictive focusing and gives more priority to speed of shooting than to accuracy of focusing. With the Focus setting for Focus/Release Priority when using AFF or AFC, focusing results may be better, depending on other conditions. With continuous autofocus, I got more shots before slowdown than with single autofocus, but at a slower maximum burst speed. (With the AFS option, the setting for Focus/Release Priority should not affect the speed of continuous shooting, because focus is fixed with the first shot in the burst.)

The burst-shooting options are available in every shooting mode for still images, except for Panorama. However, there are several limitations on the use of burst shooting. You cannot use it with flash, or with the Rough Monochrome, Silky Monochrome, Miniature, Soft Focus, Star Filter, or Sunshine filter effect settings. You also cannot use it with some of the other special settings such as Multiple Exposure, White Balance Bracket, Handheld Night Shot, Glistening Water, Glittering Illuminations, or Soft Image of a Flower settings, or during motion picture recording.

After shooting with any of the burst options, you are likely to see for at least a few seconds the red icon on the left side of the display screen indicating that the camera is writing images to the memory card; while that icon is displayed, you should not try to take any more pictures, and you should not open the battery compartment cover or otherwise interfere with the camera's operation.

4K Photo

The third position for drive mode dial, labeled 4K, gives you access to the powerful 4K Photo features. The term 4K originated with 4K video recording, which is available with the FZ2500 and other modern cameras. 4K is a video format that has about 4,000 (4K) pixels in the horizontal dimension, as opposed to the more standard HD (high-definition) formats that have about 1,920 (2K) pixels in that dimension. The 4K format is sometimes referred to as ultra-HD or UHD.

With the FZ2500 camera, a single frame of 4K video has 3840 horizontal pixels and 2160 vertical ones, for a total of about 8.3 megapixels. So, a single frame of 4K video has about the same resolution as a still image taken with aspect ratio set to 16:9 and picture size set to M. Because of the relatively high resolution of each frame of 4K video, you can use the 4K capability of the camera as another alternative for taking a high-speed burst of single images.

The difference from normal burst shooting is that, with 4K Photo, the camera actually records a video sequence at its normal rate of 30 frames per second, and it can record continuously at that fast rate, rather than for the relatively short time the camera can record at a fast rate with normal burst shooting. As a result, you can record thousands of medium-resolution still images and then select the best ones from that group.

In addition, you are not limited to using the 16:9 aspect ratio of video footage. You can set the Aspect Ratio item on screen 1 of the Recording menu to any of its values: 4:3, 3:2, 16:9, or 1:1. In that way, you can take advantage of the rapid shooting of video recording while still using an aspect ratio that lets you compose still photographs in a traditional format.

All of the 4K Photo options are available for use in all still-image shooting modes except Panorama. Therefore, you can shoot these high-quality bursts in the more advanced modes, including Shutter Priority and Manual exposure. In that way, you can set the shutter speed to a value that avoids the motion blur that often is present in still frames captured from video scenes. To do that, set the shooting mode to Shutter Priority or Manual and set the shutter speed to a value such as 1/1000 second using the rear dial. Of course, in order to capture usable shots with that setting, there will have to be strong lighting, presumably in an outdoor location.

Figure 5-7 is a sample shot I took using 4K Photo, with aspect ratio set to 3:2 and shutter speed set to 1/1000 second to avoid motion blur.

Figure 5-7. Image Taken Using 4K Photo Feature

In order to use the 4K Photo option, as with 4K video recording, you need to use a memory card that is rated in UHS Speed Class 3.

The 4K Photo option has three sub-options with somewhat different functions, as discussed below. You select these settings using the 4K Photo option on screen 2 of the Recording menu. Under that option, there are two sub-options, Recording Method and Loop Recording, as shown in Figure 5-8. To select one of the three recording types, choose the first option, which has three choices, as shown in Figure 5-9: 4K Burst, 4K Burst (S/S), and 4K Pre-burst. These are described below.

Figure 5-8. 4K Photo Menu Options Screen

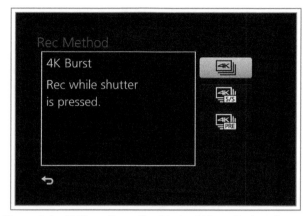

Figure 5-9. 4K Photo Recording Method Menu Options Screen

4K Burst

The basic option for the 4K Photo feature, highlighted in Figure 5-9, is called 4K Burst. With this option, the camera records a 4K video sequence while you press the shutter button and hold it down. This approach is useful when you are trying to capture a burst of shots of an activity with a fairly clear duration. For example, if a group of bicycle racers is nearing your position, when the cyclists get close, you can press the shutter button and hold it down until they have passed out of view. With this setting, the camera can record for as long as the camera is powered and the memory card has capacity.

4K Burst (S/S)

The second selection is 4K Burst (S/S), for Start and Stop. With this option, the camera starts recording its 4K video sequence when you press and release the shutter button, and it records continuously until you press and release the button again.

The idea with this approach is to let the camera run so it can capture a burst of shots of an unpredictable activity. For example, if you are photographing a group of geese on a pond and you want to catch them in flight, you can start the camera recording and not stop it until they have taken off and flown away. Here, again, the camera can record for an indefinite period, depending on power and memory card capacity. If you see a scene you may want to save later as a single frame, press the Fn5 button to insert a marker in the file. You can add as many as 40 markers for each 4K Burst (S/S) sequence.

With the 4K Burst (S/S) setting, you can also turn on the Loop Recording option, which is the second option under the main 4K Photo menu item. If you turn on Loop Recording, then, when the 4K Burst (S/S) option is in use, the camera will continue to record for as long

as 12 hours, provided the power and memory card capacity permit, but it will record the scene in a loop, erasing the older scenes and retaining only about the last ten minutes of video. In that way, you won't have to search through hours of video to find the few shots that you were attempting to capture.

4K Pre-burst

With this final option the camera actually records continuously, even before you press the shutter button. It retains only a short amount of action in its memory—about one second. When you press the shutter button fully down and release it, the camera records the scene for the one second that is already in its memory and for about one additional second, resulting in a sequence lasting about two seconds.

You can use this option for a situation when you believe an action is about to happen, and you don't want to miss the beginning of it. For example, if you are watching a batter at a baseball game, you can press the shutter button as soon as the bat hits the ball, and you should catch the entire swing and impact.

With this option, because the camera records continuously even when you are not pressing the shutter button, the battery is run down more quickly than usual. So, you should not activate this setting until you are ready to use it.

If you use autofocus with any of the 4K Photo settings, focus will be adjusted continuously, regardless of whether AFS, AFF, or AFC is selected for focus mode. (This is because the camera is actually recording video, and in that mode, focus always is adjusted continuously when autofocus is in use.)

With the 4K Burst and 4K Pre-burst options, no audio is recorded. However, with the 4K Burst (S/S) option, audio is recorded through the camera's built-in microphone or an external microphone, if one is used. This audio is not played back when you play back the sequence in the camera. However, if you copy the sequence's .mp4 file to a computer and play it back, the audio track will be present. So, if you want to capture both still images and video along with audio, this option can be a useful one.

Extracting a 4K Photo Still Image

Once you have recorded a 4K Photo sequence, you need to take further steps to extract a still image from it.

After you press the Playback button and find the sequence, press the Up button to enter 4K Photo playback mode, as indicated in Figure 5-10.

Figure 5-10. 4K Photo Playback Mode

The camera will display a screen with a group of image icons stacked near the bottom center of the display. With your finger, swipe along that stack to drag through the series of images, or press the Right and Left buttons, or turn the front or rear dial, to move through the stack. A vertical yellow line will move through the progress bar at the top of the display to show how far through the group of images you have moved. If there are more than 45 images in the group, you can touch the right or left arrow icon on the screen, on either side of the stack of image icons, to move to the next or previous group. (You also can press the Menu/Set button when the arrow pointing to the next or previous group is highlighted in yellow.)

If the sequence is long, you can play through it with DVR-like controls. To do that, press the Fn4 button and the camera will display a screen like that in Figure 5-11, with playback control icons.

You can touch those icons (or press the button associated with each icon, as indicated by the yellow arrow next to each icon, to play or rewind, or to advance or go backward a frame at a time. (For example, to play through the frames at normal speed, press the Up button, or touch the play icon next to the upward-facing yellow triangle.)

If you added markers to a 4K Burst (S/S) sequence, you can press the Fn5 button to switch to marker mode. In that mode, pressing the Right or Left button (or touch icon) moves to the next or previous marker.

Figure 5-11. 4K Photo Playback Screen with Playback Controls

When the camera is displaying the single frame you want to extract from the 4K Photo sequence as a still image, press the Menu/Set button, or touch the icon at the far right of the bottom of the screen. The camera will display the message shown in Figure 5-12, asking if you want to save the image. If you highlight and select Yes, the camera will save that frame.

Figure 5-12. Confirmation Screen to Save 4K Photo Image

I have found the 4K Photo feature to be of great use, especially when I am trying to capture an image of a bird at a birdfeeder. The birds come and go rapidly and unpredictably. With this option, I can set up the camera on a tripod, activate 4K Photo (S/S), and leave the camera alone for several minutes. When I return, the chances are good that I will have captured an image like that in Figure 5-13, showing a bird in flight.

Figure 5-13. 4K Photo Image of Bird in Flight

Post Focus

The fourth icon on the drive mode dial represents the powerful Post Focus option. As its name indicates, this setting lets you choose the focus point of an image after it was captured. In order to accomplish this feat, the camera records a short 4K video sequence, adjusting focus for different parts of the scene throughout the recording. When the recording is finished, you can select a frame with the sharpest focus on the area you are most interested in, and the camera will save that frame as a JPEG image. In addition, you can combine multiple frames with different focus points to create a composite image with sharp focus throughout most or all of its area. That operation, called focus stacking, is discussed later in this section.

The only initial setting for Post Focus is to turn the feature on or off, by turning the drive mode dial to select the fourth icon. You can use this option in any shooting mode except Creative Video and Panorama.

Once Post Focus is turned on, aim the camera at the subject and press the shutter button halfway. Because the camera is using 4K video mode, which crops the frame somewhat, you will see that the camera has zoomed in slightly. You may have to adjust the framing of the image to account for the increased focal length.

If the camera finds a focus point, it will display a steady green circle in the upper right corner. If it cannot find a focus point, the green circle will blink. When you are ready, hold the camera as still as possible and press the shutter button all the way down and release it. The camera will record a video sequence for several seconds, during which it will change the focus to every focus point it can find throughout the scene.

When the recording has finished, press the Play button to enter playback mode. You will see a screen like that in Figure 5-14, with a Post Focus icon in the upper left corner.

Figure 5-14. Post Focus Initial Playback Screen

Press the Up button or touch that icon, and you will see a screen like that in Figure 5-15, with various icons including a plus sign, a return arrow, Fn4, Fn5, and an icon in the lower right corner for saving an image from the sequence.

Figure 5-15. Post Focus Playback Screen with Control Icons

On this screen, move your finger to any point where you would like focus to be fixed. If the camera is able to show an image with that focus point, it will briefly display a green frame at that point and it will change the focus to that location. For example, in Figure 5-16, after I touched the screen over the yellow vase in the foreground of the scene, the camera displayed the image with sharp focus at that point.

Figure 5-16. Post Focus Playback: Focus on Yellow Vase

In Figure 5-17, after I touched the screen over the blue vase in the background, the camera displayed a frame with focus fixed on that point.

Figure 5-17. Post Focus: Focus on Blue Vase

To adjust focus at any point in more detail, press the magnifying glass icon with the plus sign, or move the zoom lever to the right, to enlarge the image. The camera will then display a sliding scale at the bottom of the screen, as seen in Figure 5-18.

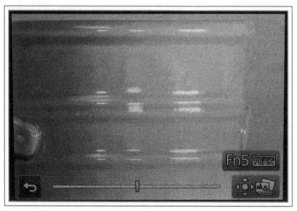

Figure 5-18. Sliding Control to Fine-tune Focus

Slide your finger along that scale, or use the Left and Right buttons or the rear dial, to adjust the focus point on the enlarged image in small increments until you have adjusted the focus as precisely as possible. Then touch the return arrow in the lower left corner of the screen, or move the zoom lever to the left, to return the image to normal size.

You also can press the Fn5 button or its on-screen icon, which causes the camera to turn on its peaking display, placing colored pixels at the areas of sharpest focus to help you determine where focus is sharp. Successive presses of that button or icon cycle through various levels of peaking, which the camera indicates with Off, L, and H labels in the upper left corner.

When you have focus adjusted as you want it, touch the yellow icon in the lower right corner of the screen, or press the Menu/Set button, and the camera will display the message shown in Figure 5-19, asking if you want to save this image. If so, highlight and select Yes, and the camera will save a JPEG image with the focus point set as you have selected. You can repeat this process as often as you want, to save more images with this or another focus point.

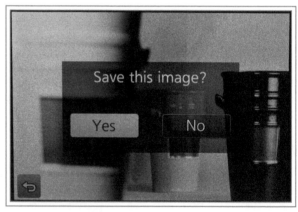

Figure 5-19. Confirmation Screen to Save Post Focus Image

Focus Stacking

Once you have recorded a set of images with the Post Focus option, you also can use those images to create a composite image using shots with different focus points, which has sharp focus throughout much or all of the area in the scene. To do this, when you are viewing a Post Focus series in playback mode, press the Up button to call up the Post Focus editing screen, as shown in Figures 5-15 and 5-16, earlier. On that screen, press the Fn4 button or touch its icon in the upper right corner of the display. The camera will display the screen shown in Figure 5-20, with choices of Auto Merging or Range Merging.

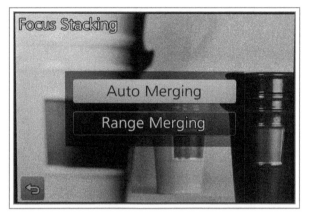

Figure 5-20. Focus Stacking Merging Options Screen

If you choose Auto Merging, the camera will automatically select the shots that it deems to be the best for merging into a final image, giving preference to shots with focus points closer to the lens. The camera will create and save a final image that should have sharp focus in many or all areas, as shown in Figure 5-21.

Figure 5-21. Focus Stacking Final Image

If you choose Range Merging, the camera displays the screen shown in Figure 5-22.

Figure 5-22. Focus Stacking: Range Merging Options Screen

On that screen, touch a point to select it for inclusion in the range of focus points to be used for the final image. Touch it again to deselect it. You can keep touching more points, or drag on the screen to include an area of the scene. You also can use the direction buttons to move a green selection frame around the screen and press the Fn5 button to select or deselect the point within that frame. When you have selected two or more focus points, the camera will display those points and all other points between those focus points in a green shade, to show that they will be included in the final image, as shown in Figure 5-23. The camera will display gray frames for points that are not included in the focus area. You can press the Display button to select or deselect all points in the image at any time, to start over with a completely full or empty set of focus points.

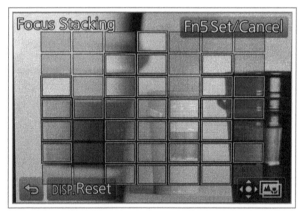

Figure 5-23. Screen to Select Range Merging Focus Points

When you have finished selecting the focus points you want to be included in the final image, press the yellow focus stacking icon in the lower right of the image, or press the Menu/Set button, and the camera will display the message shown in Figure 5-24, asking you to confirm the merging of the focus points. Choose Yes if you want to proceed.

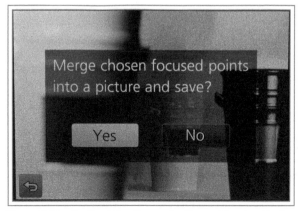

Figure 5-24. Confirmation Screen for Range Merging Option

Post Focus and Focus Stacking cannot be used with several settings of Scene mode and Creative Control mode, or when the Multiple Exposure option is being used. The camera cannot use the Raw setting for Quality, and the image will be limited to a size of eight megapixels. The camera will use the electronic shutter with a limited range of shutter speeds. However, you still can adjust many settings, and these features are very useful in situations where focus is critical or uncertain, such as macro photography. In a sense, Post Focus acts for focus as the Raw format does for white balance and exposure, which can be adjusted after the fact in a Raw image.

Self-timer

The next-to-last icon on the drive mode dial represents the self-timer. When you activate the self-timer, the camera delays for a specified number of seconds (ten or two) after you press the shutter button, before taking a picture. The ten-second setting is useful when you need to place the camera on a tripod and press the shutter button, and then run around to join a group of people the camera is aimed at. The two-second setting is helpful when you need to avoid jiggling the camera by pressing the shutter button as the exposure is taken. This is the case when taking extreme closeups or other shots for which focus is sensitive.

To select a timer setting, use the Self-timer option on screen 3 of the Recording menu, as shown in Figure 5-25.

Figure 5-25. Self-timer Menu Options Screen

From top to bottom, these selections are ten-second self-timer; ten-second self-timer with three images taken; and two-second self-timer. Select the setting you want with the Up and Down buttons, by turning the rear dial, or by touching its icon on the screen. Then

press the Menu/Set button to confirm the selection and press the Fn6 button to return to the recording screen. To activate the self-timer, turn the dial to the next-to-last drive mode icon. The camera's display will have an icon in the upper right corner showing the current self-timer setting, as seen in Figure 5-26.

Figure 5-26. Icon for Self-timer on Shooting Screen

Now you can wait as long as you want before actually taking the picture (unless the camera times out by entering Sleep Mode). Compose the picture and press the shutter button. The AF assist lamp, which also serves as the self-timer lamp, will blink and the camera will beep until the shutter is automatically tripped at the end of the specified time. The beeps and blinks speed up for the last second as a warning, when the timer is set to ten seconds. For the two-second option, the camera beeps four times and blinks five times as it counts down. You can cancel the shot while the self-timer is running by pressing the Menu/Set button.

If you choose the option with which the camera takes three pictures after the ten-second timer runs, the three shots will be spaced about two seconds apart, so tell your subject(s) to maintain the pose until all three images have been captured.

You cannot use the self-timer option with multiple images when the camera is set for any type of bracketing or Multiple Exposure, or when Simultaneous Record Without Filter is turned on. You cannot use the self-timer at all when recording motion pictures or in Panorama mode.

Time Lapse Shot/Stop Motion Animation

The final position on the drive mode dial activates the camera's Time Lapse Shot and Stop Motion Animation features. In order to make the settings for either of those options, you use the Time Lapse/Animation item on screen 3 of the Recording menu.

Time Lapse Shot

The Time Lapse Shot option lets you shoot a time lapse series of photographs. You probably have seen sequences in the movies or on television in which an event that takes a fair amount of time, such as a sunset, a flower opening, clouds moving across the sky, or a parking lot filling up with cars, is shown in a speeded-up series of images, so it appears to happen in a few seconds.

The FZ2500 can use its time lapse feature with any shooting mode, including the Intelligent Auto modes, except for Creative Video and Panorama. If you use the more advanced shooting modes, you have access to all of the major settings for your images, including Raw quality, white balance, ISO, and others.

To use this feature, select the Time Lapse/Animation menu item. On the next screen, select Mode, and select Time Lapse Shot for that option. You will then see the setup screen shown in Figure 5-27.

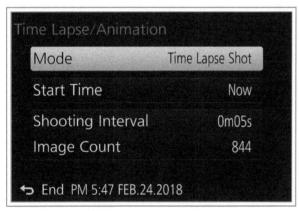

Figure 5-27. Setup Screen for Time Lapse Shot Option

On that screen, use the direction buttons, the front or rear dial, or the touch screen to move through the various options. Select a start time, the interval between shots, and the total number of shots. The start time can be set to Now, or to any time within the next 23 hours 59 minutes. The interval between shots can be set to any value from one second to 99 minutes 59 seconds. One point to bear in mind when setting the interval is that, if the lighting is very dim, the camera may need to set a long shutter speed. For example, if the camera is set to use a shutter speed of one minute, which requires a long time for in-camera processing after the exposure is made, this system will not succeed

if the interval between shots is set to less than two minutes. The total number of shots can be any number up to 9,999.

When you have made all of the settings as you want them, exit from the menu screen using the Fn6 button, and make sure you are ready to start shooting your time lapse sequence. Then turn the drive mode dial to the last position, for interval shooting. When you are ready to start the sequence shooting, press the shutter button.

When you press the shutter button, the camera will take the images at the specified intervals and will repeat the process until the total number of images has been recorded. Of course, if the battery runs down or the memory card fills up, the process will end prematurely. (You can use an optional AC adapter to avoid a power issue; see Appendix A.) At any time (except when the screen is dimmed between shots), you can press the Fn5 button and the camera will display a screen asking if you want to continue, pause, or end the process. Highlight your choice and press Menu/Set to select it.

When the sequence is complete, either after the full series has been taken or after an interrupted series, the camera will display a message asking if you want it to create a movie using the recorded images. If you say yes, it will take some time to process the movie, which you can then play like any movie.

If you say no to creating the movie, assuming you have a detailed display screen selected in playback mode, the first image in the series will be displayed with indications like those in Figure 5-28, showing that you can press the Up button to play back the sequence quickly, like a short movie.

Figure 5-28. Time Lapse Shot Playback Screen

If you press the Down button, you will see a screen that lets you choose a sub-menu that gives you the options of displaying the images sequentially one by one or uploading them by Wi-Fi. (The uploading process is discussed in Chapter 9.)

If you don't create a movie from the shots at this point, you can do so later using the Time Lapse Video option on screen 3 of the Playback menu, as discussed in Chapter 6.

Stop Motion Animation

The other choice for the Mode option of the Time Lapse/ Animation menu item is Stop Motion Animation. This feature is similar to the Time Lapse Shot option, because it involves taking a series of still images that the camera combines into a movie. The difference is that this option is intended for use in animating objects, such as clay figures or puppets. You also can use it to make an animated movie based on drawings, as is done for cartoons and animated feature films. You need to move the figure or change the drawing very slightly for each new shot. You will need a large number of images to create a movie of any length. For example, if the final movie is to be shown at 30 frames per second, you will need to take 30 images for every second of the movie, changing the position or other aspect of the subject slightly for each successive image.

When you select this option for Mode, you will see a screen with options for Add to Picture Group, Auto Shooting, and Shooting Interval. The interval option will not be available unless you first select Auto Shooting. If you turn on Auto Shooting, the camera will capture images on its own at the interval you specify, from one second to 60 seconds. Otherwise, you will have to trigger the camera yourself for each shot. Because it is critical to keep the camera absolutely still throughout the image-taking process, it is advisable to use Auto Shooting so you will not have to touch the camera for each shot. If you do not use Auto Shooting, you can control the camera from a smartphone or tablet, as discussed in Chapter 9, or from a wired remote control, as discussed in Appendix A.

You also may want to use an optional AC adapter, discussed in Appendix A, to make sure the camera does not lose power during the shooting. However, if the camera does turn off, you can resume the series of shots when it is turned back on. It will prompt you to do so if the series has been interrupted.

While the shooting is in progress, the camera will display an icon showing a series of frames at the right side of the display with the cumulative number of shots taken so far, as shown in Figure 5-29.

Figure 5-29. Shooting Screen During Stop Motion Animation

It also will display an overlaid image of the previous two shots, to help you line up the next shot properly with the figure or drawing in the proper position.

If you want, you can include in your animation a group of pictures that you previously recorded using the Stop Motion Animation feature. To do that, select the Add to Picture Group menu option. The camera will then display any groups of such pictures, and you can select a group to include. In that way, you can build up a stop motion sequence from images captured in various shooting sessions.

When you have finished your series of shots, press the Menu/Set button and go back to the Stop Motion Animation menu item. Press Menu/Set when that item is highlighted, and the camera will ask whether you want to stop the shooting series. If you say yes, it will ask if you want to create the video now. If so, it will prompt you for the settings to use, including recording quality, frame rate, and whether to run the sequence forward (normal) or in reverse. For the best quality, you should select 30 frames per second for the frame rate (in the United States), but 15 frames per second will still provide a reasonably smooth flow of action. Select OK when the settings are made as you want, and the camera will create the video. You can play it back in the camera by pressing the Up button.

If you don't create a movie from the shots at this point, you can do so later using the Stop Motion Video option on screen 3 of the Playback menu, as discussed in Chapter 6. As with the Time Lapse Shot option, you can view the shots in playback mode as a quick sequence using the Up button or individually from the sub-menu called up by the Down button.

Controls on Back of Camera

Figure 5-30 shows the controls on the camera's back.

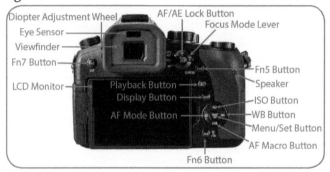

Figure 5-30. **Controls on Back of Camera**

Focus Mode Lever

This lever at the top of the camera's back, to the right of the viewfinder, controls the basic focus mode used for capturing still images and videos. You use the small handle at the right of the control to move the white indicator line on the left to one of three positions: AFS/AFF, AFC, or MF.

AFS/AFF

If you choose AFS/AFF, the camera will use its autofocus mechanism, along with the settings you make for other focus-related options such as AF Mode, AFS/AFF, and others. I discussed the AFS/AFF setting in Chapter 4, and I will discuss the AF Mode setting later in this chapter. The camera will use its normal autofocus distance range of 11.8 inches (30 cm) to infinity at the wide-angle setting and 3.3 feet (1 meter) to infinity at the full telephoto setting. AFS/AFF is the normal setting to use for most everyday shooting.

AFC

If you choose AFC, the camera will continuously adjust the focus, even if the subject is not moving. This option uses more battery power than either AFS or AFF. If you are taking photographs of subjects in motion, such as pets or children at play, using the AFC setting will keep the focus approximately correct as the subjects move,

and it should result in more accurate focusing when you press the shutter button to take the picture. If you are photographing stationary subjects, stick with the AFS or AFF setting to save battery power.

Manual Focus

If you move the lever to the MF position for manual focus, you will need to adjust the focus manually using the focus ring. The process for using manual focus involves several possible steps, which depend on the settings for several Custom menu options. I will discuss the details of those options in Chapter 7. For now, to discuss the basics of using manual focus, I will assume that the MF Assist option on screen 4 of the Custom menu is turned on, and that Touch Screen is set to On under the Touch Settings item on screen 10 of the Custom menu. I will also assume that the MF Assist Display item on screen 4 of the Custom menu is set to Full, and that the MF Guide and peaking items on that screen are also turned on.

With the above settings in place and the focus mode lever at the MF position, start turning the focus ring (the thin ridged ring around the lens, farthest from the camera's body) to adjust the focus.

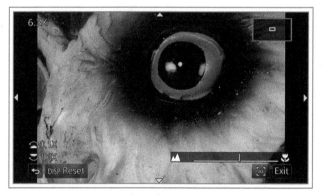

Figure 5-31. **Enlarged Screen with MF Assist**

As soon as you start turning the ring, you will see a screen like that in Figure 5-31, showing an enlarged area on the display, with yellow arrows at the edges. You can move that area around the screen with your fingers, and you can pinch or pull on the screen or turn the rear dial to change the enlargement factor to anywhere between 3.0x and 10.0x normal. You also can use the direction buttons to move the enlarged area. When you have the enlarged area located where you want it, turn the focus ring to get the focus as sharp as you can. The peaking feature will place an increasing density of colored pixels at the locations that are in sharpest focus.

You can press on the touch icon that looks like a rectangle with a small, solid rectangle in its upper right corner to switch from the Full setting to a PIP (picture-in-picture) view, with the entire display enlarged between 3.0x and 6.0x normal. You can press on the small AF icon to cause the camera to use autofocus in the center of the enlarged display. You can touch the DISP. Reset icon to return the focus point to the center. You can touch the EXIT icon to return to the normal-sized display. While you are adjusting focus, the MF Guide will appear near the bottom of the display, showing roughly where the focus point is located between the minimum distance and infinity.

When the focus is as sharp as you need it to be, press the shutter button to capture an image or press the red movie button to start recording a video.

I will discuss the menu options for assisting with manual focus further in Chapter 7.

AF/AE Lock Button

This button, located in the center of the focus mode lever, is permanently assigned to carry out either the autofocus lock or autoexposure lock function, or both, or the AF-On function. Those settings are controlled by the AF/AE Lock option on screen 1 of the Custom menu, as discussed in Chapter 7. By default, the button is assigned to the AE Lock option. With that setting, when you press the button the current exposure setting is locked, in all shooting modes except Manual exposure and the two Intelligent Auto modes.

By default, you have to hold the button down to keep the focus or exposure locked. However, you can change that behavior using the AF/AE Lock Hold option on screen 1 of the Custom menu. If you turn that option on, you can press and release the AF/AE Lock button, and its assigned operation will stay in place until you press and release the button a second time. (That option does not work when the button is assigned to AF-On.)

Fn5 Button

By default, the Fn5 button is assigned as the Q.Menu button, though you can assign this button to a different function using the Function Button Set option on screen 7 of the Custom menu. I recommend leaving it as it is, because the Q.Menu label is printed on the camera next to the Fn5 button. As discussed in Chapter

4, when you press the Q.Menu button while the camera is in recording mode, a mini-version of the camera's menu system opens up, allowing you to choose settings for various menu options without having to use the standard menu system.

The Fn5 button also has some miscellaneous functions permanently assigned to it. When you are setting up the autofocus area using the Custom Multi option of AF Mode, in which you select one or more of 49 possible focus zones, you press this button to lock in your selections after highlighting the desired zones. When you are recording a 4K Burst (S/S) sequence, you can press the Fn5 button to insert markers at promising spots. During playback, you can press the button to find those markers. When you are using the Post Focus feature, you can press this button to highlight the in-focus part of the image with focus peaking.

Playback Button

This button, located below the Fn5 button, is marked by a small triangle. You press this button to put the camera into playback mode. Press it again to switch back into recording mode. When the camera is placed into playback mode, the lens barrel will retract automatically after about 15 seconds, because the lens is not needed during playback operations. If you don't want that automatic retraction to take place, you can turn it off using the Lens Retraction item on screen 9 of the Custom menu.

Display Button

The Display button is in the center of the camera's back, to the right of the LCD screen. It has several functions, depending on the context. Its primary function is to switch among the several available display screens for the LCD screen and the viewfinder, in both recording mode and playback mode.

In recording mode, following are the screens you see on the LCD monitor from repeated presses of the Display button. I will not include the touch screen icons in describing these screens, because the touch screen can be turned off, removing all such icons from the display.

- As shown in Figure 5-32, full display, with battery status, Picture Size, Quality, aspect ratio, Photo Style, flash status, ISO (if set to a specific value), exposure compensation amount, movie quality and format, recording mode, metering mode, focus mode, AF mode, AFS/AFF setting, number of pictures or length of video that can be shot with the remaining storage, ND Filter status, and the histogram (discussed later), if it is turned on through screen 4 of the Custom menu. The aperture and shutter speed also will display briefly after exposure is evaluated, and one or both of those values will remain on the screen in some shooting modes. The focus frame will appear if the current AF Mode setting displays a frame.

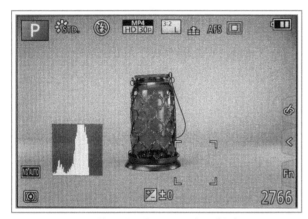

Figure 5-32. Shooting Screen with Full Information

○ Blank display showing the live view, along with the focus area (if using a focus mode that displays a focus frame, such as 1-Area AF or AF Tracking). The aperture, shutter speed, ISO value, and exposure compensation scale also will display briefly after exposure is evaluated.

○ As shown in Figure 5-33, full information with level gauge (sometimes called the tilt sensor display by Panasonic), as well as histogram and focus frame if applicable.

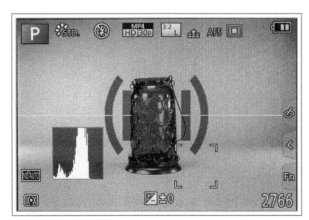

Figure 5-33. Shooting Screen with Full information, Level Gauge, and Histogram

○ As shown in Figure 5-34, level gauge with focus frame if applicable.

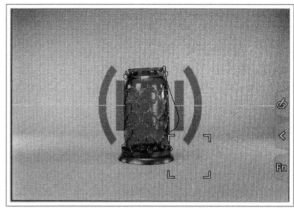

Figure 5-34. Shooting Screen with Level Gauge and Focus Frame

○ As shown in Figure 5-35, screen with no live view, but with shooting information. Panasonic calls this the on-monitor information screen. When this screen is displayed, you can touch many of the icons on the screen to adjust the settings represented by those icons. For example, if you touch the ISO icon, the camera will display the ISO menu, letting you choose a new setting for ISO. When the adjustment is done, the on-monitor information screen returns.

Figure 5-35. On-monitor Information Screen

○ Finally, another press of the Display button produces a black screen with no live view and no information.

In the basic Intelligent Auto mode, the Display button produces the screens listed above, but the histogram does not appear even if it was turned on through the Custom menu. There also are other items that will appear on the information screens, such as the Guide Line grid if selected on screen 5 of the Custom menu, and icons for items such as the self-timer when they are activated.

When you are using the viewfinder, the display screens are similar, but there is no screen with a black background and shooting information, and no blacked-out screen, neither of which would be useful with the viewfinder.

When the camera is in playback mode, repeated presses of the Display button produce the following screens.

○ As shown in Figure 5-36, image with battery status, Picture Size, Quality, aspect ratio, recording mode, aperture, shutter speed, exposure compensation, ISO, white balance, and icon showing that you can press the Down button to upload images via Wi-Fi. (As with the recording mode displays, I am not including touch icons, because the touch screen may be turned off).

Figure 5-36. Playback Screen with Basic Information

○ As shown in Figure 5-37, a smaller image with the same information, plus date and time of image capture, image number, and some other settings, including metering mode, Photo Style, Intelligent Dynamic, and Photo Style.

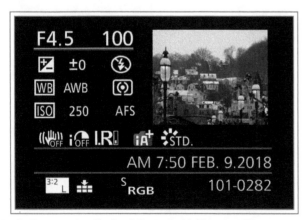

Figure 5-37. Playback Screen with Thumbnail Image

As shown in Figure 5-38, the smaller image with basic recording information and the histogram, which is discussed in Chapter 7. Basically, the histogram is a graphic display that shows the brightness of the image through peaks and dips. A normal histogram should have most peaks in the middle portion of the graph, for each color.

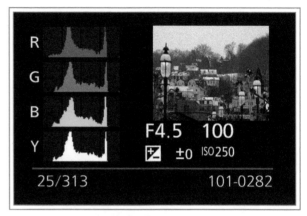

Figure 5-38. Playback Screen with Histogram

○ Just the recorded image, with no other information, but flashing the highlights in areas that are overexposed. (This screen appears only if the Highlight option is turned on through screen 5 of the Custom menu. The highlights also will flash on the detailed information screens; this screen is added so you can see the overexposed areas without interference from information items.)

○ Just the recorded image with no other information, and with no flashing highlights.

If you are playing back a motion picture, the display is similar, except for some added information that applies to that mode, including an icon showing that you can press the Up button to start the motion picture playing.

After about one minute of no activity with the controls, the camera removes the playback information from the screen. To restore it, press the Playback button or the Display button.

The Display button also has several other functions. When you are adjusting ISO and ISO Limit, you can press this button to switch those adjustments between the rear dial and the front dial. You can press it to restore the focus frame to normal after you have moved it off center or resized it when using the 1-Area focus mode or one of the other modes that allow you to move or resize the focus point or points. If you need a reminder of the current date and time, with the camera in recording mode, press the Display button enough times to cycle back to the screen with the most recording information, and the date and time will appear on the lower left of the screen for about five seconds.

When you are viewing a menu screen, you can press the Display button to cycle through the menu in the forward direction by a full screen at a time, the same way you can by pressing the zoom lever to the right. When the exposure compensation adjustment screen is displayed, you can press the Display button to switch the functions of the rear dial and front dial between controlling exposure compensation and controlling flash compensation. When the Highlight Shadow screen is displayed, pressing the Display button switches the format of the display of the adjustment graph. When you are using a wireless flash setup, you can press the Display button to test the communication between flash units.

Menu/Set Button and Direction Buttons

An important control group on the FZ2500 is the set of five buttons on the back of the camera, arranged in a circular pattern. Each of the buttons is marked with an icon that indicates its primary function. In the center of the pattern is a fifth button, labeled Menu/Set. I generally refer to the four outer buttons as direction buttons or cursor buttons (Left, Right, Up, and Down), and to the center button as the Menu/Set button.

Direction Buttons

The direction buttons act as cursor keys do on a computer keyboard, letting you navigate up and down and left and right through menu options. However, each of the four direction buttons also performs at least one additional function, as indicated by the icon or label on the button. I will discuss those functions for each button in turn.

Up Button: ISO

The Up button doubles as the ISO button, which lets you set the camera's ISO, or sensitivity to light. On the FZ2500, the available ISO settings range from 125 to 12800, though the range varies in some situations. With the lower settings, the camera produces the best image quality, but exposures require more light. With higher settings, the camera can produce good exposures in dim

light, but there is likely to be an increasing amount of visual "noise" in the image as the ISO value increases.

Generally speaking, you should shoot images with the lowest ISO that will allow them to be exposed properly. (An exception is if you want the grainy look that comes with a high ISO value.) For example, if you are shooting indoors in low light, you may need to set the ISO to a high value (say, 800) so you can expose the image with a reasonably fast shutter speed. If the camera were set to a lower ISO, it would need to use a slower shutter speed to take in enough light for a proper exposure, and the resulting image would likely be blurry and possibly unusable.

The ISO setting is available only when the camera is set to one of the advanced shooting modes, including the PASM modes, Panorama, and Creative Video. To make the setting, press this button and a horizontal menu will appear at the bottom of the display, as shown in Figure 5-39.

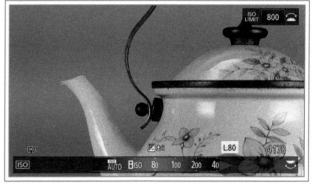

Figure 5-39. ISO Menu

You can scroll through the values on this menu by pressing the Left and Right buttons, by turning the rear dial, or by scrolling the menu with the touch screen. (If you prefer, you can use the front dial to select an ISO setting; to do that, press the Display button, and the functions of the rear dial and front dial will be switched.)

The possible numerical values are 125, 200, 400, 800, 1600, 3200, 6400, and 12800, unless you change some menu settings, discussed below, to add values below 125 and above 12800, as well as intermediate values. With Creative Video mode and when using the 4K Photo or Post Focus option, ISO can be set only to Auto or a specific value from 125 to 6400.

As I discussed in Chapter 4, when ISO is set to Auto ISO or Intelligent ISO, the camera will choose an ISO setting based on the exposure conditions, up to the value set with the ISO Limit Set option. That limit can be set using the ISO Limit Set menu item on screen 5 of the Recording menu. It also can be set when the ISO adjustment screen is displayed. By default, the front dial adjusts the ISO Limit Set value, but, as noted above, if you press the Display button when the ISO adjustment screen is displayed, the front dial will adjust the basic ISO value, and the rear dial will adjust ISO Limit Set.

If no value has been entered for ISO Limit Set, the camera uses 3200 as the Auto ISO/Intelligent ISO upper limit unless the flash is in use, in which case the limit will be 1600. When you set a numerical value for the ISO, the ISO Limit Set value has no effect. As discussed in Chapter 3, you can use Auto ISO with Manual exposure mode for still images, which lets you keep shutter speed and aperture fixed while the ISO varies.

When you use the Intelligent ISO setting, the camera adjusts the ISO based on the movement of the subject as well as the brightness, so the camera can set a higher shutter speed to stop the motion. Intelligent ISO is available with the Program and Aperture Priority modes, but not with the Shutter Priority or Manual exposure modes, or when using the 4K Photo or Post Focus option, or in Creative Video mode. It is automatically turned on in Intelligent Auto mode.

When would you want to use a numerical value for the ISO setting, rather than setting it to Auto ISO or Intelligent ISO? One example is if you want the highest quality for your image, and you aren't worried about camera movement, either because you are using a tripod so a slow shutter speed won't result in blur, or the lighting is bright enough to use a fast shutter speed. Then you could set the ISO to its lowest possible setting of 125 (or 80 if Extended ISO is turned on) to achieve high quality. On the other hand, if you definitely want a grainy, noisy look, you can set the ISO to 3200 or even higher to introduce noise into the image. You also might want a high ISO setting so you can use a fast shutter speed to stop action or in low light. In many cases, though, you can just leave the setting at Auto or Intelligent and let the camera adjust the ISO as needed.

It is important to be aware of how much a high ISO value can affect the quality of your images. For example,

Figure 5-40 was taken at ISO 125 and Figure 5-41 was taken at ISO 25600. (I am showing small portions of each image here, so the effects of the ISO setting will be more obvious.) As you can see, the second image shows noticeable deterioration, both in the figurine itself and in the plain background. You can use this high setting when absolutely necessary to get a shot, but it's advisable to avoid the highest ISO values when possible.

Figure 5-40. Image Taken with ISO Set to 125

Figure 5-41. Image Taken with ISO Set to 25600

As was discussed in Chapter 4, you can use the Extended ISO option on screen 6 of the Recording menu to include ISO values as low as 80 and as high as 25600. You also can use the ISO Increments option on screen 5 of that menu to include values between the major settings, including values such as 160, 250, and 1000.

In playback mode, the ISO/Up button is used to start playing a motion picture or a panorama when the initial frame is displayed on the screen. The button also serves as a play/pause button once a movie has started playing, and it has various duties to move among settings on certain screens, such as the screen for saving Highlight Shadow values on the Recording menu, the screen for setting a custom white balance setting, and the screen for saving a Custom Multi frame for AF Mode. You can use the Up button to set exposure bracketing from the exposure compensation setting screen.

Right Button: White Balance

The Right button calls up the menu for setting the camera's white balance. The white balance menu option is needed because cameras record the colors of objects differently according to the color temperature of the light source that illuminates those objects.

Color temperature is a value expressed in Kelvin (K) units. A light source with a lower K rating produces a "warmer," or more reddish light. A source with a higher rating produces a "cooler," or more bluish light. Candlelight is rated about 1,800 K, indoor tungsten light (ordinary light bulb) is rated about 3,000 K, outdoor sunlight and electronic flash are rated about 5,500 K, and outdoor shade is rated about 7,000 K. If the camera is using a white balance setting that is not calibrated for the light source that illuminates the scene, the colors of the recorded image are likely to be inaccurate.

The FZ2500, like most digital cameras, has an Auto White Balance setting that attempts to set the proper color correction for any given light source. The Auto White Balance setting works well, and it will produce good results in many situations, especially if you are taking snapshots whose colors are not critical.

If you need more precision in the white balance of your shots, the FZ2500 has settings for common light sources, as well as options for setting white balance by color temperature and for setting a custom white balance based on the existing light source.

The white balance setting is available for adjustment in all shooting modes except for the two Intelligent Auto modes and the Creative Control mode. You get access to this setting by pressing the Right button, which calls up the white balance menu screen at the bottom of the display, as shown in Figure 5-42.

This menu includes the following choices for the white balance setting, most of them represented by icons: Auto White Balance (AWB); Daylight (sun icon); Cloudy; Shade; Incandescent; Flash; White Set 1; White Set 2; White Set 3; White Set 4; and Color Temperature Set (WB K Set) 1 through 4. (Only the first six options are shown in Figure 5-42; you need to scroll to the

right to reach the others.) You can scroll through these selections using the front or rear dial, the Left and Right buttons, or the touch screen.

Most of these settings are self-explanatory. You may want to experiment to see if the named settings (Daylight, Shade, Incandescent, etc.) produce the results you want. If not, you'll be better off setting the white balance manually. To do that, you can use any one of the four White Set options, which let you measure the white balance based on the light that is actually illuminating your subject, and save a custom setting to that numbered slot in the camera's memory. Then, you can use that custom setting whenever you are faced with the same lighting situation in the future.

Figure 5-42. White Balance Menu

Figure 5-43. White Set Icon Highlighted on Menu

To set white balance manually, press the Right button to activate the white balance menu and scroll to highlight one of the four White Set icons, as shown in Figure 5-43. Press the Up button, and a yellow rectangle will appear in the middle of the display, as shown in Figure 5-44.

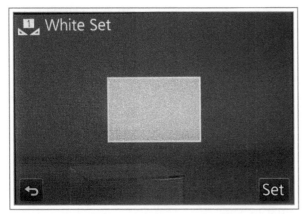

Figure 5-44. Screen for Setting Custom White Balance

Aim the camera at a white or gray surface illuminated by the light source you will be using, and fill the rectangle with the image of that surface. Then press the Menu/Set button (or you can press the shutter button or the Set icon on the touch screen if you prefer) to lock in that white balance setting.

The camera will display a Completed message if the setting was successful. Now, until you change that setting, whenever you select that preset value (White Set 1 or another slot, as the case may be), it will be calibrated for the white balance you have just set. This system is useful if you often use a particular light source and want to have the camera set to the appropriate white balance for that source.

To set the color temperature directly by numerical value, choose one of the four Color Temperature Set (WB K Set) options from the white balance menu, as shown in Figure 5-45.

Figure 5-45. Color Temperature Set Icon Highlighted

Then press the Up button to pop up a screen with a value such as 2500K displayed. You then can press the Up and Down buttons, turn the front or rear dial, or slide your finger on the touch screen to adjust that value anywhere from 2500K to 10000K in increments of 100K, as shown in Figure 5-46, where the value is set to 4700K.

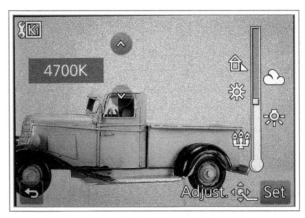

Figure 5-46. Scale for Setting Color Temperature

With this approach, you have to know the color temperature of the light source in order to make the setting. One way to find that value is to use a color temperature meter like the Sekonic C-700 color meter shown in Figure 5-47.

Figure 5-47. Sekonic C-700 Color Meter

If you don't have a meter available, you can still use the Color Temperature option using guesswork or your sense of color. For example, if you are shooting under lighting from incandescent bulbs, you can use 3,000 K as a starting point, because, as noted earlier, that is the approximate color temperature of that light source. Then you can try setting the color temperature figure higher or lower, and watch the camera's display to see how natural the colors look. As you lower the color temperature, the image will become more "cool" or bluish; as you raise it, the image will appear more "warm" or reddish. Once you have found the best setting, leave it in place and take your shots.

Once you have made the white balance setting, either using one of the preset values such as AWB, Daylight, Incandescent, or Cloudy, or using a custom-measured setting or a color temperature, you can still fine-tune the setting to an additional degree.

To make this further adjustment, after you make your white balance setting, before pressing the Menu/Set button to return to the recording screen, press the Down button, and you will be presented with a screen for fine adjustments, as shown in Figure 5-48.

Figure 5-48. White Balance Color Adjustment Screen

You will see a box containing a pair of axes that intersect at a zero point, marked by a circle with a plus sign inside it. The four ends of the axes are labeled G, B, M, and A, for green, blue, magenta, and amber.

You can use all four direction buttons, or slide your finger over the colored square, to move the circle away from the center toward any of the axes, to adjust these four values until you have the color balance exactly how you want it. The camera will remember this value whenever you select the white balance setting that you fine-tuned.

When you have fine-tuned the setting using this screen, the white balance icon on the camera's display changes color and/or adds an indicator to show what changes you have made along the color axes. If there was an adjustment to the amber or blue side, the icon changes color accordingly. If there was an adjustment to the green or magenta side, the icon will have a plus sign added for green or a minus sign added for magenta.

For example, Figure 5-49 shows the icon, in the upper left corner of the screen, after the white balance setting was adjusted toward the blue and magenta sides of the axes. To reset the adjustment axes to the zero point, press the Display button (or touch the Reset icon) while the axes are displayed, and the circle will return to the center of the adjustment area.

When the color adjustment screen is displayed, you can also get access to the white balance bracket feature. As I discussed in Chapter 4, you can use the Bracket item on screen 2 of the Recording menu to set the camera to take a series of three shots using a different white balance setting for each. You can also activate that feature from the white balance setting screen.

When the color axes are displayed, just turn the front or rear dial to set up bracketing, and the circles will spread apart on the color chart to indicate the bracket settings. (If bracketing is not available because of a conflicting setting, the BKT icon next to the icon for the rear dial, as seen in Figure 5-49, will not appear on this screen.)

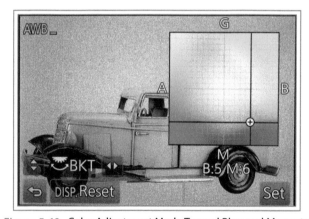

Figure 5-49. Color Adjustment Made Toward Blue and Magenta

If you're shooting with Raw quality, you don't have to worry about white balance so much, because, once you load the Raw file into your software, you can change the white balance however you want. This is one of the advantages of using Raw. If you had the camera's white balance setting at Incandescent while shooting under a bright sun, you can just change the setting to Daylight in the Raw software, and no one need ever know about the error of your shooting.

Finally, the chart in Figure 5-50 shows how the different white balance settings affect the images taken by the FZ2500. The images in this chart were taken under artificial light balanced for daylight, with the camera set for each available white balance setting, as indicated on the chart. In my opinion, the best results were obtained with the Auto White Balance, Daylight, Color Temperature, and White Set settings. The Flash setting also appeared to match the actual color temperature quite closely, and the Cloudy and Shade settings did not do badly. The Incandescent setting is the only one that yielded a result that clearly is incorrect.

Panasonic Lumix FZ2500 White Balance Chart

Auto White Balance   Incandescent

Daylight   Flash

Cloudy   White Set

Shade   Color Temperature: 5000K

Figure 5-50. White Balance Comparison Chart

Besides giving access to white balance settings, the WB/Right button has some miscellaneous functions. For example, when playing movies and slide shows, the Right button acts as a navigation control to move

through the images, and it is used to navigate among the various portions of screens with settings, such as the Highlight Shadow and Photo Style screens. When you have selected a filter effect in Creative Control mode or with the Filter Settings menu option, you can press the Right button to get access to a screen for making an adjustment to that setting. In Intelligent Auto Plus mode, pressing the Right button brings up the Color Tone scale, with which you can adjust the tone of your images from red to blue.

Left Button: AF Mode

The Left button is marked with a focus frame icon indicating that it calls up the options for AF Mode, which controls what area of the scene the camera focuses on when using its autofocus capability. (As a reminder, you select autofocus or manual focus with the focus mode lever at the top center of the camera's back. As I will discuss later in this chapter, you select AF Macro or Macro Zoom focus by pressing the Down button to bring up the Macro Mode menu.)

When you press the AF Mode button with the focus mode set to AFS, AFF, AFC, AF Macro, or Macro Zoom, the camera displays a line of icons representing the six choices available for the AF Mode setting: Face/Eye Detection; AF Tracking; 49-Area; Custom Multi; 1-Area; and Pinpoint, as shown in Figure 5-51.

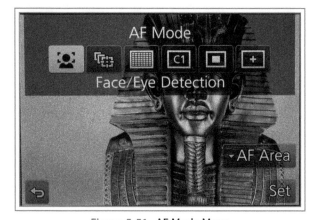

Figure 5-51. AF Mode Menu

Use the front or rear dial or the Left and Right buttons (or the touch screen) to highlight your choice, then press the Menu/Set button (or touch the Set icon), or press the shutter button halfway to select that setting and return to the recording screen.

In the Intelligent Auto and Intelligent Auto Plus modes, only two of these options are available: Face/Eye

Detection and AF Tracking. Following are details about all six options that are available in other recording modes.

Face/Eye Detection

When you select this setting, the camera does not display any focusing brackets or rectangles until it detects a human face. If it does, it outlines the general area of the face with a yellow rectangle. Then, after you press the shutter button halfway down, the rectangle turns green when the camera has focused on the face. If the camera detects more than one face, it displays white rectangles for secondary faces, as shown in Figure 5-52. (In this image, face recognition was also turned on, and the camera recognized a face I had registered earlier. That option was discussed in Chapter 4.)

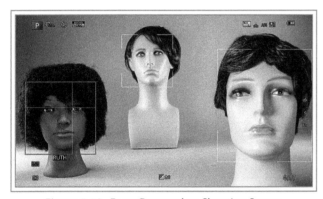

Figure 5-52. Faces Detected on Shooting Screen

Any faces that are the same distance away from the camera as the face within the yellow rectangle will also be in focus, but the focus will be controlled by the face in the yellow rectangle. If Metering Mode is set to Multi, the camera will also adjust its exposure for the main detected face.

With this setting, the camera also will look for human eyes. It will place a set of crosshairs across the closest eye it finds and fix focus there. To change the eye the camera focuses on, when the camera is displaying frames over detected faces, press the touch screen over the eye you want the camera to focus on, then press the shutter button halfway to focus. (Touching a different eye does not work in Intelligent Auto mode; in that mode, if you touch the screen, the AF Mode setting will change to AF Tracking.)

You also can change the face the camera focuses on. To do that, go to the Touch Settings item on screen 10 of the Custom menu and make sure Touch AF is set to

AF. Then touch the screen outside of the yellow frame over the main face. The camera will display the Face/Eye Detection frame on the screen, and you can move the frame around with your finger, or you can press any of the four cursor buttons to move the frame where you want it. When the frame is being moved, you can also turn the rear dial to change the frame's size in large increments, or the front dial to resize it in small increments. You can press the AF Off icon on the left side of the screen to cancel the focus operation.

When the focus frame is sized and located as you want, press the Menu/Set button to lock it in place. The camera will then shift its focus to the area inside that frame. You might want to use this option if you are aiming at two faces, but you want to focus on the one that is farther away from the camera. Ordinarily, the camera will focus on the closest face, but if you move the frame over the other face, the camera will direct its focus there.

AF Tracking

This next setting for AF Mode allows the camera to maintain focus on a moving subject. After pressing the AF Mode button, highlight the second icon, which is a group of offset focus frames designed to look like a moving focus frame. Press the Menu/Set button or half-press the shutter button to select this option.

The camera will then display a special focus frame with spokes sticking out of it, in the center of the display, as shown in Figure 5-53.

Figure 5-53. AF Tracking Focus Frame

Move the camera to place this focus frame over your subject and press the shutter button halfway, then release the button. If the camera can identify a subject at this location, the frame will turn yellow. The camera will then do its best to keep that target in focus, even as it (or the camera) moves. The yellow bracket should stay close to the subject on the display.

When you are ready, press the shutter button to take the picture. To cancel AF Tracking, press the Menu/Set button.

If the camera is not able to maintain focus on the moving subject, the focus frame will turn red and then disappear. AF Tracking will not work with certain settings, such as Time Lapse Shot and several Creative Control and Scene mode settings, including the Monochrome options in those modes. It also will not work with the Monochrome setting for Photo Style. With those Creative Control, Scene mode, and Photo Style settings, the camera will use 1-Area mode instead.

To use this option with the touch screen, touch the subject on the screen to select it, and press the AF Off icon on the screen to cancel the tracking focus.

Using AF Tracking can reduce the time it takes for you to be able to take a picture of a moving subject. If you are trying to snap a picture of a restless four-year-old or a fidgety pet, AF Tracking can give you a head start, so the camera's focus is close to being correct and the focusing mechanism has less work to do to achieve correct focus when you suddenly see the perfect moment to press the shutter button.

49-Area

This next option for AF Mode causes the camera to focus on a particular subset of 49 small focus zones within the overall autofocus area, which is the same area as that of the current aspect ratio setting. The camera looks within the selected focus zones and selects however many subjects it detects that are at the same distance from the camera and can be focused on.

To make this setting, select the third icon on the AF Mode menu, which looks like a screen with multiple focus points. Then, when you press the shutter button down halfway, the camera will display green rectangles to show you which of the multiple focus areas it has selected to focus on, as shown in Figure 5-54.

The name of this setting is somewhat misleading, however, because, even though the camera has 49 focus zones, it will only use a few of those zones at any one time in this mode. By default, the camera uses the nine

zones in the center of the screen. So, with the default setting, if you focus on a scene with a prominent object at the far right, the camera will choose whatever object it can find in the center of the display to focus on, and will ignore the object at the right.

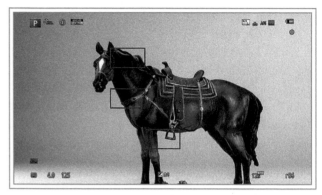

Figure 5-54. Focus Frames with 49-Area AF Mode Setting

If you want the camera to direct its focus somewhere other than the center of the scene, press the Down button while the 49-Area icon is highlighted on the menu screen, and then move the block of focus zones where you want them using the cursor buttons, as shown in Figure 5-55.

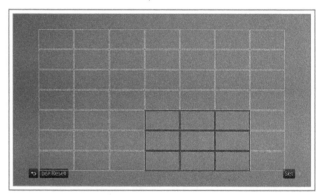

Figure 5-55. Screen to Move 49-Area Focus Zones

If the Touch AF option is turned on through the Touch Settings item on screen 10 of the Custom menu, you can touch the screen in shooting mode to select the area for the focus zone.

When you have set the focus area using the touch screen or cursor buttons, the camera displays a small white cross on the screen to indicate the center of the block of focus zones it is currently using. (The cross will disappear if you press the Menu/Set button or the AF Off icon.) The blocks near the center of the overall focus area have nine zones each, but the blocks near the edges of the display area have only six or four blocks.

The 49-Area method can be useful if your subject is likely to be located within a predictable area, and you want to have the option to adjust that area somewhat. It is a good mode to use when you are shooting landscapes or general scenes that do not require you to focus on faces or on any one particular object.

Custom Multi

This setting lets you create a custom-tailored focus zone out of the 49 available blocks. For example, you can create a horizontal focus area that is seven blocks across, or a vertical one of the same size. You can create a zone that has 21 blocks arranged in three lines of seven, either horizontally or vertically. Or, you can create a completely free-form zone with any arrangement of blocks. Somewhat oddly, with the free-form option you can create a focus area that uses all 49 of the focus blocks, resulting in a true 49-Area focus mode, unlike the mode with that name, which can use only up to nine blocks. The process for using this option is a bit complicated, so I will lay out the steps below.

1. Press the AF Mode button and scroll to the fourth icon from the left, with the label Custom Multi below it, as shown in Figure 5-56.

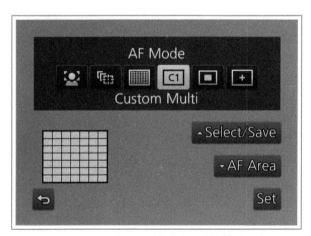

Figure 5-56. Custom Multi Icon Highlighted

2. Press the Up button to move to the line of possible patterns for the focus zone, as shown in Figure 5-57.

3. Scroll through these icons to select the one you want. The first three are for a horizontal, vertical, or central pattern. The last three—C1, C2, and C3— are for free-form custom patterns you can create and save to these slots.

4. When you have selected either horizontal, vertical, central, or free-form for the shape, press the Down button to move to the AF Area option. There you will see a screen with all 49 blocks, some of which will be highlighted in yellow for the horizontal, vertical, or central choices, but all of which will be blank for the free-form options.

Figure 5-57. Highlight in Line of Patterns for Custom Multi

5. For the horizontal, vertical, or central option, turn the front or rear dial to the right to increase the size of the focus area, or turn the dial to the left to reduce it. You can move the line or lines across the display by pressing the appropriate direction buttons or by touching the screen. When you have the focus area positioned where you want it, press the Fn5 button, at the upper right corner of the LCD screen, to set the focus area in place. The blocks will display for a moment and then disappear, and this focus area will be in effect.

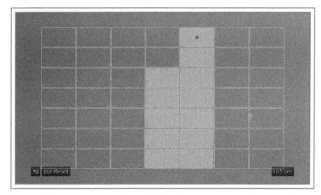

Figure 5-58. Some Blocks Highlighted for Custom Multi Pattern

6. For any of the three free-form options, after pressing the Up button, scroll to the icon that says C1, C2, or C3, then press the Down button to move to the AF Area screen. You will then see a display with all 49 blocks, none of which are highlighted, with a cross in

the center block. Use the direction buttons to move the cross to a block you want to add to the focus pattern, and press the Menu/Set button to highlight it. You also can touch a block with your finger to highlight it. Figure 5-58 shows this screen after several blocks have been selected in this way.

7. The blocks do not have to be contiguous; they can be in any pattern, up to and including selecting all 49 blocks. When you have finished selecting blocks, press the Fn5 button to lock in the pattern you have created.

8. To create and save a custom focus pattern, use the same procedure as in Steps 5 through 7. When you have finished, press the AF Mode button to bring the AF mode menu back on the screen. Then scroll to the Custom Multi option. Press the Up button to move to the line of options, and scroll to the focus pattern you just created, whether horizontal, vertical, or free-form, then press the Up button. The camera will display a screen like that in Figure 5-59, asking which Custom slot you want to save it to.

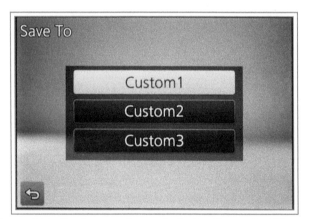

Figure 5-59. Confirmation Screen for Saving Custom Multi Pattern

9. Highlight the one you want and press Menu/Set, then select Yes when asked if it should overwrite the existing settings. To select the saved pattern in the future, just select C1, C2, or C3, depending on what slot the pattern was saved to.

The Custom Multi option is useful if you have a need for specially shaped focus zones. You might want to use a horizontal zone if you are focusing on a group of artifacts that are displayed in a straight line, to make sure the camera does not accidentally focus on an object outside of that line. You also might want to create a pattern that uses all 49 focus zones, so the camera will focus on the closest object, regardless of whether it is in the center of the image, or in a particular sector of the image.

However, there is one quirk with this setting that should be noted: If you don't select any blocks at all, the camera will treat the focus area as containing all 49 blocks, and will focus on any object in its view. So, if you want to use all 49 blocks for the focus area, just select a Custom Multi option and leave all blocks unselected. If you select any one or more blocks, the camera will focus only on an object within those blocks, but if you select no blocks at all, the camera will use all 49 blocks.

1-Area

This AF Mode setting is selected with the next-to-last icon on the AF Mode menu, as shown in Figure 5-60. With this option, the camera uses a single focus frame, which by default is in the center of the screen. You can customize the setting by moving the single frame to any position on the display and changing its size.

Figure 5-60. 1-Area Icon Highlighted on AF Mode Menu

When you have highlighted the 1-Area icon on the AF Mode menu, press the Down button to move directly to setting the location of the autofocus frame using the direction buttons or the touch screen, as shown in Figure 5-61. You can change the size of the frame in large increments by turning the rear dial or in small increments by turning the front dial. You also can change its size by pulling or pinching on the touch screen.

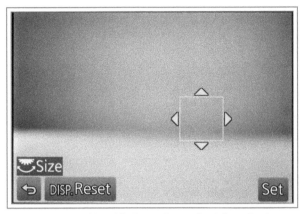

Figure 5-61. Movable Focus Frame for 1-Area Setting

When you have finished moving and resizing the focus frame, press the Menu/Set button or press the Set icon with your finger to fix the frame in place. To move the frame back to the default location in the middle of the screen or reset its size to normal, press the Display button at the bottom right of the camera's back while the frame is yellow. If the frame has been both moved and resized, you have to press Display once to reset the location and once more to reset the size.

The 1-Area method is a good setting for general shooting, because it lets you quickly position the focus area just where you want it. It is particularly helpful when you need to make sure the camera focuses on a fairly small item that is not in the center of the scene.

Pinpoint

The last icon at the right of the line of AF Mode icons, highlighted in Figure 5-62, is used to select the Pinpoint option. With this setting, you can move a single focus frame around the display and resize it, and the camera will enlarge the focus area to help you get the focus frame positioned precisely where you want it.

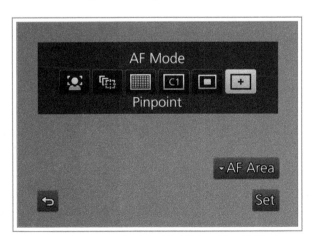

Figure 5-62. Pinpoint Icon Highlighted for AF Mode

After pressing the AF Mode button, highlight the Pinpoint icon and press the Down button to move to the AF Area screen. Move the focus area around the display using the four direction buttons and resize it using the rear dial for large increments and the front dial for small increments. You also can move and resize the focus area using the touch screen. Then press the Menu/Set button to set the focus area's location and size.

You can control the amount of enlargement for this display using the Pinpoint AF Display item on screen 2 of the Custom menu. If you select Full for that item, the image will be enlarged from three times to ten times and the enlargement will fill the display. If you select PIP, for picture-in-picture, as shown in Figure 5-63, the enlarged area will not take up the entire display, and the enlargement will only range from three times to six times. When the display is enlarged, you can vary the amount of enlargement within the specified range by turning the rear dial for large increments and the front dial for small increments. When the focus frame is located where you want it, press the Menu/Set button to exit to the shooting screen.

Figure 5-63. Pinpoint Option in Use with PIP Setting

When you focus on an item using this setting, place the small white cross over the subject and press the shutter button halfway. The camera will enlarge the display at that area for a short time while you keep the shutter button half-pressed, to help you determine whether focus is sharp. The length of time that the display remains enlarged with this option is determined by the Pinpoint AF Time option on screen 2 of the Custom menu; the time can range from 0.5 second to 1.5 second. The display then returns to normal size so you can evaluate the entire scene before pressing the shutter button to take the picture.

Moving the Focus Frame or Focus Area

With all of the AF Mode options except AF Tracking, you have the ability to move the focus frame or zones. There are several ways to do this after you have returned the camera to the shooting screen. One way to do this is to press the AF Mode button and select the current AF Mode option. Then press the Down button (or touch the AF Area icon on the screen) to go to the screen for moving the frame. Move the frame with the cursor buttons or touch screen and resize it with the front and rear dials or touch screen if necessary, then press Menu/Set and you're ready to focus again with the frame in a new location.

For a faster way to move the focus frame (or broader focus area, for the 49-Area or Custom Multi setting), there are other options. First, you can set one of the function buttons to the Focus Area Set option through screen 7 of the Custom menu, as discussed in Chapter 7. Then, if you press the assigned function button, the screen for moving the focus area will appear immediately. Second, you can turn on the Direct Focus Area option on screen 3 of the Custom menu. Then, from the shooting screen, as soon as you press any of the four direction buttons, the focus area moving screen will appear. (A drawback of that option is that you cannot then use the direction buttons to call up options such as white balance, AF Mode, and drive mode. You can use the Quick Menu to activate those items, though, or you can assign function buttons to those settings.)

Another way to move the focus frame or focus area is to use your finger to move the focus frame or area, if the Touch AF option is turned on through the Touch Settings item on screen 10 of the Custom menu.

Use of Left Button in Manual Focus Mode

If you press the Left button when the focus mode lever is set to the MF position for manual focus, the button activates the MF Assist frame so you can move it around the screen to determine the area to concentrate on for adjusting manual focus. Pressing the button also can immediately enlarge the manual focus area, depending on the setting of the MF Assist option on screen 4 of the Custom menu.

Down Button: Macro Mode

The Down button, marked with a flower icon and the letters AF, activates the Macro Mode menu, which lets you select an option for shooting objects close to the lens. When you press this button in recording mode, the camera displays the array of three choices for Macro Mode, as shown in Figure 5-64: from left, AF Macro, Macro Zoom, and off.

AF Macro

If you choose AF Macro, the camera can focus as close as about 1.2 inch or 3 cm, when the lens is zoomed back to its wide-angle setting, instead of its normal minimum distance of one foot or 30 cm. At the extreme telephoto setting, the lens can focus as close as 3.3 feet (1 meter), the same as with normal autofocus mode.

Figure 5-64. **Macro Mode Menu**

Macro Zoom

If you choose Macro Zoom, the camera can focus at the same closeup distance as with AF Macro, but the camera will let you use Digital Zoom, at a magnification factor of up to three times normal, while still focusing at the minimum focus distance. When you move the zoom lever, the image will be enlarged but the lens will not move. The Macro Zoom setting is not available with certain other settings, including Raw quality, Multiple Exposure, Handheld Night Shot, Panorama mode, or with the HDR, Impressive Art, Toy Effect, Toy Pop, or Miniature Effect settings. This setting results in reduced image quality because of the use of Digital Zoom, but it may be useful in letting you focus clearly on the subject before capturing an image, or it may be worth the trade-off in quality to get a super closeup shot.

Besides activating AF Macro mode, the Down button has various other duties. For example, pressing this button takes you to the screen for fine-tuning a white balance setting, and it provides access to the screen with options for setting the location of focus areas from the AF Mode screen. When the camera is in playback mode, pressing the Down button initiates the process to upload images by Wi-Fi, as discussed in Chapter 9. When you are playing a slide show or a movie, the Down button acts like a Stop button on a DVR to stop the playback completely. When you use the Video Divide function from the Playback menu, the down button is used to "cut" a movie at your chosen dividing point. When you are viewing a group of images that were taken with the Time Lapse or Stop Motion Animation options, you can press the Down button to view the images individually rather than as a group.

Center Button: Menu/Set

The last item to discuss in the cursor buttons group is the button in the center of the pattern, labeled Menu/Set. You use this button to enter the menu system, and to make or confirm selections of menu items or other settings. In addition, when you are playing a motion picture and have paused it, you can press the Menu/Set button to select a still image to be saved from the motion picture recording.

Fn6/Delete/Cancel Button

The Fn6 button, located to the lower left of the cursor buttons, has two built-in functions. First, as indicated by the trash can icon next to the button, it serves as the Delete button. When the camera is set to playback mode, press this button while an image is displayed, and you are presented with several options on the camera's display: Delete Single, Delete Multi, and Delete All, as shown in Figure 5-65.

Figure 5-65. Delete Screen from Pressing Fn6 Button

Use the direction buttons, the front or rear dial, or the touch screen to navigate to your choice. If you select Delete Single, the camera will display a confirmation screen; if you confirm the action, the camera will delete the currently displayed image (unless it is protected, as

discussed in Chapter 6).

If you select Delete Multi, the camera presents you with a display of recent pictures, up to nine at a time per screen, as shown in Figure 5-66.

Scroll through these thumbnail images and press the Menu/Set button to mark any picture you want to include in the group for deletion, up to 100 in total (counting a grouped set of images taken with a setting such as Focus Bracket as one image). Press Menu/Set a second time to unmark a picture for deletion. When you have finished marking pictures for deletion, move the highlight to the OK block at the left of the display and press Menu/Set to start the deletion process; the camera will ask you to confirm, and one more press of Menu/Set will delete the marked images.

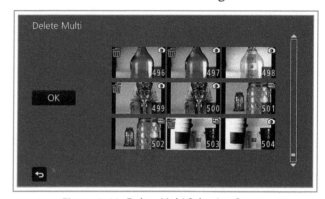

Figure 5-66. Delete Multi Selection Screen

The Delete All option deletes all images on the memory card, unless you have marked some as Favorites and choose to delete all except Favorites (indicated by stars), as prompted by the camera. You can interrupt a deletion process with the Menu/Set button, though some images may have been deleted before you press the button.

The Fn6 button also serves as a Cancel button, as indicated by the backward-curving arrow next to the button. When you are viewing menu screens, you can press this button to cancel out of a selection or other event, such as the use of the Format command on the Setup menu to erase and reformat a memory card. When the Fn6 button can be used to cancel an action and return to a previous screen, the camera displays the curving arrow, as shown in Figure 5-66, for example.

When the camera is in Intelligent Auto Plus mode or Creative Control mode, the Fn6 button activates the defocus control option, which lets you choose a different aperture setting for the lens, as discussed in Chapters 2 and 3. The Fn6 button has that assignment permanently in those two shooting modes, no matter what function is assigned to it for other shooting modes. (As with all function buttons, you can assign another option to this button using the Function Button Set option on screen 7 of the Custom menu, as discussed in Chapter 7.)

VIEWFINDER, EYE SENSOR, DIOPTER ADJUSTMENT DIAL, AND FN7 BUTTON

The last items to be discussed on the back of the camera all have to do with displaying the live view, camera settings, and recorded images through the viewfinder. When you look through the viewfinder's eyepiece, you will see the view seen by the camera's lens, overlaid with whatever information you have selected by pressing the Display button. As I discussed earlier in this chapter, pressing that button cycles through several screens of information, in both recording mode and playback mode. If you need to adjust the view in the viewfinder for your vision, use the diopter adjustment dial located on the left of the viewfinder's eyepiece.

The Fn7 button by default is assigned as the LVF button, which controls how the camera switches the view between the viewfinder and the LCD screen. When you press this button, the camera cycles through three settings: LVF/Monitor Auto, Viewfinder, and LCD. With LVF/Monitor Auto, the eye sensor, located in the slot at the top of the viewfinder's eyepiece, switches the view to the viewfinder when your head approaches the viewfinder. With Viewfinder, the camera switches the view to the viewfinder. With LCD, the camera switches the view to the LCD monitor.

LCD MONITOR

The FZ2500 is equipped with an LCD monitor that has a diagonal dimension of three inches or 76mm, with a resolution of about one million dots. The screen can tilt and swivel to assist with various types of shots. First, the screen can rotate all the way forward so it faces in the same direction as the lens for self-portraits, as shown in Figure 5-67. This orientation also is useful if you need to see yourself as you record a video blog.

Figure 5-67. LCD Monitor Rotated for Self-portraits

If you need to take images from a vantage point near ground level, you can rotate the screen so it tilts upward toward your eye, as shown in Figure 5-68, and hold the camera down as far as you need to get a mole's-eye view of the world. It can be helpful to shoot upward like this when your subject is in an area with a busy, distracting background. You can hold the camera down low and shoot with the sky as your background to reduce or eliminate the distractions. This angle of the tilting display also is useful for street photography: You can rotate the screen upward and look down at the camera while taking photos of people without drawing undue attention to yourself, particularly when the lens is zoomed in to a telephoto setting.

Figure 5-68. LCD Monitor Rotated Upward for Low-angle Shots

You also can tilt the LCD so it is facing downward, as shown in Figure 5-69, and hold the camera above your head to view the scene as if you were an arm's length taller or were standing on a small ladder. If you attach the camera to a monopod or other support and hold it up in the air, you can extend the height even farther and still view the LCD screen quite well. You can activate the self-timer before raising the camera up in the air to take the photo. You also can use a smartphone or tablet connected to the camera by Wi-Fi to trigger the camera by remote control while it is raised overhead, as discussed in Chapter 9, or use a wired remote control, as discussed in Appendix A.

Figure 5-69. LCD Monitor Rotated Downward for Overhead Shots

In addition, the FZ2500's LCD monitor has an excellent set of features as a touch screen. I will provide an overview of those features here. I will also discuss them as I cover the various menu options and other camera functions that rely on the touch screen.

Finally, when you are using only the viewfinder or are storing the camera in a case, you can rotate the LCD into a closed position to protect the screen from damage.

Using the Touch Screen

A few basic pointers can be helpful in understanding the use of the touch screen. First, the Touch Settings menu option, on screen 10 of the Custom menu, controls several important touch screen settings. I will discuss the details in Chapter 7. If the Touch Screen sub-option of Touch Settings is turned off, none of the normal touch screen functions will be available. (However, the Silent Operation option on screen 6 of the Motion Picture menu will still operate if turned on, and the Clear Retouch option on screen 2 of the Playback menu will still work.)

If the Touch Tab sub-option is turned off, there will be basic touch options, but none of the special tabs that appear at the right edge of the shooting screen. The Touch AF and Touch Scroll sub-options control other aspects of the camera's touch screen functions.

Second, watch for icons that appear to be touchable, and try them out. It can't hurt to experiment, and you will eventually come to realize which icons on the screen are responsive to your touch and which ones are there only to provide information.

Third, don't forget that the touch screen operates in playback mode and with menu screens, not just with recording functions. In this discussion, though, I will concentrate on using the touch screen in recording mode.

Figure 5-70. Touch Screen Icons on Shooting Screen

Figure 5-70 shows the shooting screen in Program mode with the touch screen settings turned on. At the right edge of the screen are three icons. From the top, these are the touch icons for controlling filter effects, for activating the touch tab, and for getting access to the virtual function buttons. In this image, all three of those icons are white.

Figure 5-71. Filter Effect Icon Activated

If you touch the top icon, the icons change, as shown in Figure 5-71. You will now see a larger filter effect icon with an X beside it. That icon means that filter effects are turned off. If you touch that icon, the currently selected filter effect, in this case Impressive Art (IART), turns on, and the icons change again. To change the effect, touch the IART icon, and the camera will display a screen for selecting a different filter effect. When you are done with filter effects, touch the top icon again to turn off the effect. Then touch the small, yellow filter effect icon to collapse the touch tab area.

The second of the three icons at the right of the screen in Figure 5-70 is the left-facing arrow, which is the touch tab icon. When you touch that icon, the display changes as seen in Figure 5-72, to show various items in the touch tab area. From the top, these are the touch zoom icon, the touch shutter icon, the touch AE icon, and the peaking icon.

Figure 5-72. Touch Tab Icons Activated

If you touch the touch zoom icon, it will turn yellow to show that it is active and the camera will display the touch zoom controls, as shown in Figure 5-73. You can then touch those controls to zoom the lens in or out.

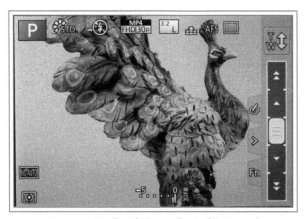

Figure 5-73. Touch Zoom Control Activated

Touch the yellow icon again to turn off touch zoom and get access to other items in the touch tab area.

The icon below the touch zoom icon is the touch shutter icon. If you touch it, it turns yellow to show that it is

active. You can then touch the screen on any object you want the camera to direct its focus on, and the camera will take a picture without your having to press the shutter button. Touch the yellow icon to turn touch shutter off.

The next icon is the touch AE icon. When you touch that icon, a small blue cross appears on the display, as shown in Figure 5-74. Use your finger to move that cross over the subject where you want the exposure to be evaluated, or just touch that area, then touch the Set icon. Touch the touch AE Off icon at the left of the screen to cancel touch AE.

Figure 5-74. Blue Cross for Touch AE on Display

The last of this group of icons is the peaking icon, which functions only when manual focus is in use. When manual focus is turned on, touch this icon repeatedly to cycle from peaking being off, low, or high.

When you have finished with the touch tab icons, press the yellow arrow to collapse that area of tabs, leaving only the three main tabs shown earlier.

Finally, you can press the Fn icon at the bottom of the touch tab area to open up the area for the virtual function buttons, Fn8 through Fn12.

The display will then look like Figure 5-75, with the icons for those buttons visible. Touch any one of those icons to activate the function assigned to it. In Chapter 7 I will discuss how to assign a function to a function button. In this illustration, Fn8 is assigned to Wi-Fi, Fn9 to the level gauge (tilt sensor), Fn10 to the histogram option, Fn11 to snap movie, and Fn12 to 4K Photo. When you have finished using the virtual function buttons, press the yellow Fn icon to collapse the Fn tab.

I discuss the various other touch screen functions in connection with the appropriate menu items and camera operations as they come up in other chapters of this book.

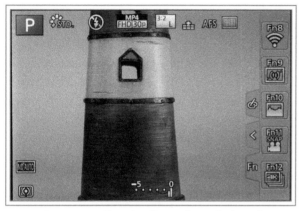

Figure 5-75. Function Button Icons Activated

Items on Left Side of Camera

Items on the left side of the camera are shown in Figure 5-76.

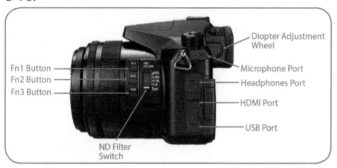

Figure 5-76. Items on Left Side of Camera

FUNCTION BUTTONS FN1, FN2, AND FN3

These three function buttons are located on the left side of the lens housing, within easy reach by a finger on your left hand. By default, the Fn1 and Fn2 buttons are assigned to the Slow Zoom function. When you press the Fn1 button, the lens zooms in under electronic control by the camera; when you press Fn2, it zooms back out. This method of zooming is more controlled than zooming with the zoom ring or zoom lever, which depend on the speed with which you operate the control. So, for a smooth, slow zoom, you can use these buttons. Of course, as with all function buttons, you can assign them to other functions, or you can assign other buttons to the Slow Zoom function, but it makes sense to use these buttons for this option because of their location.

You can control the speed of the Slow Zoom feature using the Slow Zoom Speed option on screen 8 of the Custom menu. On that same screen, you can use the Slow Zoom Button Setting option to choose whether you have to hold down the button to zoom the lens, or whether you can just press the button once to start the zoom and a second time to stop it.

The Fn3 button is assigned by default to the Dial Operation Switch option. With that option assigned, when you press the Fn3 button the front and rear dials are temporarily given new assignments, so you can quickly make adjustments to the settings temporarily assigned to the dials. The assignments can include settings such as Photo Style, Filter Effect, aspect ratio, flash mode, and others. These assignments are made using the Dial Operation Switch Setup option, which is found under the Dial Settings menu item on screen 9 of the Custom menu.

Figure 5-77. Icons for Dial Operation Switch on Shooting Screen

For example, using the Dial Operation Switch sub-option on the menu, you can assign the front dial to control white balance and the rear dial to control ISO. Then, assuming that the Fn3 button remains assigned to the Dial Operation Switch item, when you press Fn3, the camera will display icons showing the items controlled by the dials, as seen in Figure 5-77. While that display remains on the screen (a few seconds), you can turn either dial to adjust the item it is temporarily assigned to. Once those adjustments are made, the dials revert to their normal operations. I will discuss the applicable menu items in Chapter 7.

ND FILTER SWITCH

Located directly behind the Fn1, Fn2, and Fn3 buttons is the ND filter switch. You can operate this switch to activate the camera's built-in neutral density filter. That filter reduces the amount of light reaching the image sensor without changing the color of the light, which is why it is a "neutral" filter. This option is useful when you are shooting in bright conditions but need to use a slow shutter speed or a wide aperture. For example, if you are shooting images of a waterfall, you may want to use a shutter speed of one second in order to blur the flowing water into a smooth-looking stream. In bright sunlight, you might not be able to set values for ISO and aperture that would permit the use of such a long shutter speed. If you activated the ND filter, though, you probably could find values that would result in a properly exposed image.

In addition, when you are recording video footage, the filter can be very useful because of the relatively fast shutter speeds that are generally used, such as 1/30 second. If you want to use a wide aperture when shooting at 1/30 second, it may be helpful to have the ND filter available to expose the video properly.

The operation of this switch is simple. If you choose Off, the filter will never be activated. For specific values, slide to the indicators for 1/64, 1/16, or 1/4, to reduce the amount of light to that fraction of the normal amount. For example, the 1/64 setting cuts the light down to 1/64 of normal.

If you choose the Auto setting, the camera will activate the ND filter as needed, depending on the lighting conditions. However, the Auto setting does not operate when the camera is set to Manual exposure or Creative Video mode, when it is recording movies, or when Silent Mode is turned on through screen 1 of the Custom menu. In those cases, the ND filter will remain off at all times with the Auto setting, even if the lighting conditions might call for its use. If you want to use the ND filter with any of those settings, you have to set it to a specific value.

Ports for Microphone, Headphones, HDMI, and USB

Also located on the left side of the camera, hidden under small flaps, are several ports. The top one is where you can plug in an external microphone with a standard 3.5mm plug, to improve the sound quality for video recordings. The port below that one lets you plug

in a 3.5mm headphone jack, so you can monitor the sound for video recordings.

The bottom flap covers the HDMI and USB ports. The HDMI port is where you can plug in a micro-HDMI cable to send the camera's images and videos in playback mode to an external HDTV set or monitor. You also can use this port in recording mode to connect the camera to an external monitor, or to a video recorder to record HD or 4K video. I will discuss that process in Chapter 8. The USB port is where you can plug in the micro-USB cable that comes with the camera to upload images and videos from the camera to a computer. You also can use it to connect the camera to a printer to print images.

Items on Right Side of Camera

The right side of the camera, shown in Figure 5-78, has two flaps that conceal ports. Under the small, upper flap is the Remote port, where you can plug in a wired remote control such as the Panasonic DMW-RSL1, which can operate the shutter from a distance. I will discuss that item in Appendix A.

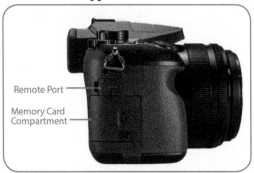

Figure 5-78. Items on Right Side of Camera

The larger, lower flap covers the compartment for inserting a memory card. Pull the flap back and it will flip open. Insert the card with its label facing the front of the camera. To remove a card, press down on it until it pops up so you can grab it and pull it out.

Items on Front of Camera

Although the focus ring and zoom ring are located on the front of the camera, they are more clearly visible in the view of the top of the camera, so they were discussed earlier in this chapter. The other items on the front of the camera, shown in Figure 5-79, are discussed below.

Figure 5-79. Items on Front of Camera

AF Assist/Self-timer Lamp

This small lamp gives off a bright reddish light when it carries out either of its two functions. First, when the camera is set to use autofocus, this light turns on when lighting is dim, to assist the autofocus mechanism in observing the scene and detecting focus points. You can control that behavior using the AF Assist Lamp item on screen 3 of the Custom menu. If you set that option to Off, the lamp will never turn on for autofocus assistance. You might want to make that setting in order to avoid disturbing a child or pet, or to avoid drawing attention to your camera. Even with that option set to turn the lamp off, the lamp will still illuminate when the self-timer is used. The lamp will blink several times during the self-timer countdown.

Lens

The lens of the FZ2500 camera is a variable focal length (zoom) lens, with an aperture range from f/2.8 to f/11.0 when the lens is zoomed back to its wide-angle setting of 24mm. When it is zoomed in to a focal length of 250mm or more, its widest aperture setting is f/4.5. Using normal autofocus settings, the lens can focus as close as 11.8 inches (30 cm) at the wide-angle zoom setting and as close as 3.3 feet (1 meter) at the telephoto end of the zoom range. Using the AF Macro setting, the lens can focus as close as 1.2 inch (3 cm) at

the wide-angle zoom setting and as close as 3.3 feet (1 meter) at the telephoto setting.

In normal shooting mode with aspect ratio set to 3:2, the lens has an optical focal length range from 24mm to 480mm. The focal length range varies, though, with factors such as aspect ratio, use of the Stabilizer option, and use of 4K shooting. For example, with aspect ratio set to 4:3, the effective focal length range is 26mm to 520mm. For a list of the focal length ranges under various conditions, see the Panasonic specifications at http://shop.panasonic.com/cameras-and-camcorders/cameras/lumix-point-and-shoot-cameras/DMC-FZ2500.html (scroll to the bottom of the page).

Items on Bottom of Camera

On the bottom of the camera, the items of note are the tripod socket and the battery compartment, as shown in Figure 5-80. At the outer edge of the battery compartment is a flexible flap that can be moved aside when you use an AC adapter to power the camera. The cord connecting the adapter to its "dummy battery" can pass through the small channel covered by that flap, so you can close and latch the battery compartment door with the dummy battery inside and connected to the power cord. I discuss AC adapters in Appendix A.

Figure 5-80. Items on Bottom of Camera

Chapter 6: Playback

In this chapter I'll discuss the playback operations of the FZ2500, including the features on the Playback menu and options for printing images directly from the camera to a printer.

Normal Playback

First, you should be aware of the setting for Auto Review on screen 7 of the Custom menu. The setting for Duration Time under this menu option determines whether and for how long the image stays on the screen for review when you take a new picture. If your major concern is to check images right after they are taken, this setting is all you need to use. As discussed in Chapter 7, you can leave Auto Review turned off or set it to one, two, three, four, or five seconds, or to Hold. If you choose Hold, the image will stay on the display until you press the shutter button halfway to return to recording mode.

There is another sub-option under Auto Review, called Playback Operation Priority. If that option is turned on, you can perform operations on images while they are being displayed with Auto Review, if you press a button while the image is displayed. For example, you can delete an image by pressing the Fn6 button. If that option is turned off, you cannot perform playback operations in Auto Review mode; pressing a button while an image is displayed will perform the operation assigned to that button for recording mode. Both settings for Auto Review are discussed in Chapter 7.

To control how images are viewed later on, you need to use the options available in playback mode. For ordinary review of images, press the Playback button, marked by a small triangle, located below the Fn5 button. Once you press the Playback button, the camera is in playback mode, and you will see the most recent image that was viewed in playback mode. To move back through older images, press the Left button or turn the front or rear dial to the left. To see more recent images,

use the Right button or turn the front or rear dial to the right. To speed through the images, hold down the Left or Right button.

You also can use the touch screen to scroll through images and videos, if the Touch Settings item on screen 10 of the Custom menu has Touch Screen turned on. Just drag across the screen with your finger in either direction to scroll backward or forward through the items. You can adjust the speed of this scrolling using the Touch Scroll option on screen 10 of the Custom menu.

Index View and Enlarging Images

When you are viewing an individual image in playback mode, press the zoom lever once to the left, and you will see a screen showing 12 images, one of which is outlined by a yellow frame, as shown in Figure 6-1. You also can touch the index screen icon, located above the trash can icon on the individual image.

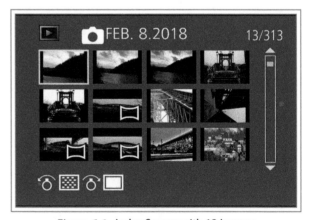

Figure 6-1. Index Screen with 12 Images

Press the zoom lever to the left once more, or touch the index screen icon in the lower left of the index screen, to see an index screen with 30 images.

You can press the Menu/Set button to view the outlined image, or you can move through the images and videos on the index screen by pressing the four direction buttons or by turning the front dial or the rear dial. You can also drag on the touch screen to scroll the images.

From the 30-image index screen, one more press of the zoom lever to the left or a touch of the CAL icon brings up a calendar display, as seen in Figure 6-2.

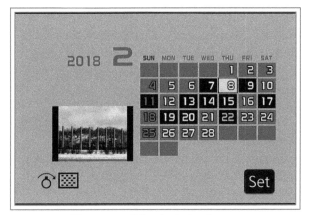

Figure 6-2. Calendar Index Screen

On that screen, you can move the yellow highlight to any date with a black background and press the Menu/Set button or touch the Set icon to bring up an index view with images from that date.

When you are viewing a single image or video, one press of the zoom lever to the right enlarges the image (or the first frame of the video). You will briefly see a display in the upper right corner showing a green frame with an inset yellow frame that represents the area of the image that is filling the screen in enlarged view. When that inset frame disappears, you will just see the enlarged image with a few icons, as shown in Figure 6-3.

Figure 6-3. Enlarged Image

If you press the zoom lever to the right repeatedly, the image will be enlarged to greater levels, up to 16 times normal. While it is magnified, you can scroll in it with the four direction buttons or by dragging on the touch screen. The yellow inset frame will reappear and will move around inside the green frame. To reduce the image size again, press the zoom lever to the left as many times as necessary or press the Menu/Set button to revert immediately to normal size. To move to other images while the display is magnified, turn the front dial or the rear dial.

You can enlarge an image to two times normal size by tapping on the touch screen twice. If you tap twice again, an enlarged image returns to normal size. You also can pinch and pull on the screen with your fingers to enlarge and reduce the size of an image.

The Playback Menu

The Playback menu is represented by a triangle icon that turns green when highlighted. It is the last icon at the bottom of the line of menu icons at the left of the main menu screen, as seen in Figure 6-4.

Figure 6-4. Playback Menu Icon Highlighted at Left

This menu has five screens of options that control how playback operates and that give you access to special features. The first menu screen is shown in Figure 6-5.

SLIDE SHOW

The first option on the Playback menu is Slide Show. Navigate to this option, then press Menu/Set or the Right button (or press the menu option on the touch screen), and you are presented with the choices All, Picture Only, or Video Only, as shown in Figure 6-6. Following are details for each of these choices.

Figure 6-5. Screen 1 of Playback Menu

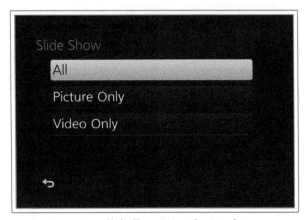

Figure 6-6. Slide Show Menu Options Screen

[Play] All

If you choose All from the Slide Show menu, you are taken to a menu with the choices Start, Effect, and Setup, shown in Figure 6-7.

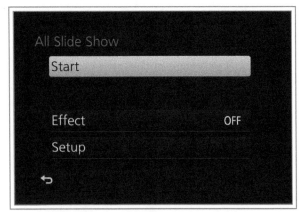

Figure 6-7. Slide Show Setup Options Screen

You can choose Start to begin the slide show, or you can select Effect or Setup first and make some selections. Setup lets you choose a duration of one, two, three, or five seconds for each still image, but you can only set the duration if Effect is set to Off. If you turn on any

effect, the camera will automatically set the duration to two seconds per still image.

You can also choose to set Sound to Off, Audio, Music, or Auto, but only if some effect is selected. If no effect is selected, the Sound option can be set only to Audio or Off. With Off, no sound is played. With the Auto setting, the camera's music is played for still images, and motion pictures have their own audio played. The Music setting plays music as background for all images and movies, and the Audio setting plays only the movies' audio tracks.

Also, you can set Repeat On or Off. Note that you can set a duration even when there are videos included along with still images; the duration value will apply for the still pictures, but not for the videos, which will play at their normal, full length.

For effects, you have the following choice of styles: Natural, Slow, Swing, Urban, or turning effects off altogether. If you choose Urban, the camera not only plays "urban" music, it uses a somewhat more dramatic visual style, with a variety of transitions, including converting some color images to black and white. So choose Urban only if you don't mind having a slide show with altered images.

Once the slide show has begun, you can control it using the direction buttons as a set of playback controls, the same as with playing motion pictures. The Up button controls play/pause; the Left and Right buttons move back or forward one slide; and the Down button is like a stop button; pressing it ends the slide show. The rear dial adjusts audio volume. A small display showing these controls appears briefly on the screen at the start of the show. After it disappears, you can press the Display button to make it appear again. You also can use touch screen icons to control playback.

[Play] Picture Only/Video Only

These next two options for playing the slide show are self-explanatory; instead of playing all images and videos, you can play either just still images or just videos. If you select videos, the camera will also include photos recorded in 4K burst mode or with the Post Focus feature. For Post Focus, though, the camera will only include one, well-focused image for each group of images.

The only difference between the options for these two choices is that, as you might expect, you cannot select an effect or a duration setting for a slide show of only videos; the slide show will just play all of the videos on the memory card, one after the other. You can use the Setup option to choose whether to play the videos with their audio tracks or with the sound turned off.

PLAYBACK MODE

The second option on the Playback menu, Playback Mode, is similar to the Slide Show option, in that it provides choices for which images and videos are played. This option, though, controls which items are viewed when you are viewing them outside of a slide show. The FZ2500 offers three choices for this option: Normal Play, Picture Only, or Video Only.

Normal Play is the playback mode for ordinary display of your images and videos. This mode is automatically selected whenever the camera is first turned on or switched into playback mode. With this mode, you can scroll through images and videos, enlarge them, and display index screens, as discussed earlier in this chapter. The Picture Only and Video Only options work for playback just as they do for the Slide Show option, discussed above.

LOCATION LOGGING

The next option on the Playback menu provides a way for you to add location information to the images saved to your memory card, using a smartphone. To do this, you have to first establish a Wi-Fi connection between the FZ2500 and the smartphone; I discuss that process in Chapter 9. To do that, you can use the Wi-Fi option on screen 1 of the Setup menu or press a button assigned to the Wi-Fi option. (The Fn8 virtual function button is assigned that option by default.) You also need to download the Panasonic Image App to your smartphone. Once the Wi-Fi connection is established, follow the steps below.

1. Open the Panasonic Image App on the smartphone and, if the app is not on the Home screen, select the Home icon, on the left at the bottom of the screen, as shown in Figure 6-8. On the Home screen, shown in Figure 6-9, select Geotagging.

Figure 6-8. Panasonic Image App: Home Icon at Left

Figure 6-9. Panasonic Image App Home Screen

2. On the smartphone, select the Start Geotagging option, as shown in Figure 6-10.

Figure 6-10. Panasonic Image App Geotagging Screen

3. The phone will display the screen shown in Figure 6-11, saying it is getting location data.

Figure 6-11. Screen When App Getting Location Data

4. Leave the smartphone in this status while you take photos with the FZ2500. The smartphone will be recording location data that can later be synced with the images you are capturing at the same time. (Note: With some Panasonic camera models, you need to select the Time Sync option before the Start Geotagging option, so the camera and phone will synchronize their times. This step is not necessary with the FZ2500 and some other models.)

5. After you have finished taking photos with the camera, select the Stop Geotagging option on the smartphone. Re-establish the Wi-Fi connection between the camera and the smartphone if it was disconnected. Then go to the Geotagging screen on the smartphone and select the Batch Send option, with an icon that looks like an arrow going to a camera, as shown in Figures 6-10 and 6-11.

6. When the app asks if it should send location data to the camera, say yes. The camera will display a message saying Location Data Received. After the data has been sent, answer yes to the question in the app whether the data can be erased. When the app asks if it should save the location information to the picture files, choose the Write option. The smartphone will display a screen saying Saving Location Data and the camera's display will say Writing Location Data. When that operation is complete, you can terminate the Wi-Fi connection.

7. When you load the images from your memory card into appropriate software, such as Adobe Bridge,

you will see the latitude and longitude information recorded in the metadata for the images, as seen in Figure 6-12.

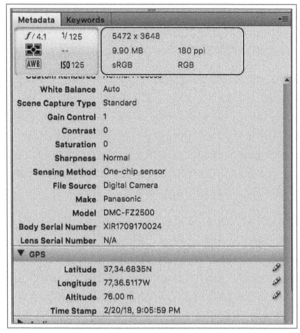

Figure 6-12. Location Data for Image Viewed in Adobe Bridge

8. You can use that information in mapping software, or in general-purpose software such as Adobe Lightroom, to map the locations of your images, or you can copy the GPS data into a resource such as Google Maps to view the locations. Images that have had location data written to them will have the letters GPS at the top in playback mode on the detailed display screen in the camera, as shown in Figure 6-13.

Figure 6-13. GPS Label on Image Viewed in Camera

RAW PROCESSING

The Raw Processing option gives you tools for processing your Raw files right in the camera. As I discussed in Chapter 4, the Raw format gives you great flexibility for adjusting settings such as exposure, white balance, sharpening, and contrast in post-processing software. But with the FZ2500 you don't have to transfer your images to a computer to convert Raw files to JPEGs. You can adjust several settings in the camera and save the altered image as a JPEG, or just convert the Raw file to a JPEG with no alterations if all you need is a file that is easier to send by e-mail or view on another device.

If you're not certain whether a given image was shot with Raw image quality, press the Display button until one of the detailed information screens appears; the Raw label will appear next to the aspect ratio for all Raw shots, as shown in Figure 6-14.

Figure 6-14. Raw Label on Image in Camera

Once you have a single Raw image displayed on the screen in playback mode, highlight Raw Processing on the Playback menu, then press the Menu/Set button twice (or press the Set icon on the touch screen once the initial Raw Processing screen is displayed). The camera will display the Raw Processing screen, as shown in Figure 6-15, overlaid on the image you selected for processing.

Figure 6-15. Initial Raw Processing Screen

At the left of the display will be a series of thumbnail images, each with a label displayed to the right. Scroll through those thumbnail images using the front or rear dial, the Up and Down buttons, or the touch screen, and press Menu/Set or the Set icon when the block for that thumbnail is highlighted with a yellow frame. Each of those thumbnail images represents an action you can take or a setting you can adjust.

Figure 6-16. White Balance Main Setting Screen

For any setting other than Noise Reduction, Intelligent Resolution, and Sharpness, you can press the Display button to switch between the main setting screen, as shown in Figure 6-16, and a comparison screen, as shown in Figure 6-17, on which the camera displays several thumbnail images on the same screen so you can compare the effects of different settings as you scroll through them. Also, for any setting, you can press the zoom lever or pinch/pull on the touch screen to enlarge the image on the main setting screen so you can see the effects of the adjustment with a magnified view.

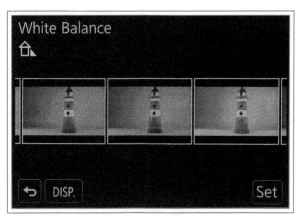

Figure 6-17. White Balance Comparison Screen

Following are descriptions of the individual items you can adjust.

Setup. If you select this item, the camera will display a sub-menu with three items: Reinstate Adjustments, Color Space, and Picture Size. If you select Reinstate Adjustments, the camera will show you the image as it now stands with any adjustments you have made with the other settings. You can then proceed to cancel all of those adjustments if you want. The Color Space option lets you keep the color space setting the image was shot with, or change it to the other option, either Adobe RGB or sRGB. The Picture Size option lets you set the Picture Size to L, M, or S.

Begin Processing. If you select this block, the camera will process all of the adjustments you have set using the other blocks. Before it proceeds to make those changes, it will show you a preview of how the processed image will look before you confirm the operation, as shown in Figure 6-18.

If you choose Yes, the camera will save a new JPEG image using all of the settings you have made. The new image will appear right after the existing Raw image on the camera's display, but it will have an image number at the end of the current sequence on the memory card.

White Balance. With this item, the camera will display the Raw image with the complete line of white balance adjustment icons at the bottom of the screen. (If you don't see that screen, press the Display button to make it appear.) As you scroll through those icons, the display will change to show how the image would look with the selected setting. If you select the color temperature option, you can press the Up button to select the numerical color temperature. For any setting, you can press the Down button to get to the screen with color axes for fine-tuning the white balance appearance.

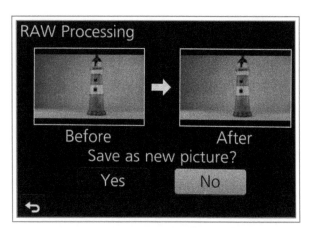

Figure 6-18. **Raw Processing Preview Screen**

Exposure Compensation. If you select this adjustment, you will be able to increase or decrease the exposure of the image, but only by up to plus or minus one EV level, in 1/3 EV increments.

Photo Style. With this item, you can change the Photo Style setting to any of the basic options for still images. You cannot select a Custom setting or any of the video-oriented settings. If you choose Monochrome, you will also be able to set the Color Tone adjustment and the Monochrome Filter Effect adjustment that simulates the use of a glass filter for black-and-white film. (Those two adjustments will appear later in the list of Raw Processing options.) If you select any other Photo Style setting, the Color Tone and Filter Effect adjustments will not be available. (The Saturation and Hue items will be available in place of the Color Tone adjustment.)

Intelligent Dynamic. The Intelligent Dynamic, or i.Dynamic screen lets you set this adjustment at a level of Off, Low, Standard, or High, regardless of how it was set when the image was captured.

Contrast. This adjustment is somewhat unusual because, ordinarily, it is made as part of the Photo Style adjustment. With the Raw Processing option, it is separated out. With this item, you can adjust the contrast of your Raw image by as many as five units positive or negative.

Highlight. On the Recording menu, the Highlight item is included as one aspect of the Highlight Shadow item. With the Raw Processing option, Highlight and Shadow are provided as two separate adjustments. If you select this item, you can alter the brightness of the highlights in the image by up to five units in either direction.

Shadow. This item is similar to the previous one, but deals with shadow rather than highlight adjustments.

Saturation. As noted earlier, this item is available for adjustment if you have selected a Photo Style other than Monochrome. If you selected Monochrome, the Raw Processing menu option includes Color Tone as an adjustment in place of Saturation.

Hue. As with Saturation, this item appears for adjustment if you have selected a Photo Style other than Monochrome. With Monochrome, Color Tone takes the place of Saturation and Hue.

Color Tone. As noted above, if you choose Monochrome for Photo Style, this item is provided for adjustment in place of Saturation and Hue; otherwise, it does not appear.

Filter Effect. As discussed earlier, if you choose Monochrome for Photo Style, the Filter Effect item is available to adjust; otherwise, it does not appear.

Noise Reduction. With this item, you can adjust Noise Reduction up to five units positive or negative.

Intelligent Resolution. With the Intelligent Resolution, or i.Resolution item, you can set this feature to Off, Extended, Low, Standard, or High.

Sharpness. The last item in the line of boxes for adjustment is Sharpness, which, like Contrast and Resolution, is separated out from the Photo Style adjustment. You can change the level of this item up to five units in either direction.

4K PHOTO BULK SAVING

This option gives you a way to save a portion of a 4K Photo burst as a group of individual pictures. As discussed in Chapter 5, the ordinary way to extract a single image from a 4K Photo burst is to scroll through the 4K Photo burst and select a single image to extract and save.

With 4K Photo Bulk Saving, instead of extracting a single image, you can extract a segment of images lasting up to five seconds, and save that group of 100 or more images as a burst, just as if it had been taken using the Focus Bracket, Time Lapse Shot, or Stop Motion Animation option. That is, the burst of images will be displayed as a single image in playback mode, until you press the Up button to view the individual images in the burst one by one. Here are the steps to use this feature:

1. Select the 4K Photo Bulk Saving menu option.

2. At this point, the camera will display all 4K Photo bursts that are available. Scroll through them to find the one you want to use, and press Menu/Set (or touch the on-screen Set icon) when it is displayed. If the sequence of shots is longer than five seconds in duration, the camera will display a message on a black screen saying it can produce a crop of five seconds' length, and telling you to select the start position. (If the sequence is shorter than five seconds, the camera will display a message asking if you want to proceed with 4K Photo Bulk Saving; there is no need to select a start position in that case.)

3. Use the on-screen controls to move through the burst of images and stop when the yellow cursor at the top of the screen is at the place where you want to start the five-second group of images. Press the Menu/Set button to select that position, and confirm it when the camera prompts you.

4. The camera will then extract and save the five-second segment you identified, and save the individual frames from that 4K footage as images within a burst group. This process will take a fairly long time, probably several minutes.

5. When the process is complete, you will have a set of up to 150 images (125 for PAL cameras) with an icon in the upper left corner indicating that you can press the Up button for burst play and an icon in the lower left corner indicating that you can press the Down button to play the images individually.

6. If you press the Up button, the images will play back in a continuous stream, though you can pause and resume with the Up button. If you press the Down button, you can use the normal playback controls to scroll through the images one by one.

Screen 2 of the Playback menu is shown in Figure 6-19.

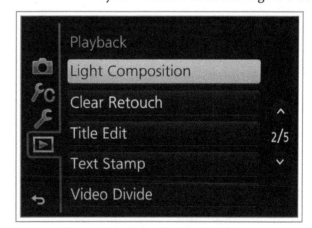

Figure 6-19. **Screen 2 of Playback Menu**

LIGHT COMPOSITION

This next menu option gives you a way to select and combine multiple frames from a sequence that was shot using 4K Photo mode. This feature lets you build a composition with dramatic areas of light in different locations, such as from a series of fireworks bursts. Figures 6-20 through 6-22 illustrate this effect. Figures 6-20 and 6-21 are two images from a 4K Photo burst; Figure 6-22 is a composite that resulted from combining those two images together using the Light Composition option.

Figure 6-20. First Image for Light Composition

To use this option, select it from the menu, and the camera will display any 4K Photo bursts on the memory card in the camera. Scroll through those choices and press the Menu/Set button or the Set icon on the screen to select an image. On the next screen, select Composite Merging or Range Merging. With Composite Merging, you can select any images from the 4K Photo burst. With Range Merging, you select the beginning and ending images of a range, and the camera includes all images within that range.

Then use the on-screen icons to select the images you want to include in the final composite. When you have finished, select Save, and the camera will display a message asking you to confirm, and telling how long it will take to produce the composite. If you confirm, the camera will create the composite image.

Figure 6-21. Second Image for Light Composition

Figure 6-22. Final Light Composition Image

Apart from fireworks displays, traffic lights and similar light displays, I have not found situations in which this feature would be useful, though I'm sure a creative photographer will find other applications for it. You should have the camera on a tripod to achieve good results, so the backgrounds of the combined images will blend together seamlessly. Also, note that the camera will create the image using only the brightest parts of the component images, so, if the parts you want to combine are not the brightest parts, they will not be included in the composite image. Of course, if you are shooting a fireworks display, the fireworks bursts almost certainly will be the brightest parts of the image, but in other contexts this feature may not work as expected.

CLEAR RETOUCH

This feature lets you erase parts of a recorded image by touching them with your finger on the camera's screen. It works only with normal JPEG images, not with Raw images, panoramas, movies, 4K Photo burst shots, or shots taken with the Post Focus option.

To use this feature, select it from the Playback menu and scroll through your images until you find one to retouch. When that image is displayed, press the Menu/Set button or touch the Set icon on the screen. The camera will display a screen with Remove and Scaling icons at the right. Touch Remove and then drag or tap your finger on areas you want to erase from the image. The camera will color those areas, as shown in Figure 6-23.

Touch Scaling to enlarge the screen before or after designating areas to remove. After you touch Scaling, you can enlarge the image further by pinching the screen apart with your fingers, using the zoom lever, or using the rear dial. You can then press Remove to activate or resume the removal process.

Figure 6-23. **Clear Retouch Option in Use**

When you have finished touching areas to be removed, press the Set icon or press the Menu/Set button to finish the process. The camera will display a preview screen; touch the Save icon or press the Menu/Set button to save that version of the image. The camera will display a final confirmation screen for you to save the image as a new picture. Figures 6-24 and 6-25 show the before and after versions of an image that I edited with this option to remove the person on the left from the scene. This feature could be useful if you are preparing some images for a quick presentation and need to remove an object from one or two shots, but it is no substitute for editing with a program such as Photoshop using a computer.

Figure 6-24. **Clear Retouch: Original Image**

Figure 6-25. **Clear Retouch: After Retouching**

TITLE EDIT

This next option on the Playback menu lets you enter text, numerals, punctuation, and a fairly wide range of symbols and accented characters for a given JPEG image or group of images through a system of selecting characters from several rows.

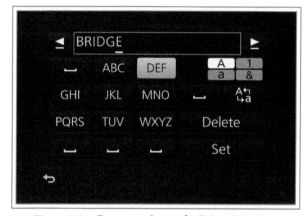

Figure 6-26. **Text-entry Screen for Title Edit Option**

After you select this option from the Playback menu, choose one or more images to have text added and press Menu/Set or touch the Set icon to go to the screen with tools for entering text, shown in Figure 6-26. Navigate using the direction buttons to the block that contains the character to be entered. Then cycle through the choices in each block, such as ABC, using the Menu/Set button, and advance to the next space using the rear dial. You can toggle between displays of capital letters, lower case letters, and numerals and symbols using the Display button. You also can touch the letters and icons using the touch screen to select them.

The maximum length for a caption or other information is 30 characters. You can use the Multi option to enter the same text for up to 100 images. You cannot enter titles for motion pictures, images from 4K Photo bursts, Post Focus images, protected images (see discussion later in this chapter), or Raw images.

Once you have entered the title or caption for a particular image, it does not show up unless you use the Text Stamp function, discussed below, or the PHOTOfunSTUDIO software supplied with the camera. The title is then attached to the image, and it will print out as part of the image. There is no way to delete the title other than going back into the Title Edit function and using the Delete key from the table of characters, then deleting each character until the title disappears.

TEXT STAMP

The Text Stamp function takes information associated with a given image and imprints it on the image in a visible form.

For example, if you have entered a title or caption using the Title Edit function discussed above, it does not become visible until you use this Text Stamp function to "stamp" it onto the image (or use the PHOTOfunSTUDIO software, as discussed above).

Once you have done this, the text or other characters in the title will print out if you send the picture to a printer. Besides the information entered with the Title Edit function, the Text Stamp function gives you the choice of making the following other information visible: shooting year, month, and day, with or without time; travel date (if set); and location (if set). Also, you can use this function to imprint names for Baby 1, Baby 2, or Pet, if you have entered those names and taken pictures using the Profile Setup menu option; and to imprint names registered with the Face Recognition function, if you have taken pictures of people whose faces were recognized by the camera.

To use this function, highlight Text Stamp on the menu screen and press Menu/Set. On the next screen, choose Single or Multi, and then select the image or images you want to add text to. When you have selected one or more images, press Menu/Set, highlight Set on the next screen, and press Menu/Set. You will then see a screen where you can select the items to be imprinted on the image or images, including shooting date, name, location, travel date, and title.

When you have made the selections, press the Fn6 button to return to the previous screen, select OK, and press Menu/Set. The camera will ask if you want to save the stamped image as a new picture; select Yes and press Menu/Set to carry out the operation. The text will be set in small, orange characters in the lower right corner of the image, as shown in Figure 6-27.

This function cannot be used with Raw images, movies, 4K Photos, Post Focus images, or panoramas. The camera saves the text-stamped image to a new file, so you will still have the original. I have never needed to use this function, but if you have an application that could benefit from it, it is available to assist you.

Figure 6-27. Text Stamp in Use on Image

VIDEO DIVIDE

The Video Divide option gives you a basic ability to edit or trim videos in the camera. Using this procedure, you can, within limits, pause a video at any point and then cut it at that point, resulting in two segments of video rather than one. You can then, if you want, delete an unwanted segment.

To do this, highlight Video Divide on the Playback menu and press the Right button or Menu/Set to go to the playback screen. If the video you want to divide is not already displayed, scroll through your images and videos using the Left and Right buttons, the front or rear dial, or the touch screen, until you locate it.

You can recognize videos because they display the length of the video in the upper right quarter of the screen and a movie camera icon with an up arrow in the upper left, as shown in Figure 6-28.

Figure 6-28. Movie Ready to Play in Camera

The camera displays all of your images here, including stills, so you may have to scroll through many non-videos until you reach the video you want. If you want to narrow the choices down to videos only, choose Video

Only for Playback Mode on screen 1 of the Playback menu before selecting the Video Divide menu option.

With the desired movie on the screen, press Menu/Set to start it playing. When it reaches the point where you want to divide it, press the Up button to pause the video. While it is paused, move through it a few frames at a time using the Left and Right buttons or the touch screen icons for frame advance and reverse, until you find the exact point where you want to divide it.

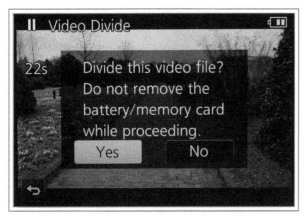

Figure 6-29. Confirmation Message for Video Divide

Once you reach that point, press the Down button to make the cut. You will see an icon of a pair of scissors in the display of controls at the bottom of the screen. After you press the Down button, the camera will display the message shown in Figure 6-29, asking you to confirm the cut.

Highlight Yes and press Menu/Set to confirm. Now you will have two new videos, divided at the point you chose.

As I noted above, this is a rudimentary form of editing. It can't be used to trim a movie too close to its beginning or end, or to trim a very short movie at all. But it's better than nothing, and it gives you some ability to delete unwanted footage without having to edit the video on your computer. Note, though, that this operation does not save a copy of the original video, so use it only if you are sure you want to divide the video file.

The options on screen 3 of the Playback menu are shown in Figure 6-30.

Figure 6-30. Screen 3 of Playback Menu

TIME LAPSE VIDEO

This option lets you create a movie from a series of shots taken using the Time Lapse Shot feature that is activated with the drive mode dial. As I discussed in Chapter 5, when you use that feature, the camera will ask at the end of the process if you want to create a movie from the group of time lapse shots. If you say no, you can use this option on the Playback menu at a later time to create the movie.

When you select this option, the camera will display any groups of images that were taken with the Time Lapse Shot option. Scroll through those and select the one you want to make into a movie. Then press the Menu/Set button, and the camera will display the screen shown in Figure 6-31, where you can set the recording quality, frame rate, and whether to play the sequence normally or in reverse. Make your choices and press Menu/Set; the camera will then create the video.

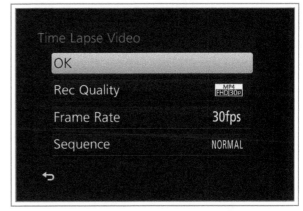

Figure 6-31. Time Lapse Video Menu Options Screen

STOP MOTION VIDEO

This option, similar to the previous one, is for creating a video from images you took using the Stop Motion

Animation feature discussed in Chapter 5. As with the Time Lapse Video option, select this option, scroll to the group of shots you want to use to create the video, and select your desired options from the screen that appears, which has the same options as in Figure 6-31.

RESIZE

This function on the Playback menu is useful if you don't have access to software that can resize an image, and you need to generate a smaller file to attach to an e-mail message or upload to a website. After selecting this menu item, on the next screen you choose whether to resize a single image or multiple ones. Then navigate to the image you want to resize, if it's not already displayed on the screen.

Once an image to be resized is on the screen, press the Menu/Set button or touch the Set icon to start the resizing process. Following the prompts on the screen as shown in Figure 6-32, highlight the size to reduce the image to. The choices may include M and S for Medium and Small, or just S for Small, depending on the size of the original image. When the option you want to use is highlighted in yellow, press Menu/Set to carry out the resizing process. The camera will ask you to confirm that you want to save a new picture at the new size.

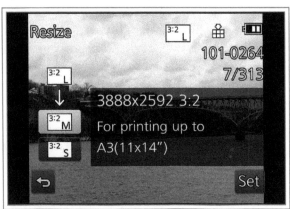

Figure 6-32. Resize Options on Image

As with the Text Stamp function, resizing does not overwrite the existing image; it saves a copy of it at a smaller size, so the original will still be available. The new image will be found at the end of the current set of recorded pictures. Raw images, 4K Photo or Post Focus images, panoramas, protected images, and motion pictures cannot be resized, nor can pictures stamped with Text Stamp. If you want to convert up to 100 images at the same time, select the Multi option and follow the same procedure.

CROPPING

This function is similar to Resize, except that, instead of just resizing the image, the camera lets you crop it to show only part of the original image. To do this, select Cropping from the Playback menu and navigate to the image to be cropped, if it isn't already displayed, and press the Menu/Set button or touch the Set icon. Then use the zoom lever or touch the zoom icon to enlarge the image, and use the direction buttons or scroll with the touch screen to position the part of the image to be retained.

Figure 6-33. Image Ready to Crop with Cropping Option

When the enlarged portion is displayed as you want, as shown in Figure 6-33, press Menu/Set or the Set icon to lock in the cropping, and select Yes when the camera asks if you want to save the new picture. Again, as with Resize, the new image will be saved at the end of the current set of recorded images, and it will have a smaller size than the original image, because it will be cropped to include less information (fewer pixels) than the original image. The Cropping function cannot be used with Raw images, motion pictures, 4K Photo or Post Focus images, panoramas, or pictures stamped with Text Stamp.

ROTATE

When you take a picture in a vertical (portrait) orientation by holding the camera sideways, you can set the camera to display it so it appears upright on the horizontal screen, as in Figure 6-34.

The setting to make such images appear in this orientation is the Rotate Display option on screen 4 of the Playback menu, which is discussed next, after the Rotate option. If you have the Rotate Display option turned on, then the Rotate option becomes available, so you can manually rotate the image back to the way it was taken. If the Rotate Display option is not turned on, then the Rotate option is dimmed and unavailable for selection.

Figure 6-34. Vertical Image Displayed on Horizontal Screen

To use the Rotate option, select it from the menu and scroll to the image you want to rotate. Then press Menu/Set and the camera will display two arrows, as seen in Figure 6-35. Select the top arrow to rotate the image 90 degrees clockwise or the bottom one to rotate it 90 degrees counter-clockwise and press Menu/Set to do the rotation.

Figure 6-35. Rotate Screen with 2 Arrows

The options on screen 4 of the Playback menu are shown in Figure 6-36.

Figure 6-36. Screen 4 of Playback Menu

ROTATE DISPLAY

As I noted above in connection with the Rotate option, when the Rotate Display option is turned on, images taken with the camera turned sideways are automatically rotated so they appear upright on the horizontal display. If you want to rotate such an image so you can see it at a larger size, taking up the full display, use the Rotate menu option, discussed above.

FAVORITE

You have the ability to mark selected images and videos as Favorites. Then, if you later select the option to delete all images on the memory card, the camera will offer you the option to delete all except Favorites, as shown in Figure 6-37.

Figure 6-37. Option to Delete All Images Except Favorites

To use this feature, choose Favorite from the Playback menu, and then choose the images and videos to mark as Favorites, either a single item or multiple items (up to 999). The camera will display your images and videos, either singly or as thumbnails, and you can mark any image as a Favorite by pressing the Menu/Set button or touching the Set/Cancel icon when the image or its thumbnail is displayed. A star will appear on the marked image, as shown in Figure 6-38.

Once the star appears, press the Fn6 button or the Cancel icon to exit from this screen. (Don't press Menu/ Set on this screen; if you do, the star will be removed.)

When you later display an image or video that was marked as a Favorite, a star appears in its upper left corner if you are viewing the playback screen that displays full information and the full-sized image. You cannot mark Raw images as Favorites.

Figure 6-38. Image Marked with Star as Favorite

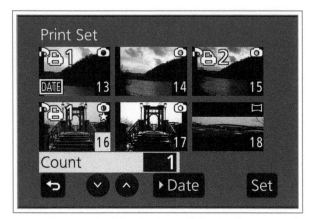

Figure 6-39. Print Set Image Selection Screen

PRINT SET

The next option on the Playback menu, Print Set, lets you set your images for Digital Print Order Format (DPOF) printing. DPOF is a process developed by the digital photography industry to allow users of digital cameras to specify, on the camera's memory card, which pictures to print and other details, then take the card to a commercial printing shop to have them printed according to those specifications. You also can print them directly from the camera to a printer that supports the PictBridge protocol, by connecting with the camera's USB cable or a compatible micro-USB cable.

With the FZ2500, you select this option from the Playback menu and then select Single or Multi. If you select Multi, the camera displays six images at a time on the screen. Using the direction buttons, the front or rear dial or the touch screen, navigate through the images. When you arrive at one you want to have printed, press the Menu/Set button or the Set icon, and you will then see a box with the word "Count" followed by a number and up and down arrows. Use the Up and Down buttons or the screen icons to raise (or, later, lower, if you change your mind) the number of copies of that image you want to have printed, as shown in Figure 6-39.

In addition, if you press the Right button or touch the Date icon on the screen, the word "Date" is added to the thumbnail image, and the date will be printed on that picture. Press Menu/Set when you have set the number of copies and date or no date for an image, then navigate to another image if you want. When you are finished setting copies to be printed, press the Fn6 button to exit from the selection screen. You can follow the above procedure for a single image by selecting "Single" when you first choose the DPOF option.

The DPOF settings cannot be used for Raw images, videos, or 4K Photo or Post Focus images. Once you have set one or more images to print using this menu option, you can use the Cancel option from the Print Set menu to go back and cancel the printing setup.

PROTECT

The next option on screen 4 of the Playback menu is Protect, which is used to lock selected images or videos against deletion. The process is essentially the same as that for the Favorite function: Select the Protect option, and then select Multi or Single. Mark the files you want to protect using the Menu/Set button. Press that button again to unmark a file. When a picture or video is protected in this way, a key icon appears on the left side of the display, as shown in Figure 6-40.

Figure 6-40. Key Icon on Protected Image

The Protect function works for all types of images, including Raw files and motion pictures. Note, however, that all images, including protected ones, will be deleted if the memory card is re-formatted.

Face Recognition Edit

This Playback menu option is of use only if you have previously registered one or more persons' faces in the camera for face recognition and taken one or more pictures for which the camera has recognized a face and placed a name on the image. If you have, use this option to select a picture with a recognized face, then follow the prompts to replace or delete the information for the person or persons you select. Once deleted, this information cannot be recovered.

The items on screen 5 of the Playback menu are shown in Figure 6-41.

Figure 6-41. Screen 5 of Playback Menu

Picture Sort

With this option, you can choose the order in which the camera displays your images from the memory card. If you choose the default option, File Name, the camera arranges them in order by folders and then by numbers within the folders. For example, the file names of your images might include entries such as P1000003, P1000010, P1020023, P1030425, etc.

If you have taken all of your images with the same camera, all of these images should also appear in chronological order according to when they were taken. However, if you have taken images with several different cameras you may have multiple images with the same file names, or with file names that do not match the order in which the images were taken. In that case you can choose the other option for this menu item, Date/ Time. In that case, the images will be displayed in order by the dates and times they were taken.

Delete Confirmation

This option lets you fine-tune the way the menu system operates for deleting images. Whenever you press the Fn6/Delete button and choose the option to delete an image or video in playback mode, the camera displays a confirmation screen, as shown in Figure 6-42, with two choices: Yes or No.

One of those choices will be highlighted when the screen appears; you can then just press the Menu/ Set button to accept that choice and the operation will be done. Of course, you also can use the front or rear dial, the Left or Right button, or the touch screen to highlight the other choice.

Figure 6-42. Confirmation Message for Delete Screen

With the Delete Confirmation menu item, you can choose whether the camera highlights "Yes" or "No" on the confirmation screen. Which option you choose depends on your habits, and how careful you want to be to guard against the accidental deletion of an item. If you like to move quickly in deleting images and videos, choose "Yes" first. Then, as soon as the confirmation screen appears you can press the Menu/Set button to carry out the deletion. If you prefer to have some assurance against an accidental deletion, choose "No" first, so that, if you press the Menu/Set button too quickly when the confirmation screen appears, you will only cancel the operation, rather than deleting an image.

Unless you use this process often and need to save time, I recommend you leave this menu item set at the "No" First setting to be safe.

Chapter 7: The Custom Menu and the Setup Menu

The Custom and Setup menus include options for controlling things such as focus, zoom, and the appearance of the display, as well as date, time, formatting memory cards, and audio options. As a reminder, you enter the menu system by pressing the Menu/Set button on the camera's back.

The Custom Menu

After pressing Menu/Set, press the Left button to move the highlight into the left column of menu choices, then use the Up and Down buttons or the front or rear dial to move to the wrench icon with the letter C, as shown in Figure 7-1. (You also can use the camera's touch screen features to navigate through the menu system.)

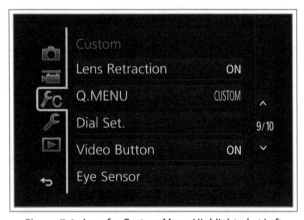

Figure 7-1. Icon for Custom Menu Highlighted at Left

Once that icon is highlighted, navigate to the list of menu options, which occupy ten menu screens, discussed below. (If the camera is set to the basic Intelligent Auto mode, the Custom menu displays only one screen with two items.) If necessary, navigate to the top of the menu's first screen.

If you have to move forward or backward through several menu screens, you can press the zoom lever to move through them a screen at a time in either direction, or press the Display button to move a screen at a time in the forward direction only.

I will discuss all of the Custom menu items below, starting with the first screen, shown in Figure 7-2.

Figure 7-2. Screen 1 of Custom Menu

Custom Set Memory

This feature gives you a way to quickly change several shooting settings without having to remember them or use menus or physical controls to set them individually. The camera lets you save three different groups of settings, each of which can be recalled instantly using the Custom (C) position on the mode dial.

Here is how this works. First, set the camera to Program, Aperture Priority, Shutter Priority, Manual exposure, Scene, Panorama, Creative Control, or Creative Video mode (You can't use the Custom Set Memory feature in the Intelligent Auto or Intelligent Auto Plus modes.)

Next, make all of the menu settings that you want to have stored for quick recall, such as Photo Style, ISO, AF Mode, exposure metering method, i.Dynamic, and the like. Your custom set can include all of the items on the Recording Menu except Face Recognition and Profile

Setup; all items on the Custom Menu except for Touch Scroll and Menu Guide; all items on the Motion Picture menu; and all items on the Playback menu except for Rotate Display, Picture Sort, and Delete Confirmation. You cannot include any items from the Setup menu.

You can include exposure compensation, white balance, macro focus, and AF Mode settings, even though they are not set from the menu. However, you cannot save settings that are controlled by a switch that remains in position for the setting, such as the focus mode lever or the drive mode dial. In addition, you cannot add inconsistent settings. For example, you cannot adjust white balance if you have selected a filter effect. So, if you try to add both a white balance setting and a filter effect setting to a saved group, only the filter effect setting will be effective.

Once you have all of the settings as you want them, leave them that way and go to the Custom menu. Navigate to Custom Set Memory and select it, which gives choices of C1, C2, and C3, as shown in Figure 7-3.

Figure 7-3. Custom Set Memory Menu Options Screen

Highlight the slot you want to save your settings in and press Menu/Set. The camera will display a message asking you to confirm this action; highlight Yes and select it to confirm.

When, at a later time, you want to use this set of saved settings, turn the mode dial to the C position and press the Menu/Set button. On the sub-menu that appears, shown in Figure 7-4, select C1, C2, or C3. Once you have selected the custom mode you want, you are still free to change the camera's settings, but those changes will not be saved into a Custom Set Memory slot unless you go back to the Custom menu and save the changes there with the Custom Set Memory option.

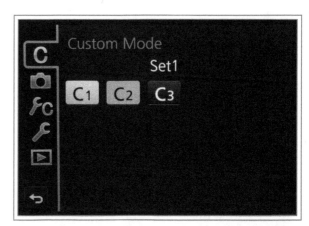

Figure 7-4. Screen to Select Custom Set Memory Slot for Shooting

Although it has some limitations, Custom Set Memory is a powerful capability, and anyone who has or develops some favorite groups of settings would be well advised to experiment with this option and take advantage of its power.

SILENT MODE

The Silent Mode option is a quick way to turn off the lights and sounds made by the camera that might distract a subject or cause a disturbance in a quiet area. When you turn this option on, the camera switches to using the electronic shutter, which is quieter than the mechanical shutter; silences all beeps and other sounds for matters such as focus and shutter operation; forces the flash off; and turns off the AF assist lamp. However, the lamp will still light up to indicate use of the self-timer (though the self-timer will not beep), and the blue Wi-Fi connection lamp on top of the camera will illuminate if you start a Wi-Fi connection. If the ND Filter switch is set to Auto, it will be changed to Off. If you will often use Silent Mode, you can include it as part of a group of saved settings with the Custom Set Memory option, or you can assign it to a function button.

AF/AE LOCK

This menu item lets you choose the function of the AF/AE Lock button, as well as the function of any other function button to which the AF/AE Lock option is assigned using the Function Button Set option on screen 7 of the Custom menu. You can use the AF/AE Lock menu option, whose screen is shown in Figure 7-5, to control how the assigned button locks autofocus (AF) and autoexposure (AE) settings. If you select AE Lock or AF Lock, the camera locks only the one designated setting. If you choose AF/AE Lock, the camera locks both settings at the same time.

Figure 7-5. AF/AE Lock Menu Options Screen

The camera will place icons on the recording display to indicate which of the values are locked, once you press the assigned button and the values are locked in. The AF Lock icon will appear in the upper right corner and the AE Lock icon in the lower left corner. Figure 7-6 shows the display when both values are locked.

Figure 7-6. Icons for AFL and AEL on Shooting Screen

It is not possible to lock exposure using the AF/AE Lock function in Manual exposure mode. None of the AF/AE Lock settings function in Intelligent Auto mode.

If you select AF-On, the final option on the AF/AE Lock menu, pressing the button assigned to AF/AE Lock will cause the camera to use its autofocus system to focus on the subject, using whatever AF Mode setting is in effect to determine what area to focus on. If manual focus is in effect, the camera will still use the autofocus system when you press this button. This is a useful option as backup when you are using manual focus. You also can use it if you have set the Shutter AF option to Off, as discussed below, so pressing the shutter button

halfway does not cause the camera to use its autofocus. You will then be able to press the assigned AF/AE Lock button when you need to get the camera to focus again quickly. The ability to use a button on the back of the camera for focusing is sometimes called "back button focus." (You also can assign this function to a button on the top or left side of the camera, of course.)

AF/AE Lock Hold

This next menu option determines how a button assigned to the AF/AE Lock function operates. If you set AF/AE Lock Hold to On, then, when you press the assigned button and release it, the camera retains the locked value(s). If you set this option to Off, then you have to hold the button down to retain the value(s); when you release it, the locked value(s) will be released. This option is dimmed and unavailable for selection when AF/AE Lock is set to AF-On. With that setting, pressing the assigned AF/AE Lock button causes the camera to use its autofocus, but not to lock focus, so it is not possible to "hold" the locked setting.

Shutter AF

This option lets you choose whether or not the camera will use autofocus when you press the shutter button halfway. With the default setup, with Shutter AF turned on, when the camera is set to an autofocus mode, it will evaluate focus when you half-press the shutter button. With single autofocus (AFS), focus will be locked as long as you hold the button in that position; with flexible autofocus (AFF), the camera will refocus if it detects movement, and with continuous autofocus (AFC), the camera will constantly attempt to adjust focus.

If you use this menu option to turn Shutter AF off, then the camera will not use its autofocus at all when you half-press the shutter button. There are several reasons why you might choose that setting. First, if you are taking a series of shots at the same distance, such as when you have the camera on a tripod and are taking shots of flat objects for auctions, you might focus once and then have no need to keep focusing. You can avoid using up the camera's battery for repeated uses of the autofocus system by turning Shutter AF off.

Another reason for using this option is if you prefer using the "back button focus" method to adjust autofocus. To do that, first assign a function button to AF/AE Lock (or just use the AF/AE Lock button, which already is assigned to that option.) Then, on screen 1 of the Custom menu, set the AF/AE Lock option to AF-On. (Or, just assign the function button to AF-On, which is available as a separate choice with the Function Button Set menu option.)

Then, when you press the function button assigned to AF/AE Lock (or AF-On), the camera will adjust autofocus. With this setup, you can adjust the focus whenever you want, and once you have it set as you want it, you can compose your shot and have the camera evaluate exposure without worrying that the camera will reset the focus to a different subject. You will be able to trigger the shutter to take another shot at any time.

Some photographers use this system with the autofocus mode set to AFC for continuous autofocus. Then, they can adjust focus at any time using the AF/AE Lock button, and press the shutter at any time without being concerned about focus. It's probably a good idea to give this setup a try and see if it works well for your type of shooting.

The next items to be discussed are on screen 2 of the Custom menu, which is shown in Figure 7-7.

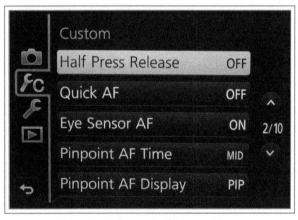

Figure 7-7. Screen 2 of Custom Menu

HALF PRESS RELEASE

This option lets you set the camera to capture an image when the shutter button is pressed halfway down, rather than requiring a full press, as is the normal situation. If you turn this setting on when Shutter AF is turned on, the camera will still adjust focus just before the image is captured, so the half-press of the button carries out both the autofocus operation and the image capture. If you have Shutter AF turned off, then you could use a button assigned to AF/AE Lock to adjust

autofocus, with the AF-On option turned on for that button, as discussed above. (Or, of course, you could use manual focus.)

Using the Half Press Release option can speed up your shooting, because you don't have to go through the sequence of half-press followed by full press of the shutter button; you can just touch the button lightly to capture an image, or a burst of images if the camera is set for burst shooting. This system can work well if you won't be needing to make adjustments to focus or exposure after half-pressing the shutter button. When you are shooting in predictable, steady lighting at a constant distance and you need to shoot quickly, this option can be useful. Also, the ability to trigger the shutter with a light touch can help reduce the risk of motion blur from camera shake.

QUICK AF

This next option on the Custom menu, Quick AF, can be turned either on or off. If you turn this setting on, the camera will focus on the subject whenever the camera has settled down and is still, with only minor movement or shake. You do not need to press the shutter button halfway down to achieve focus; the camera focuses on its own, as long as an autofocus mode is in use.

The advantage of turning Quick AF on is that you will have a slight improvement in focusing time, because the camera does not wait until you press the shutter button (or a button assigned to AF-On for focusing) to start the focusing process. The disadvantage is that the battery will run down faster than usual. So, unless I believe a split second for focusing time is critical, I usually leave this menu option turned off. The camera will still focus automatically when you press the shutter button halfway down; it just will take a little bit longer to bring the subject into focus. This option is not available when using the Preview Mode function or in dim lighting.

EYE SENSOR AF

When this option is turned on and the camera is set to an autofocus mode, the camera will automatically use its autofocus mechanism to adjust focus as soon as your head approaches the eye sensor and turns on the electronic viewfinder. However, the autofocus system will work only once with this system, even if the camera is set for continuous autofocus. So, when you first put the camera up to your eye, the focus will be adjusted for whatever subject the camera is aimed at at that instant. The camera will not readjust the focus unless you then press the shutter button halfway or use the AF/AE Lock button, if that button is set up to adjust focus.

This option can give the autofocus system a head start by bringing the scene into focus with an approximate setting, so it can quickly reach an exact focusing position when you press the shutter button halfway or use the AF/AE Lock button to make the final focus adjustments. I generally leave it turned off, but for snapshots it can be useful to have an approximate first cut at focusing take place as soon as you use the viewfinder.

This option works only when the viewfinder is turned on, either permanently or as your eye approaches it, through use of the LVF button or the Eye Sensor option on screen 9 of the Custom menu. The camera does not beep when focus is achieved with this option; the focus is adjusted silently.

PINPOINT AF TIME

As I discussed in Chapter 5, one of the options for AF Mode is Pinpoint AF, with which you can set a precise point for the focus area. Then, when you press the shutter button halfway to evaluate focus, the camera focuses at that point and enlarges the display briefly with that point centered, so you can judge the sharpness of the focus. The Pinpoint AF Time menu option controls how long the display stays enlarged when you press the shutter button halfway. The choices are Short (0.5 second), Mid (1.0 second), or Long (1.5 second). If you release the shutter button before the specified time has passed, the display will revert to normal size. Because of that behavior, I prefer to set this option to Long. Then, the display will stay enlarged for a long enough time to let me judge the focus, but I can always release the shutter button early to return the display to its normal size.

PINPOINT AF DISPLAY

This setting lets you choose one of two options for the size of the enlarged display that appears when you use the Pinpoint option for AF Mode—Full or PIP (picture-in-picture). With Full, the entire display is enlarged by a factor of between three and ten times; with PIP, only the central part of the display is enlarged, by a factor of between three and six times. You can vary the

enlargement factor by turning the rear dial when the enlargement is active as you are setting the focus point. That enlargement factor will then take effect when you half-press the shutter button to focus using the Pinpoint AF option.

The next items to be discussed are on screen 3 of the Custom menu, shown in Figure 7-8.

Figure 7-8. Screen 3 of Custom Menu

AF ASSIST LAMP

The autofocus (AF) assist lamp is the reddish light on the front of the camera, near the lens below the mode dial. The lamp illuminates when the ambient lighting is dim, to help the autofocus mechanism work by providing enough light to define the shape of the subject. Ordinarily, this option is left turned on for normal shooting, because the light only activates when it is needed in low-light conditions. However, you have the option of turning it off using the AF Assist Lamp menu option, so it will never turn on to help with autofocus. You might want to do this if you are trying to shoot pictures without being detected, or without disturbing a subject such as a sleeping animal.

In Intelligent Auto mode, you cannot turn off the AF assist lamp using this menu option, but you can use the Silent Mode option on screen 1 of the Custom menu to turn off the lamp, along with the flash and camera sounds. The lamp does not illuminate when you are using manual focus (unless you have set a function button to use the AF-On option and you press that button to cause the camera to use its autofocus).

The AF assist lamp also serves as the self-timer lamp. Even if you set the AF Assist Lamp menu option to Off, the lamp will light up when the self-timer is used; there is no way to disable the lamp for that function.

DIRECT FOCUS AREA

This is another option that can be turned either on or off; it is off by default. If you turn it on, then, in recording mode, if you press any of the four direction buttons, the camera immediately displays a screen for adjusting the position of the autofocus area. For example, if AF Mode is set to 1-Area, Pinpoint AF, or Face/Eye Detection, then, when you press, say, the Left button, that button immediately activates the focus frame and starts moving it across the display. If you have AF Mode set to 49-Area or Custom Multi, then, when you press a direction button, the camera immediately displays the screen for selecting the focus zones to be included in the focus area. You can then keep pressing any of the direction buttons to adjust the area or use other controls to make other adjustments.

This option could be useful if you were in a situation when you need to adjust the focus area often, particularly with the 1-Area or Pinpoint AF options. I would not recommend using it with the 49-Area or Custom Multi options, because you need to do considerable adjusting with those options, and a split second of added speed will not be of that much use.

I do not use this option myself, because it is so easy to adjust the focus area without it. Just press the Left button to bring up the AF Mode option, then press the Down button to get to the screen for moving the focus frame. You also can use the touch screen to make quick changes to the focus area.

Also, if you turn on Direct Focus Area, you lose the other functions of the direction buttons while this option is in effect. So, if you wanted to set white balance or ISO, you would have to use the Quick Menu, assign those functions to another button, or turn off this menu option before making that adjustment.

FOCUS/RELEASE PRIORITY

This option determines whether the camera places more importance on taking a picture even if focus is not perfect, or on achieving the best possible focus before permitting a picture to be taken. This menu item has two main sub-options—one for when the focus mode is set to AFS/AFF, and one for when it is set to AFC.

For either of those sub-options, you can set this item to Focus or Release. If it is set to Focus, the camera will not take a picture until focus has been confirmed, when autofocus is in effect. So, if you aim the camera at a subject that is difficult for the autofocus system to bring into sharp focus, such as an area with no sharp features in dim lighting, the camera may display a red focus frame and beep four times, indicating focus was not achieved. In that situation, if this menu option is set to Focus, the camera will not take the picture when you press the shutter button. If you set this option to Release, the camera will take the picture even if it is not in focus. If you are using manual focus, the camera will take the picture regardless of focus, even if you set the priority to Focus.

The use of this option is a matter of personal preference and the situation you are faced with. If you are taking images of a one-time event, you may want to use the Release option so you don't miss a shot just because focus is slightly off. It's usually better to get an image that is slightly out of focus than no image at all. But if you have time to make sure focus is sharp, you can use the Focus option to make sure you have focus properly adjusted before you capture an image.

I almost always set this option to Release so I will not miss a shot because of a focusing issue. In particular, I choose Release when the focus mode is set to AFC, because the camera adjusts focus continuously, and I do not want the camera to avoid capturing an image because the focus is slightly off because of the continuing adjustments.

This option also has an impact on the speed of burst shooting. As I discussed in Chapter 5, if this option is set to Focus, shooting may be slowed down as the camera attempts to adjust focus before recording each image, when you are using a burst setting with continuous focus adjustments.

AF SENSITIVITY

This option lets you regulate how quickly the camera's autofocus system locks on to a new subject when the AFF or AFC setting for autofocus is in use. As shown in Figure 7-9, when you select this menu option, you will find a scale of adjustments up to two units in a positive or negative direction from the normal. If you adjust the setting in the positive direction, the camera will increase the speed with which it adjusts focus; a setting in the negative direction will have the opposite effect.

Figure 7-9. AF Sensitivity Adjustment Screen

This option is particularly useful in a situation when you are recording a video and an object or person temporarily blocks your view by walking in front of the camera. If you have AF Sensitivity adjusted to the negative (slower) side, the camera will not immediately react to the new subject, and will maintain focus on the main subject. Without this adjustment, the camera might switch its focus to the new subject, disrupting the flow of the video.

However, if you are recording a scene where there is a stream of different subjects that you want to include in the video, such as athletes in a competition, you may want to adjust AF Sensitivity in the positive direction so the camera will not hesitate to move the focus point when a new subject appears.

I usually leave this option at zero, and I only make an adjustment when there is a specific need for one.

AF+MF

This is an on-or-off option that is turned off by default. If you turn it on, then, when the autofocus mode is set to AFS, for single autofocus, once you have pressed the shutter button halfway to lock focus, while holding the button in that position, you can turn the focus ring to fine-tune the focus manually. Features such as MF Assist and peaking will operate if they are turned on through the Custom menu. This option also takes effect if you have locked focus with a button assigned to the AF-On option or to the AF/AE Lock option, when that option is set to lock autofocus or to the AF-On setting through screen 1 of the Custom menu.

This option is useful when, for example, you have locked focus on a group of small objects, and you want to make sure the focus is precisely set on one of those

objects, such as on an object behind the others, or on a portion of one of them. Once the autofocus system has locked on the group, just start turning the focus ring while keeping the shutter button pressed halfway (or the assigned AF/AE Lock or AF-On button pressed, if applicable) to adjust the focus manually until you have it set exactly as you want.

Screen 4 of the Custom menu is shown in Figure 7-10.

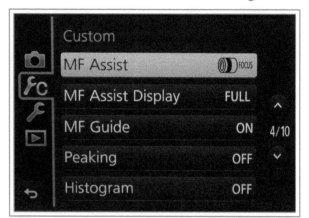

Figure 7-10. Screen 4 of Custom Menu

MANUAL FOCUS (MF) ASSIST AND MF ASSIST DISPLAY

These next two Custom menu options let you set whether and how the recording screen display is magnified when you're using manual focus. With the MF Assist option highlighted, press the Right button to pop up a sub-menu with icons for choosing one of four settings, as shown in Figure 7-11.

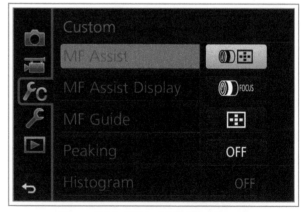

Figure 7-11. MF Assist Options Screen

If you choose the top option, which shows icons for the focus ring and the AF Mode button (Left button), then, when you start turning the focus ring to focus or you press the Left button, the screen will immediately be magnified to help you adjust the focus.

With the second option, turning the focus ring will immediately magnify the display, but pressing the Left button will not immediately magnify the screen, though it will activate the MF Assist frame so you can move the frame around the display. Once you press Menu/Set to set the frame in place, the display will be magnified in that area. With the third option, pressing the button will immediately enlarge the display, but turning the focus ring will not immediately enlarge the display, though it will still adjust the manual focus.

With the Off setting, when you press the Left button the MF Assist frame works in the same way as with the second option, discussed above, and the focus ring acts in the same way as with the third option.

The MF Assist Display option lets you set the area of magnification with MF Assist to Full or PIP (picture-in-picture). With Full, the magnification takes up the whole display and varies between three and 10 times normal. With PIP, the magnified area is smaller and the factor varies between three and six times normal.

You can use all four direction buttons to move the focus area around the display, and you can turn the front or rear dial, or pull and pinch on the touch screen, to change the magnification factor. To reset the focus point to the center of the display, press the Display button. To dismiss the MF Assist display, press the shutter button halfway or press the Menu/Set button. Or, if you turned the focus ring to start the magnification, the screen will return to normal size on its own after about 10 seconds. You can then press the Left button or turn the focus ring (depending on menu settings) to bring the MF Assist display back on the screen, or you can just press the shutter button to take the picture. You can switch between the full-screen and PIP views by touching the rectangular icon at the bottom of the display with a small inset white rectangle in its upper right corner.

The MF Assist option is not available for recording motion pictures or when Digital Zoom is activated.

MF GUIDE

If this option is turned on, then, when you are turning the focus ring to adjust manual focus, the camera

displays a scale at the bottom of the screen with an indicator that shows the approximate focus distance along the scale from far to near, with no numerical value for the distance. With this option turned off, the scale does not appear.

PEAKING

This menu option controls another feature for assisting with manual focus. The peaking feature, when it is turned on, places colored pixels on the screen at areas that the camera determines are in sharp focus. As you turn the focus ring to adjust focus, watch for the colored areas to reach their maximum intensity. When you see the largest areas of glowing pixels, focus will be sharp for the areas where those pixels appear.

Figure 7-12. Peaking Menu Options Screen

The peaking menu item has three main options: On, Off, and Set, as shown in Figure 7-12. In most cases, I leave it turned on, because it operates only when manual focus is in effect and I find it helpful for most manual focusing situations. The Set option has two sub-options: Detect Level and Display Color, as shown in Figure 7-13.

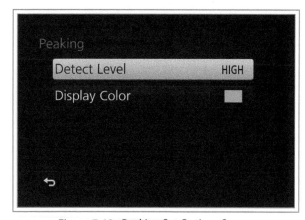

Figure 7-13. Peaking Set Options Screen

The Detect Level can be set to High or Low. If you set it to High, the camera will require a higher degree of sharpness before it places pixels at a given focus area. With that setting, there will be fewer peaking pixels displayed than with the Low setting. You may find that it is easier to gauge the focus with fewer pixels, because you can adjust focus until those few pixels appear. However, in some situations, such as with objects that are lacking in straight lines or sharp features, you may find that it is preferable to set Detect Level to Low, so there will be more peaking pixels visible.

With the Display Color sub-option, you can choose light blue, yellow, yellow green, pink, or white for the peaking color if Detect Level is set to High. You can choose dark blue, orange, green, red, or gray if the level is set to Low. It is useful to choose a color that contrasts with the scene you are photographing, so you can distinguish the peaking pixels from other parts of the image.

If the touch screen options are turned on, you can use the Peak icon in the Touch Tab area to cycle from peaking off to on with Low to on with High.

Figures 7-14 and 7-15 illustrate the use of this feature. Figure 7-14 shows the view with peaking turned off, and Figure 7-15 has peaking turned on with Detect Level set to Low.

Figure 7-14. Peaking Turned Off

Figure 7-15. Peaking Detect Level Set to Low

As noted above, peaking operates only when the camera is set to manual focus. If you assign a function button to AF-On or to AF/AE Lock using the AF-On option on screen 1 of the Custom menu, peaking pixels will appear when you press that button to cause the camera to use autofocus, if manual focus is in effect. Peaking also operates if you adjust manual focus using the AF+MF option, discussed earlier in this chapter. Peaking does not operate when the Rough Monochrome filter effect setting is in use.

Histogram

The next menu option, Histogram, controls the display of the histogram in recording mode. A histogram is a graph showing the distribution of dark and bright areas in the image that is being viewed on the camera's screen. The darkest blacks are represented by vertical bars on the left, and the brightest whites by vertical bars on the right, with continuous gradations in between.

Figure 7-16. Histogram for Underexposed Image

If an image has a histogram in which the pattern looks like a tall ski slope coming from the left of the screen down to ground level in the middle of the screen, that means there is an excessive amount of black and dark areas (tall bars on the left side of the histogram), and very few bright and white areas (no bars on the right). The histogram in Figure 7-16 illustrates this situation.

A pattern moving from the middle of the graph up to peaks at the right side of the graph would mean just the opposite—too many bright and white areas, as in the histogram shown in Figure 7-17.

Figure 7-17. Histogram for Overexposed Image

A histogram that is "just right" would be one that starts low on the left, gradually rises to a medium peak in the middle of the graph, then moves gradually back down to the bottom at the right. That pattern indicates a good balance of whites, blacks, and medium tones. An example of this type of histogram is shown in Figure 7-18.

Figure 7-18. Histogram for Normally Exposed Image

In playback mode, the FZ2500 includes one display screen with a histogram for the image being displayed. The camera does not, by default, display the histogram for the live view in recording mode. To turn on the histogram when you are shooting, you need to use this menu option.

The Histogram menu option has only two choices: On or Off. If you turn the histogram on, it will appear on the camera's display in recording mode, if a detailed display screen has been selected using the Display button, as shown in Figures 7-16 through 7-18.

The histogram does not display in Intelligent Auto mode, but it does appear in Intelligent Auto Plus mode and all other shooting modes. When the histogram is first activated, it appears in a yellow frame with arrows indicating that you can move it to any position on the display, as shown in Figure 7-19.

Figure 7-19. Histogram Ready to be Moved

You can move it with the cursor buttons or by dragging it on the touch screen. Once you have it located where you want it, press the shutter button halfway down to lock it in place. While it is movable, press the Display button to reset it to the center of the display. If you need to move it after it has been locked in place, you can touch it on the screen to reactivate it for moving. Or, you can go back to this menu option and select On for the Histogram item.

The histogram is an approximation, and you should not rely on it too heavily. It provides some information as to how evenly exposed your image is likely to be. (Or, for playback, how well exposed it was.) If the histogram is displayed in orange, that means the recording and playback versions of the histogram will not match for this image, because the flash was used, or in a few other situations.

The items on screen 5 of the Custom menu are shown in Figure 7-20.

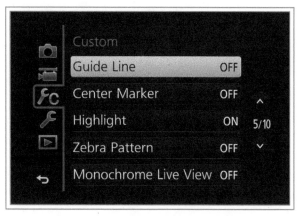

Figure 7-20. Screen 5 of Custom Menu

GUIDE LINE

This option lets you set grid lines to be displayed on the LCD and in the viewfinder to assist you with composition. Once you select Guide Line from the Custom menu, you see a screen with four options: Off, and three patterns of lines, as shown in Figure 7-21.

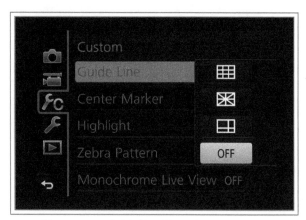

Figure 7-21. Guide Line Menu Options Screen

If you choose Off, no grid lines will be displayed. If you choose the top option, the camera will display a grid that forms nine equal rectangles on the screen. This choice can help you line up subjects, including the horizon, along straight lines. The second option is a pattern of 16 rectangles with a pair of intersecting diagonal lines, which can help you locate items along diagonals as well as along horizontal or vertical lines. With the third option, the camera displays just two intersecting lines, one horizontal and one vertical, and lets you set their positions using the direction buttons or the touch screen. This option can be useful if you need to compose your shot with an off-center subject.

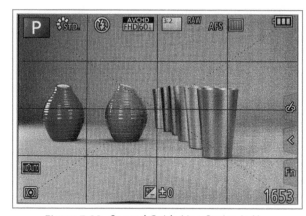

Figure 7-22. Second Guide Line Option in Use

When any of the Guide Line options is turned on, the grid lines will display whenever the camera is in recording mode, in all shooting modes except Panorama and on all display screens that include the live view. An example of the second option as displayed in shooting mode is shown in Figure 7-22.

CENTER MARKER

This option, when turned on, places a small cross in the center of the display, as shown in Figure 7-23, to help you keep the subject centered. This option can be particularly useful when recording video, because you may be distracted by the action and this marker may remind you to keep the most important part of the scene in a safe zone near the center of the display so it won't accidentally be cut off. This cross appears in all shooting modes and on all display screens that include the live view in recording mode.

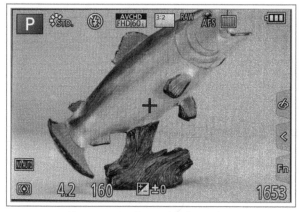

Figure 7-23. Center Marker in Use

HIGHLIGHT

This feature produces a flashing area of black and white on areas of the image that are oversaturated with white, indicating they may be too bright. The flashing effect takes place only when you are viewing the pictures in Auto Review or Playback mode, on the LCD or in the viewfinder. That is, you will see the Highlight warning only when the image appears briefly on the screen after it has been recorded (Auto Review) or when you view the picture in Playback mode. This feature alerts you that the image may be washed out (overexposed) in some areas, so you may want to reduce the exposure for the next shot. If you find that sort of warning distracting, just turn this feature off. The flashing does not occur on one playback screen that shows the image only, with no information. So, even if this option is turned on, you can see your image without the flashing, by pressing the Display button to view that screen.

ZEBRA PATTERN

This feature helps you gauge whether an image or video will be overexposed by setting the FZ2500 to place a striped "zebra" pattern on the display in recording mode. You can select either left-slanting or right-slanting stripes to match the scene as well as possible, and you can set either type of stripes to a numerical value from 50% to 105% in 5% increments. For Zebra2, though, you can also choose Off for the value. I will discuss the reason for that setting later in this section.

The numbers from 50 to 105 are a measure of relative brightness or exposure on a scale where 0 represents black and 100 represents bright white. A value of 100 or 105 indicates overexposure. To make the settings, select the menu option and pop up the menu with sub-options of Zebra1, Zebra2, Off, and Set, as shown in Figure 7-24.

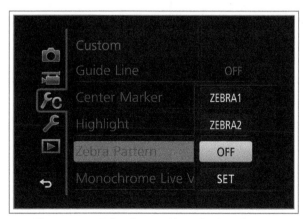

Figure 7-24. Zebra Pattern Menu Options Screen

Zebra1 generates stripes that slant from lower left to upper right and appear to move down to the right; Zebra2 generates stripes in the opposite direction. Use

the Set option to set a numerical level for either Zebra1 or Zebra2, and then choose Zebra1 or Zebra2 from the menu to display that pattern on the screen.

When you turn this option on to any level less than about 90, you very likely will see, on some parts of the display, the "zebra" stripes that give this feature its name. When you see the stripes on part of the image, that means that area is at or above the brightness level that was set for the stripes. For example, if you select stripes set to the 65% level and aim the camera at the scene, the stripes will appear on any part of the display where the brightness level reaches 65% of bright white.

There are various approaches to using these stripes, which originated as a tool for professional videographers. Some photographers like to set the zebra function to 90% and adjust the camera's exposure so the stripes just barely start to appear in the brightest parts of the image. Another recommendation is to set the option to 75% for a scene with Caucasian skin, and expose so that the stripes appear in the area of the skin.

In Figure 7-25, I set the pattern to Zebra1 at 65% and exposed to have the stripes appear on the mannequin's face.

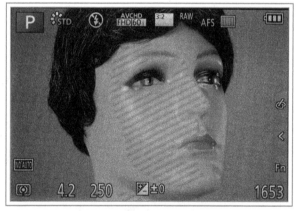

Figure 7-25. Zebra1 Pattern in Use

As I noted earlier in this section, for Zebra2, you can set the brightness to any value from 50 to 105, and also to Off, which is not available for Zebra1. The reason for this setting is that, if you assign Zebra Pattern to a function button, when you press that button the camera cycles from Zebra1 to Zebra2 and then to Off. If you want to be able to turn Zebra on and off in the quickest way possible, you can set Zebra2 to a value of Off, so pressing the button will immediately switch from Zebra1 (at a numerical value) to Zebra2, which will be equivalent to Off.

Zebra Pattern is a feature to consider, especially for video recording, but the FZ2500 has an excellent metering system, including both live and playback histograms, so you can manage without this option if you don't want to deal with its learning curve.

MONOCHROME LIVE VIEW

When you turn this feature on, the camera converts the display to a black-and-white view of the scene it is aimed at. This feature might help you concentrate on composition and geometry in your image, without being distracted by colors. You also might find it easier to adjust manual focus with this view, because you can turn on peaking with a color that contrasts clearly with all parts of the display. The monochrome view does not affect the recorded image, which will be in color unless you have also selected a monochrome setting for the final image using the Photo Style menu option or one of the monochrome Scene mode or Creative Control mode settings. This setting does not have any effect in the basic Intelligent Auto mode, but it is effective in all other shooting modes, including Intelligent Auto Plus.

The next menu options are on screen 6 of the Custom menu, shown in Figure 7-26.

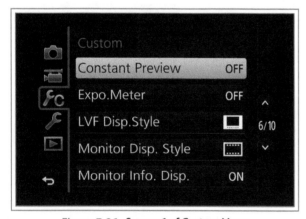

Figure 7-26. Screen 6 of Custom Menu

CONSTANT PREVIEW

This option lets you see a preview of the effects of your exposure settings when the camera is in Manual exposure mode. When you turn this option on with the camera in that recording mode and then adjust shutter speed, aperture, or ISO, the display will grow darker or brighter to show how the settings would affect the

final image. The display also will show how the aperture setting would affect the depth of field.

For example, if you set shutter speed to 1/125 second, aperture to f/8, and ISO to 1600 in a moderately lighted room with this option turned off, the camera's display will appear normal, showing the scene clearly. If you then press the shutter button halfway (assuming default settings for focus and shutter behavior), the display will grow dark and you will see more items in focus, reflecting the effects of the current settings. If you then turn this menu option on, you will see the same view you did when you pressed the shutter button halfway, even before pressing that button.

This setting can help if you need to see exactly what effect the current settings will have. However, in some situations it is better to leave this option turned off. For example, if you are shooting an image using a manually triggered off-camera flash in Manual exposure mode, the camera will not realize that you are using the external flash, and the display screen may be quite dark with the settings you are using. In that situation, you might not be able to see the display to compose your image with this option activated, so you should leave Constant Preview turned off. (If you are using the camera's flash to trigger the external flash, you don't need to bother about this setting, because it is disabled when the camera's flash is in use.)

If you have a function button set to the Preview option and have the Constant Preview option turned on, pressing the function button in Manual exposure mode will not activate the Preview function, because it is already in effect through this menu option.

EXPOSURE METER

This feature gives you the option of having the camera display its Exposure Meter feature, which is a set of two graphical dials that appear when you are adjusting shutter speed, aperture, exposure compensation, or Program Shift, as shown in Figure 7-27.

Any red zones that appears on the dials indicate values that are outside the range of normal exposure. The display disappears after about four seconds when no controls are used.

I find this display distracting and not all that helpful, so I leave it turned off, but it might be useful in some situations as a clearly visible confirmation of current exposure settings.

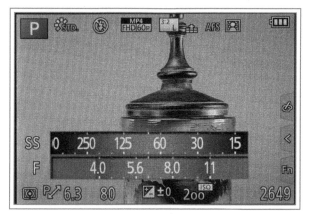

Figure 7-27. Exposure Meter Display for Program Shift

LVF DISPLAY STYLE

This option controls how various informational icons are displayed in the viewfinder. There are two choices, indicated by graphic icons. With the top choice, known as live viewfinder style, several of the icons, including those for recording mode, battery status, metering mode, and number of images remaining, are displayed outside of the live view area, so you can see more of the live view with no icons blocking the view. In addition, the Metering Mode icon and a few others remain on the display even when the no-information screen is selected. With the bottom choice, known as monitor style, all of the icons are placed within the live view area and that area extends farther down to accommodate them. I find the differences between these two views to be minimal, but this is one way to tweak the viewfinder's operation if you want to.

MONITOR DISPLAY STYLE

This option is the same as the previous one, except that it applies to the LCD display, rather than the viewfinder. For this setting, I prefer using the bottom option, which places all of the icons within the live view of the image, so you have a slightly larger view of the scene. I find that the icons do not significantly block the view.

MONITOR INFORMATION DISPLAY

This option lets you choose whether or not to include the information-only display among the screens that the camera displays on the LCD (but not in the viewfinder) in recording mode when you press the Display button. If you turn this option on, then the

camera includes the screen shown in Figure 7-28 (called the on-monitor information screen), which displays current recording settings, including recording mode, ISO, exposure compensation, Quality, Photo Style, White Balance, Metering Mode, images remaining, AF Mode, and other settings. It displays the aperture and shutter speed once they are determined by your settings or by the camera's metering.

As I discussed in Chapter 5, when this screen is displayed, you can adjust the various settings using the touch screen as you scroll through them.

This display does not include any view of the image; the idea is that you will use this display for information (or for touch screen adjustments), and use the viewfinder to view the scene. If you don't want to include this screen in the cycle of displays, just turn the option off using this menu item.

Figure 7-28. On-Monitor Information Display Screen

Next, the items on screen 7 of the Custom menu are shown in Figure 7-29.

Figure 7-29. Screen 7 of Custom Menu

RECORDING AREA

This option lets you set the camera's recording screen to display either the recording area used for still photos or the area used for motion pictures. For still pictures, that area is determined by the aspect ratio setting; for motion pictures, it is determined by the Recording Quality option on the Motion Picture menu's second screen. For still images, there are four options: 4:3, 3:2, 16:9, and 1:1. For motion pictures the aspect ratio is 16:9, for all settings for HD and 4K video. For C4K video, which is available only when System Frequency is set to 24.00 Hz on screen 5 of the Setup menu, the aspect ratio of the video frame is 256:135, or 1.90:1.

The reason for having this option available is that the FZ2500 does not ordinarily show the area available for movie recording until you press the red motion picture button to start the recording. So, if the aspect ratio menu option is set for, say, 3:2, you will not see the actual shape of the motion picture recording screen until the recording starts, so you will not be able to compose the scene on the camera's monitor properly. But, if you set the Recording Area menu option to the Motion Picture option, then you will see the available recording area on the camera's screen before you start the recording.

The choice here depends on whether you are planning to capture still images or record motion picture sequences in your shooting session. To make the choice, use this menu item to select the icon for the still camera or the icon for a movie camera. This option does not function for 4K Photo or Post Focus recording.

VIDEO-PRIORITY DISPLAY

If you turn this option on, the camera will change its display icons to reflect the settings that are available for video recording. For example, it will not display icons for settings such as Picture Size and Quality, but will display icons for settings such as Recording Format and Quality for movies. If you adjust exposure compensation while the camera is set to a still-shooting mode, the screen will display the normal exposure compensation scale, but, as shown in Figure 7-30, will place a small camera icon above the scale for any values that are available for shooting still images but not for recording movies. In the lower right corner of the display, the camera will show the remaining time available for recording movies using current settings, rather than the number of still images

that can be captured. If you are going to be shooting movies, turning on this setting is quite helpful.

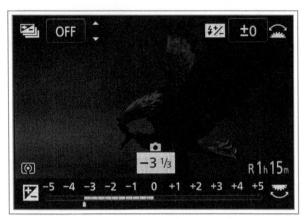

Figure 7-30. Exposure Compensation Scale with Video-Priority Display

AUTO REVIEW

This option controls how long your still images are displayed immediately after they are recorded by the camera, and how the camera behaves during that display. The Auto Review menu option has two sub-options: Duration Time and Playback Operation Priority. When you select Duration Time, the possible settings are Off, one second, two seconds, three seconds, four seconds, five seconds, or Hold. These choices are fairly self-explanatory. After the shutter button is pressed, the image appears on the screen (or not) according to how this option is set. If you choose Hold, the image stays on the screen until you press the shutter button halfway.

The second sub-option, Playback Operation Priority, controls whether you can perform playback operations on an image while it is displayed for a specific number of seconds under the Duration Time option. If Playback Operation Priority is turned on, then, when an image is displayed for one to five seconds under Auto Review, if you press a button such as Fn6 to delete an image, or a navigation button such as the Left or Right button, the camera will respond as if it were in playback mode, and carry out that operation. If Playback Operation Priority is turned off, pressing a button will have the effect it would have in recording mode. For example, if you press the Fn6 button, the camera will carry out whatever function is assigned to that button for recording mode, which, by default, is the Preview function.

If Duration Time is set to Hold, then Playback Operation Priority is automatically turned on, and the camera will act as if it were in playback mode at all times while a new image is displayed immediately after capture.

Auto Review does not work when recording motion pictures. When 4K Photo or Post Focus shooting is turned on, the only settings available for Duration Time are On and Off.

FUNCTION BUTTON SET

As I discussed in Chapter 5, the FZ2500 has seven physical function buttons labeled Fn1 through Fn7. It also has five virtual function buttons represented by icons on the touch screen, labeled Fn8 through Fn12. Each of those buttons has a particular function assigned to it by default. For all twelve buttons, though, you can choose a different function to be assigned when the camera is in recording mode. For the Fn1, Fn2, Fn3, Fn4, Fn5, and Fn7 buttons (but not Fn6), you also can choose a function to be assigned when the camera is in playback mode. You make those assignments with the Function Button Set menu option. (There also are other ways to make the assignments, discussed later in this section.)

When you highlight this option and press the Menu/Set button or the Right button, the camera displays the screen shown in Figure 7-31, letting you choose the settings in recording mode or playback mode.

Figure 7-31. Function Button Set Main Options Screen

If you select recording mode, the camera will display the special screen shown in Figure 7-32, with a graphic display of the assignable buttons. On that screen, turn the front or rear dial or press the Up and Down buttons to move the highlight to the button whose assignment you want to change, and press Menu/Set. (Or, just

touch the button's icon on the touch screen.) You will then see a display like that in Figure 7-33, which highlights the current setting for that button on a sub-menu screen. Scroll through that series of 21 screens until you find the new setting you want to assign to that button, and press Menu/Set to confirm it.

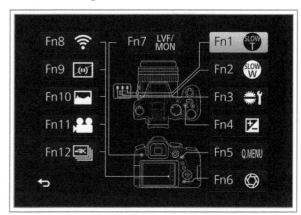

Figure 7-32. Graphic Display of Function Buttons

Figure 7-33. List of Options for a Function Button

Some of the items that can be assigned to these buttons are not available through any menu or other control, while some of them are options that can also be selected through the menu system or through another control. Table 7-1, below, lists all of the possible assignments for a button for recording mode. The first column of the table lists the functions that can be assigned to a button; the second column lists the menu option where each setting can be found, if any. The third column lists the button that is assigned to that setting by default, if any. After the table, I will discuss the settings that are not available from any menu option.

Table 7-1.   **Possible Function Button Assignments for Recording Mode**

Function	Menu/Screen or Control where Also Found	Default Setting
Exposure Compensation	None	Fn4
Wi-Fi	Setup/1	Fn8
Q. Menu	None	Fn5
LVF/Monitor Switch	Custom/9 (Eye Sensor)	Fn7
LVF/Monitor Display Style	Custom/6	None
AF/AE Lock	None (Custom/1 has related menu option)	AF/AE Lock button
AF-On	None (Custom/1 has related menu option)	AF/AE Lock button if set in menu
Preview	None	Fn6
One Push AE	None	None
Touch AE	Touch Screen	Touch Screen
Level Gauge	Display Button	Fn9
Focus Area Set	None	None
Slow Zoom T	None	Fn1
Slow Zoom W	None	Fn2
1 Shot Raw + JPG	None	None
1 Shot Spot Metering	None	None
Cursor Button Lock	None	None
Dial Operation Switch	None	Fn3
Photo Style	Recording/1	None
Filter Effect	Recording/1	None
Aspect Ratio	Recording/1	None
Picture Size	Recording/1	None
Quality	Recording/1	None
AFS/AFF	Recording/2	None
Metering Mode	Recording/2	None
Burst Rate	Recording/2	None
4K Photo	Recording/2	Fn12
Self Timer	Recording/3	None
Bracket	Recording/2	None
Highlight Shadow	Recording/3	None
i.Dynamic	Recording/3	None
i.Resolution	Recording/3	None
HDR	Recording/4	None
Shutter Type	Recording/5	None
Flash Mode	Recording/5	None
Flash Adjustment	Recording/5 (Under Flash item)	None
Wireless Flash Setup	Recording/5 (Under Flash item)	None
i.Zoom	Recording/6	None
Digital Zoom	Recording/6	None
Stabilizer	Recording/7	None
4K Live Cropping	Motion Picture/1	None
Snap Movie	Motion Picture/2	Fn11
Motion Picture Recording Format	Motion Picture/2	None
Motion Picture Recording Quality	Motion Picture/2	None

Function	Menu/Screen or Control where Also Found	Default Setting
Variable Frame Rate	Motion Picture/2	None
Picture Mode	Motion Picture/3	None
Synchro Scan	Motion Picture/5	None
Time Code Display	Motion Picture/6	None
Microphone Directivity Adjustment	Motion Picture/7 (Special Mic./Manual)	None
Color Bars	Motion Picture/8	None
Silent Mode	Custom/1	None
Peaking	Custom/4	None
Histogram	Custom/4	Fn10
Guide Line	Custom/5	None
Zebra Pattern	Custom/5	None
Monochrome Live View	Custom/5	None
Recording Area	Custom/7	None
Video-Priority Display	Custom/7	None
Zoom Lever	Custom/7	None
Zoom Ring	Custom/8	None
Touch Screen	Custom/10 (Under Touch Settings)	None
Headphone Volume	Setup/2	None
Sensitivity	ISO Button	ISO Button
White Balance	WB Button	WB Button
WB AWB (Auto White Balance)	WB Button	WB Button
WB Daylight	WB Button	WB Button
WB Cloudy	WB Button	WB Button
WB Shade	WB Button	WB Button
WB Incandescent	WB Button	WB Button
WB Flash	WB Button	WB Button
WB White Set 1	WB Button	WB Button
WB White Set 2	WB Button	WB Button
WB White Set 3	WB Button	WB Button
WB White Set 4	WB Button	WB Button
WB Color Temperature 1	WB Button	WB Button
WB Color Temperature 2	WB Button	WB Button
WB Color Temperature 3	WB Button	WB Button
WB Color Temperature 4	WB Button	WB Button
AF Mode/MF	AF Mode Button	AF Mode Button
Macro Mode	AF Macro Button	AF Macro Button
Restore to Default	None	None

Most of the settings in Table 7-1 are self-explanatory; they are options that also can be activated from one of the menus or with a dedicated control, as noted in the second column of the table. For example, if a button is assigned to the Photo Style option, pressing the button calls up a menu or settings screen for that option from screen 1 of the Recording menu. The screen that is called up by pressing the function button may look different from the screen that is called up from the menu, but it will let you make the basic selections for the menu option. The level gauge is normally activated by pressing the Display button until a screen with that item appears. I will not discuss those assignments here; you can find details about those settings in the chapters that discuss the menu systems and physical controls.

However, there are several possible button assignments that are not found on the regular menus and are not normally activated by any control button. I will discuss those functions below.

AF/AE Lock

The first non-menu setting, AF/AE Lock, lets you assign the AF/AE Lock function to a function button. Note that this function is also permanently assigned to the AF/AE Lock button, so there is not that much need to assign it to a function button, but the possibility exists.

Once the function is assigned to a button, you can use the AF/AE Lock item on screen 1 of the Custom menu to set the assigned button to lock both autofocus and autoexposure, or just one or the other. Then, you can press the assigned button to lock whichever of those settings have been selected through the menu option. When either AF Lock or AE Lock is in effect, the camera displays an icon in the lower left corner of the display. For example, Figure 7-34 shows the display when AE Lock is in effect.

Figure 7-34. Shooting Screen with AE Lock in Effect

With the AF/AE Lock menu option, you also can select AF-On. If you turn on that option, pressing the button assigned to AF/AE Lock operates the camera's autofocus system. That option gives the camera a capability for "back button focus," so named because you can press a button on the camera's back to focus the lens. If you want to turn off the shutter button's focusing function, you can do that by turning off the Shutter AF option on screen 1 of the Custom menu.

You cannot lock exposure with a button assigned to AF/AE Lock when the camera is set to Manual exposure mode, and the button will not function at all in either variety of Intelligent Auto mode. When manual focus is

in use, the button cannot lock focus with AFL, but you can use the AF-On option. Zooming the lens cancels either type of lock. You can set the button to hold its setting without keeping it pressed, using the AF/AE Lock Hold item on screen 1 of the Custom menu.

AF-On

As noted above, you can select AF-On as the function for the button assigned to the AF/AE Lock function, using the AF/AE Lock option on screen 1 of the Custom menu. You also can assign AF-On directly to a function button, by selecting AF-On from the Function Button Set options. This is just another way to select the AF-On option; it does not operate differently if you select it using this procedure.

Preview

The next non-menu setting, Preview, lets you see the effects of the current aperture and shutter speed settings on the final image before you take a picture. Ordinarily, when you aim the camera at a subject, the live view on the camera's display is set to provide a clear view of the scene, without giving effect to the current settings.

For example, suppose you are using Manual exposure mode for an indoor shot of two objects at different distances. Suppose you have set the aperture to f/8.0 to keep both items in focus with a broad depth of field and you have set the shutter speed to 1/125 second. If you aim the camera at the subjects, you will see a view like that in Figure 7-35, which does not show the effects of these settings.

Figure 7-35. Preview Example: Before Pressing Button

Now, if Preview is assigned to the Fn6 button (as it is by default), press that button once and you will see a screen like that in Figure 7-36. For this view, the Preview feature has caused the camera to close the aperture down to the actual setting of f/8.0, which shows the effect of the broad depth of field, bringing the background into sharper focus. The message on the screen, Fn6 Shtr Speed Effect Added, means that the camera is currently displaying the effect of the aperture setting; if you press Fn6 again, the camera will also display the effect of the shutter speed setting.

Figure 7-36. Preview Example: After First Button Press

After you press Fn6 the second time, the recording screen will look like Figure 7-37. In this case, the camera is displaying the effects of both the aperture and shutter speed settings. The recording screen is quite dark, which shows that using the current shutter speed and aperture would result in a dark image. In addition, the message on the screen indicates that you can press Fn6 to end the preview.

Figure 7-37. Preview Example: After Second Button Press

If you have turned on the Constant Preview option through screen 6 of the Custom menu, the Preview function will not work in Manual exposure mode, because the preview will already be in effect. (The Constant Preview option works only in Manual exposure mode.) You can change the settings while the preview screen is displayed, to see how the changes affect the image.

One Push AE

This next non-menu setting gives you a quick way to set the camera to achieve a normal exposure. It is of use only when the camera has been unable to expose the image properly given the settings you have made, including the aperture and shutter speed. For example, if you are using Shutter Priority mode and have set the shutter speed to 1/640 second with ISO set to 200, if conditions are fairly dark the camera may not be able to expose the image within a normal range. In that case, the aperture and shutter speed values will blink red on the display. At that point, press the function button assigned to One Push AE and the camera will change its settings to correct the exposure problem. When I tried these settings in a normally lighted room, the camera changed the shutter speed to 1/15 second, which produced a normal exposure.

I find this function to be of limited practical use, though it could be useful in a particular situation when it is important to get a well-exposed shot and you don't have time to pay attention to exposure settings. It is available only in Program, Aperture Priority, Shutter Priority, Manual and Creative Video shooting modes.

Touch AE

This option can also be activated by touching the Touch AE icon on the touch screen tabs, as I will discuss later in this chapter. If you assign Touch AE to a function button, you can turn on this option with one button push. Then, just touch the LCD display on the subject you want the camera to optimize exposure for. The camera will move a small blue cross over the area you touched, as shown in Figure 7-38.

Figure 7-38. Blue Cross on Screen for Touch AE

Then press the Set icon or press the Menu/Set button to accept the new exposure setting. You can press the Display button or touch the DISP. Reset icon to reset the exposure point to the center of the display.

Focus Area Set

If you assign this option to a function button, when you press the button, the camera will immediately display a screen for adjusting the current focus setting. The actual result of pressing the button will depend on the current setting. For example, if you are using autofocus with the 1-Area AF Mode setting, pressing the assigned button will place the focus frame on the display with arrows, ready to be moved using the direction buttons. If the current AF Mode setting is Custom Multi, pressing the assigned button will call up the screen for selecting the pattern of focus zones for that area. If you are currently using manual focus, pressing the button will call up a screen for adjusting the MF Assist area.

This option can be useful if you often adjust the area where the camera focuses, so you don't have to go through extra steps to reach the screen to adjust that area. However, it also is easy to move the focus area using the touch screen, and that system may be preferable in many cases.

Slow Zoom T and Slow Zoom W

As I discussed in Chapter 5, the Fn1 and Fn2 buttons are assigned by default to the Slow Zoom T and Slow Zoom W functions, respectively. With this setup, when you press the Fn1 button, the lens zooms smoothly in; the Fn2 button can be used to zoom the lens out at the same speed. You can control the speed of this zooming using the Slow Zoom Speed option on screen 8 of the Custom menu, and you can use the Slow Zoom Button Setting option on that same screen to determine whether you have to hold down the buttons when zooming. You also can use the Soft Zoom option on that screen to smooth out the zoom operation. Those menu options are discussed later in this chapter.

1 Shot Raw + JPG

If this option is assigned to a function button, pressing the button will set the Quality menu option to Raw & JPG for just one shot; after that, the Quality setting will be returned to what it was before.

1 Shot Spot Metering

This option operates in a way similar to the previous one. The assigned button will select Spot for the Metering Mode option, for just one shot.

Cursor Button Lock

When this function is assigned to a button, pressing that button locks out the operation of the four direction buttons and the Menu/Set button while the camera is in recording mode. You might want to use this feature if you don't want the current settings to be disturbed by the accidental press of a button. Once you have pressed this button, you will not be able to use the menu system in recording mode or make any settings using the buttons until you press the assigned function button again to cancel the lock. The camera will display a Cursor Button Lock message at the top of the screen if you press a locked button. It also will display a message telling you which button to press to cancel the lock.

The lock remains in place even when the camera is powered off and then on.

Dial Operation Switch

As I discussed in Chapter 5, when you assign Dial Operation Switch to a function button, pressing the button temporarily assigns the front and rear dials to carry out operations that you select. The camera will briefly display icons for the functions assigned to the dials. For example, Figure 7-39 shows the screen after the assigned button was pressed, with the front dial assigned to Photo Style and the rear dial assigned to Aspect Ratio. You select the options to be assigned to the two dials using the Dial Operation Switch Setup option under the Dial Settings item on screen 9 of the Custom menu, as discussed later in this chapter.

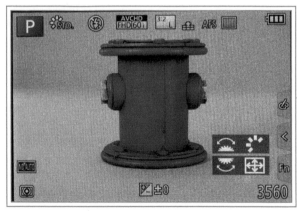

Figure 7-39. Icons on Screen for Dial Operation Switch

Restore to Default

If you choose this option for a given function button, that button will be restored to its default setting. Those defaults were shown earlier in Table 7-1.

As I noted above, you can assign any one of numerous functions to any of the seven physical function buttons using the Function Button Set option on screen 7 of the Custom menu. You can bring up that screen through the normal menu system, or you can press the Display button until the on-monitor information screen is displayed. (That is the black screen with detailed shooting information but no live view.) On that screen, if you touch the Fn icon at the far right, near the bottom, the screen for assigning function buttons will appear.

You also can change a button's assignment by pressing and holding one of the five physical function buttons from Fn3 to Fn7 for about two seconds. (That option is not ordinarily available with Fn1 and Fn2, because they are by default assigned to the Slow Zoom T and W functions, and holding either of those buttons down will zoom the lens in or out.) When you do that, the screen for assigning a function to that button will appear, and you can quickly change it to another option.

The function you assign to a button will be carried out whenever you press the assigned button, if possible. Of course, the function will be carried out only if the present context permits. For example, if you assign the Fn4 button to activate the HDR option, and then press the Fn4 button while the camera is in Intelligent Auto mode, nothing will happen, because the HDR option is not available in that recording mode. If you assign the button to activate peaking, nothing will happen unless the focus mode lever is set to manual focus, because peaking operates only for manual focus.

Similarly, if you assign the Fn5 button to activate the level gauge option, and then press that button while using the Time Lapse Shot option, the level gauge will not appear, because the Fn5 button is permanently assigned to interrupt the Time Lapse Shot operation.

With some settings, such as Aspect Ratio, Picture Size, Peaking, Flash Mode, Zebra Pattern, and Stabilizer, pressing the assigned button multiple times cycles through the possible settings.

Each of the seven physical function buttons can be assigned an option for use when the camera is in recording mode. Six of the buttons—all except Fn6, which is permanently assigned as the Delete/Cancel button—also can be assigned one of a few functions for use in playback mode. A button can have both assignments at the same time, though, of course, only one of the options can be used at a time because the camera has to be in recording or playback mode for the given function to operate.

There are four functions on Table 7-1 that cannot be assigned to the virtual function buttons, Fn8 through Fn12: LVF/Monitor Switch, AF/AE Lock, AF-On, and Touch Screen.

Don't forget that several of the items that can be assigned, including Photo Style, Quality, Flash Mode, Motion Picture Recording Quality, AFS/AFF, and Metering Mode, also can be adjusted using the Quick Menu system by pressing the Q.Menu button and then navigating through the easy-access menu that appears, as long as that button (or some other button) remains assigned to the Q.Menu function.

Assigning Options to Function Buttons for Playback Mode

As I noted earlier, the camera also lets you assign a function to six of the physical function buttons—all except Fn6—for use when the camera is in playback mode. The functions that can be assigned to any of those buttons are the following:

- Wi-Fi
- LVF/Monitor Switch
- Favorite
- Print Set
- Protect
- Delete Single
- Off
- Restore to Default

By default, in playback mode the Fn4 button is assigned to Wi-Fi, the Fn5 button is assigned to Favorite, and the Fn7 button is assigned to LVF/Monitor Switch. I find the assigned functions to be useful, but I have not yet found a need to assign a different function to any of these buttons for use in playback mode.

Zoom Lever

This last option on screen 7 of the Custom menu lets you control how the zoom lever operates. By default, this lever zooms the lens continuously through its full range of focal lengths, which ordinarily is 24mm to 480mm if no enhanced zoom settings are in use. If you choose the second option here, the zoom lever zooms the lens only to certain specific positions: 24mm, 28mm, 35mm, 50mm, 70mm, 90mm, 135mm, 160mm, 200mm, 250mm, 300mm, 400mm, and 480mm, when only the optical zoom is in use. It will not stop at any other focal length. (If 4K Photo is in use, the steps are different, because the camera uses a cropped portion of the sensor for its recording: 36mm, 42mm, 53mm, 75mm, 105mm, 135mm, 203mm, 240mm, 300mm, 375mm, 450mm, 600mm, and 720mm.)

If you turn on other options for zooming, such as Digital Zoom, Intelligent Zoom, and Extra Optical Zoom, the step zoom function will take the focal length to further stages, such as 500mm, 600mm, 800mm, and further, depending on what settings are in effect.

As I noted in Chapter 5, the zoom ring also can be assigned to use step zoom, with the Zoom Ring option on screen 8 of the Custom menu (discussed below). So, if you want to use step zoom, you can choose either the zoom ring or the zoom lever, or both, for that function, if you use the two applicable menu options.

Screen 8 of the Custom menu is shown in Figure 7-40.

Figure 7-40. Screen 8 of Custom Menu

Zoom Ring

The Zoom Ring menu option operates in the same way as the Zoom Lever option discussed above, by letting you set the zoom ring to use step zoom instead

of moving through all focal lengths for the zoom lens continuously.

Slow Zoom Button Setting

As I discussed earlier in this chapter, by default the Fn1 button is assigned to zoom the lens in slowly, and the Fn2 button to zoom it out slowly. This menu option lets you determine whether you have to hold either button down to zoom the lens (choosing the Press & Hold option), or whether you can just press and release the button to start the zoom, and press it again to stop the zoom (choosing the Start/Stop option). This is essentially a matter of preference, though, if the camera is on a tripod, it may be preferable to use the Start/Stop option, so you don't have to touch the camera, and possibly move it, during the zoom.

Slow Zoom Speed

This next option also affects the behavior of the buttons that are assigned to zoom the lens slowly (by default, the Fn1 and Fn2 buttons.) The choices are H, M, and L, for high, medium, and low speed. The choice you make depends on how quickly you want the zoom to be carried out. Even if you pick H, the lens will not zoom as quickly as you can zoom it manually, using the zoom lever or zoom ring.

Soft Zoom

This menu option is another one that controls how the zoom lens works. This menu item has four choices: Start & Stop, Start, Stop, and Off. Using these options, you can turn on Soft Zoom for the starting of the zoom process, the stopping, or both, or leave Soft Zoom turned off. When it is turned on for either end of the zoom, it causes the lens to accelerate or decelerate gradually, rather than just abruptly starting or stopping. The effect is somewhat like that of an automobile that stops at a traffic light. A car can have its brakes jammed on and come to a sudden stop, or it can coast gently to the light. In the same way, the Soft Zoom option can make the zoom seem more gentle and smooth than it otherwise would.

If the Slow Zoom Speed option, discussed above, is set to L for low speed, the Soft Zoom option is set to Off and cannot be turned on, because Panasonic presumably determined that this feature is not needed when the lens is already zooming very slowly.

Lens Position Resume

If you turn on this option, then, after you turn the camera off and back on, the lens will return to its last zoom position and focus position. If this setting is turned off, the lens will zoom out to its 24mm setting when the power is turned on. This option is convenient if you need to use a particular focal length, such as 50mm, for a series of shots that will be interrupted by turning the camera off for periods of time. The focus position is restored for either autofocus or manual focus.

Screen 9 of the Custom menu is shown in Figure 7-41.

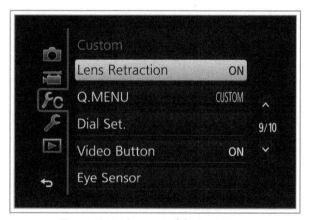

Figure 7-41. Screen 9 of Custom Menu

Lens Retraction

This menu option lets you control whether or not the lens automatically retracts after about 15 seconds when the camera enters playback mode. If you turn this option off, then the lens does not retract in that situation; if it is turned on, the retraction takes place. I usually leave this option turned on, but if you want to alternate between reviewing your images in playback mode and taking more images, you might want to turn this option off so the lens does not have to extend repeatedly every time you return to recording mode.

Quick Menu (Q.Menu)

This option gives you the ability to customize the settings that are available from the Quick Menu. As I discussed in Chapter 5, when you press the Q.Menu button, the camera displays an easy-access menu system that lets you select various settings quickly. By default, the Quick Menu includes 11 settings, which vary somewhat according to current settings: Photo Style, Flash Mode, Motion Picture Recording Quality, Picture Setting, Quality, AFS/AFF, AF Mode, Metering

Mode, Exposure Compensation, Sensitivity, and White Balance. To keep those settings in place or restore them after custom settings have been used, select the Preset option for this menu item.

If you want to set up the Quick Menu with your own selection of settings, select the Custom option for this menu item. Once you have selected Custom for the Quick Menu item, exit this menu system and press the Q.Menu button. On the screen that appears, use the Down button to move to and highlight the tool icon at the lower left of the display, as shown in Figure 7-42. (Or select that icon using the touch screen.)

Figure 7-42. Custom Icon Highlighted on Quick Menu Screen

After you select that icon, the camera will display a diagram with a message telling you to drag the icons where you want them, and then it will display the Q. Menu Customize screen, as shown in Figure 7-43.

Figure 7-43. Quick Menu Customize Screen

On that screen, navigate through the icons at the top of the display until you find the icon for a setting you want to install in the Quick Menu. With that icon highlighted, press Menu/Set and the camera will prompt you to move to the "desired position."

At that point, one of the icons in the bottom row will be highlighted; use the rear dial or the Left and Right buttons to move that highlight to the position where you want to locate the setting whose icon you selected from the top rows. If there is no blank space available in the bottom row, highlight an occupied space and press Menu/Set; the new icon will replace the existing one.

An easier way to add icons to the bottom row is simply to touch an icon with your finger and drag it to the bottom row, onto an empty spot, or drag it onto an occupied slot to replace the icon that is already there. You can add up to 15 items to the Quick Menu using this process. When you have finished adding icons to the Quick Menu, press the Q.Menu button or the Fn6 button to return to the shooting screen.

Dial Settings

This menu option has four sub-options for setting the functions of the front and rear dials, as shown in Figure 7-44: Assign Dial (F/SS), Rotation (F/SS), Exposure Compensation, and Dial Operation Switch Setup.

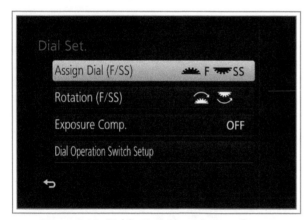

Figure 7-44. Dial Settings Menu Options Screen

With the first sub-option, Assign Dial (F/SS), you can control which dial adjusts aperture (represented by F, for f-stop) and which controls shutter speed, in Manual exposure mode. You can choose the default setting, by which the front dial controls aperture and the rear shutter speed, or you can reverse the roles of the two dials. This is strictly a matter of preference; I have not found a reason to change the default setting.

The second sub-option lets you decide in which direction to rotate the dials to increase or decrease the aperture and shutter speed settings. If you are used to a certain direction for this rotation from another camera,

or just because one direction feels more natural to you, this adjustment is easy to make.

The third sub-option lets you choose whether the front or rear dial, or neither, adjusts exposure compensation. If you choose to have one of those dials adjust exposure compensation, you can just turn that dial when the shooting screen is displayed, and the camera adjusts the value immediately, displaying only an abbreviated scale at the bottom center of the screen. This setting does not interfere with your ability to adjust aperture or shutter speed, because, in Aperture Priority or Shutter Priority mode, both rings adjust the applicable value (aperture or shutter speed), and the ring that is not assigned to exposure compensation will still adjust the aperture or shutter speed. In Manual exposure mode, exposure compensation cannot be adjusted.

The final option, Dial Operation Switch Setup, is used to assign an option to each of the two dials for use with the Dial Operation Switch function. As I discussed earlier in this chapter, you can assign Dial Operation Switch to a function button. By default, it is assigned to the Fn3 button. When you press the assigned button, the dials temporarily will carry out the functions assigned to them through this menu option. For example, if the front dial is assigned to Photo Style and the rear dial is assigned to White Balance, then, when the assigned button is pressed, the dials will adjust the values for those menu options if you turn them within a few seconds after pressing the button.

Either dial can be set to any one of the following options: Photo Style, Filter Effect, Aspect Ratio, AF Mode, 4K Photo, Highlight Shadow, i.Dynamic, i.Resolution, Flash Mode, Flash Adjustment, Sensitivity, or White Balance. If you select Highlight Shadow for either dial, it will also be assigned to the other dial, because that option requires the use of both dials, one to adjust highlights and one to adjust shadows.

Video Button

This menu option lets you keep the red motion picture button from being activated accidentally. The button is located on the top right of the camera, and it is quite possible to press it when you mean to press another control, such as the Fn4 button. If you do that, the camera will start recording a movie, which can be disruptive to your shooting, especially if you are in a hurry to capture a still image. So, if you are not planning to record movies in the near future, you can set this option to Off, and avoid the problem of accidentally starting the video recording process.

EYE SENSOR

This last item on screen 9 of the Custom menu has two sub-options with controls for the operation of the eye sensor, the small slot at the top of the viewfinder that detects the presence of your eye (or another object). Those sub-options are Sensitivity and LVF/Monitor Switch, as shown in Figure 7-45.

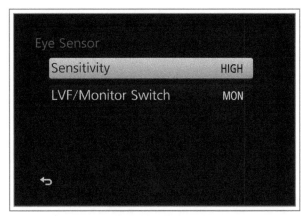

Figure 7-45. Eye Sensor Menu Options Screen

You can set Sensitivity to High or Low. I have found that the Low setting is sufficient for my needs, and it might help avoid unwanted switching to the viewfinder. However, if you want to be sure the switching happens promptly when your head approaches the camera, you can choose the High setting.

The other main setting for Eye Sensor is LVF/Monitor Switch, which has three possible choices: LVF/Monitor Auto, LVF, and Monitor. With the first choice, the camera switches automatically between using the LCD screen and using the viewfinder as your eye approaches or moves away from the eye sensor. If you choose LVF, the viewfinder will always be in use; if you choose Monitor, the LCD display will always be in use.

I find it convenient to use the LVF/Monitor Auto option, so the camera will switch to using the viewfinder whenever my head comes near to the viewfinder. However, in some cases, such as if you are doing close-up shots from a tripod, you might want to leave the monitor always in use, even though your head (or hand) may approach the eye sensor as you adjust a setting. Or, you might want to set the viewfinder to be

in effect at all times when you don't want to have the LCD display illuminate to distract those around you.

You can also switch the behavior of the eye sensor by pressing the LVF button, assuming some function button remains assigned to this option. (By default, the Fn7 button has this assignment.)

The tenth and final screen of the Custom menu is shown in Figure 7-46.

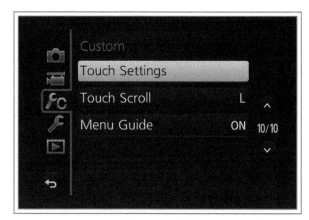

Figure 7-46. Screen 10 of Custom Menu

TOUCH SETTINGS

With the four sub-options of this menu item, you can control several aspects of the FZ2500's excellent touch screen capability.

Touch Screen

This first option can be turned either on or off. If it is on, the touch screen works as expected. If it is off, none of the main touch screen operations are active, and the normal touch screen icons do not appear at all. The next three sub-options on this menu will be dimmed and unavailable in that case.

However, even when the Touch Screen option is turned off, there are some touch operations that will still function. Specifically, if the Silent Operation option on screen 6 of the Motion Picture menu is turned on, that function allows you to use touch icons in Creative Video mode. Also, you can use the Clear Retouch option on screen 2 of the Playback menu, which requires that you touch the areas of an image that you want to remove.

If you prefer the classic operation of a camera with only traditional buttons and dials, you can leave this setting turned off and not have to worry about using touch screen options. The touch screen is very convenient, and in most situations I leave it turned on. However, when I am using the viewfinder, with my face near the LCD screen, I find that my nose sometimes activates the focus frame, moving it around the screen and creating confusion. In those situations, I sometimes turn off the Touch Screen option temporarily. Another solution is to turn off the Touch Pad AF option, discussed below.

Touch Tab

In Chapter 5, I discussed the operation of the touch tab, a set of touch controls at the right edge of the shooting screen. When you touch the small left-facing arrow, the tab opens up to reveal controls for touch zoom, touch shutter, touch autoexposure, and touch peaking (available when manual focus is in use). If you want to use the camera's other touch capabilities but not the particular functions available through the touch tab, you can turn this option off. Or, you can turn on this option and leave Touch AF, discussed below, turned off.

Touch AF

This sub-option enables or disables the use of the Touch AF and Touch AE functions. There are three possible settings for this item: AF, AF+AE, or Off, as shown in Figure 7-47. If you choose Off, then touching the screen does not have any effect on autofocus or autoexposure.

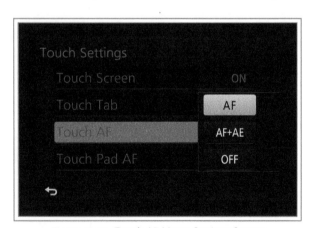

Figure 7-47. Touch AF Menu Options Screen

If you choose AF, you can change the location of the focusing area on the shooting screen just by touching the screen. If AF Mode is set to Face/Eye Detection or 1-Area, if you touch the LCD monitor, you can move the focus area around the screen. You can change the size of the focus frame by pinching or pulling the area of the frame with your fingers. When you have the frame located as you want it, press the Set icon in the lower right corner of the screen, or press the Menu/Set button.

If the 49-Area option for AF Mode is in use, touching the LCD monitor displays the screen for adjusting the area of the focus zones. You can then drag the area where you want it. With the Pinpoint AF option, you can touch the screen to move the cross that marks the area that will be enlarged when you half-press the shutter button. You can pull and pinch with your fingers to change the magnification factor within the Pinpoint AF frame.

If AF Mode is set to Tracking, you can touch a subject on the screen to start tracking that subject.

For Touch AF to operate properly, the Touch Shutter option must be turned off. (It is controlled through the touch tab settings at the right side of the screen.) Otherwise, the camera will take a picture when you touch the screen. To turn off the current AF operation, touch the AF Off icon on the left side of the screen.

The second choice for Touch AF is AF+AE. With this option, once you touch the LCD screen, the camera displays the same focus frame as with the 1-Area AF Mode setting, regardless of the AF Mode setting that is in effect. You can change the location and size of the focus frame by moving it with your fingers and resize it by pinching and pulling the screen. In addition, the camera places a small, blue cross in the center of the frame and optimizes exposure for that area. When you press the Menu/Set button or touch the AF/AE Off icon at the left side of the screen, the camera reverts to its existing setting for AF Mode.

Touch Pad AF

The last sub-option for the Touch Settings menu item is Touch Pad AF. This option is for use only when you are using the viewfinder. As you look at the scene through the viewfinder, you can move the autofocus frame around the display with your finger.

There are three sub-options: Exact, Offset, and Off. If you choose Off, this option is not activated at all. With Exact, you press on the screen in the position where you want the focus frame to be located on the viewfinder display. If you choose Offset, you can cause the focus frame to move just by moving your finger a certain distance in the desired direction, without pressing at the exact location of the frame in the viewfinder. I prefer the Exact option, because I can just press the screen where I want the focus frame to be located.

This option can be quite useful if you are taking pictures on a sunny day and need to move the focus frame around on the viewfinder display. However, if you don't need to move the focus frame often, it can be distracting, because your nose can touch the screen and put a confusing focus frame display in the viewfinder.

Touch Scroll

This next option on screen 10 of the Custom menu sets the speed for scrolling the display when you are viewing images and videos using the touch screen in playback mode. Choose High or Low for the speed with which images scroll when you drag them with your finger.

Menu Guide

This final option on the Custom menu determines what screen is displayed when you turn the mode dial to select Scene mode or Creative Control mode. If Menu Guide is turned on, then, when you turn the dial to the Scene or Creative Control position, the camera displays the selection screen for that mode. For example, if you turn the mode dial to the Creative Control position with this option turned on, the camera will display a screen like that shown in Figure 7-48, where you can immediately select a setting for this mode. (You may see a different version of the selection screen; you can press the Display button to see this and other selection screens.) For Scene mode, the camera displays the selection screen for choosing one of the numerous scene settings.

Figure 7-48. Menu Guide in Use for Creative Control Mode

If this menu option is turned off, then, when the mode dial is turned to one of those two settings, the camera displays the recording screen, so you will be ready to start shooting an image or video without pausing to select a scene type or filter effect first.

What setting you choose for this option depends in part on whether you may want to change the setting for either of these modes when you first select it. However, it is easy to change the setting from the recording screen; you can just touch the setting's icon in the upper left corner of the screen to bring up the selection screen, so I tend to leave Menu Guide turned off.

The Setup Menu

The Setup menu, designated by the solitary wrench icon, has six screens of options for adjusting settings having to do with general camera functions. Its first screen is shown in Figure 7-49.

Figure 7-49. Screen 1 of Setup Menu

Online Manual

This first option on the Setup menu provides information about where to download the online user's guide for this camera from Panasonic. The item has two sub-options, URL Display and QR Code Display, as shown in Figure 7-50.

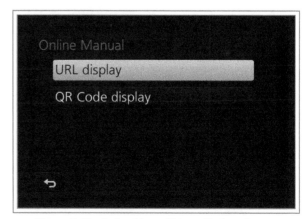

Figure 7-50. Online Manual Menu Options Screen

With the URL Display option, you can use a computer to go to the URL that is provided in this item and download the manual from that URL: http://panasonic.jp/support/dsc/oi/index.html?model=DMC-FZ2500&dest=P. With the QR Code Display option, you can display the QR code. When that code is displayed, you can aim the camera of a smartphone at the code, and, using a QR reading app on the phone, download the manual to the phone (or tablet).

CLOCK SET

When you use your FZ2500 for the first time, it should prompt you to set the clock. If it does not, or if you later need to adjust the date and time, use this menu option. When you select it and press the Right button or Menu/Set, the camera will display a screen like Figure 7-51.

Figure 7-51. Clock Set Settings Screen

On that screen, navigate through the blocks for time and date using the front or rear dial, the Left and Right buttons, or the touch screen, and adjust the settings with the Up and Down buttons or icons. You can then highlight the Style block to select the order for month, day, and year and whether to use 24-hour format for the time. When everything is set properly, navigate to the Set block in the lower right corner of the display and select it to confirm the settings. (The Set block appears only if some change has been made.)

WORLD TIME

This is a handy function when you're traveling to another time zone. Highlight and select World Time to move to the next screen, which gives you the options of choosing Destination and Home. First, select Home and use the Left and Right buttons, the front or rear dial, or the touch arrows to scroll through the world map as shown in Figure 7-52, and press the Menu/Set button or touch the Set icon to set your Home area.

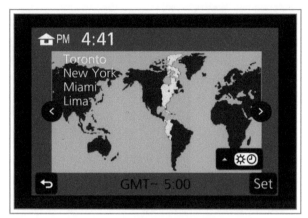

Figure 7-52. World Time Map Screen

Then, on the World Time screen, highlight Destination, and again scroll through the world map to select the time zone you will be traveling to. The map will show you the time in both locations. Press Menu/Set or touch the Set icon to select this zone for the camera's internal clock.

Then, any images taken will reflect the correct time in the new time zone. When you return from your trip, go back to the World Time item and select Home to cancel the changed time zone setting.

On both the Home and Destination screens, you can press the Up button or touch the sun and clock icon in the lower right corner to turn Daylight Saving Time on or off for that time zone.

TRAVEL DATE

This menu item has two sub-options for entering information when you take a trip, so the camera can record that information with your images. First, Travel Setup lets you set a range of dates for the trip, so the camera can record which day of the trip each image was taken. When you return from the trip, if you use the Text Stamp function to "stamp" the recorded data on the images, the images will show they were taken on Day 1, Day 2, etc., of the trip.

The camera also will remind you how many days remain before the trip, with notations such as -3 Days, etc., until the date of the trip arrives. (This reminder is shown on the recording screen above the date and time in the lower left of the screen, when that screen is first displayed. To show the reminder again, press the Display button repeatedly until the detailed information screen appears.)

The date entries for Travel Setup are self-explanatory; just follow the arrows and the camera's prompts.

After you set departure and return dates, you also can set the location, which will display along with the day number. To do that, after setting up the dates, select Location from the Travel Date menu item, enter the name of the location using the text-entry tools, and select Set from that screen, as shown in Figure 7-53.

Figure 7-53. Travel Date Setting Screen

Wi-Fi

This option is used to set up a Wi-Fi connection with the FZ2500. I will discuss the Wi-Fi operations of the camera in Chapter 9.

Screen 2 of the Setup menu is shown in Figure 7-54.

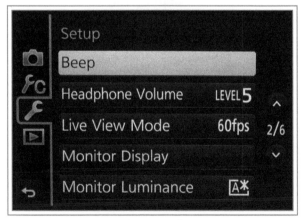

Figure 7-54. Screen 2 of Setup Menu

Beep

This first option on screen 2 of the Setup menu lets you adjust several sound items, as shown in Figure 7-55.

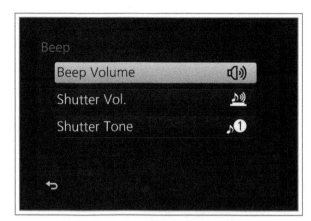

Figure 7-55. Beep Menu Options Screen

First is the volume of the beeps the camera makes when you press a button, such as when half-pressing the shutter button to evaluate focus. You can set the beeps to off, normal, or loud. It's useful to be able to turn the beeps off if you're going to be in an environment where such noises are not welcome.

Second is the volume of the shutter operation sound. Again, it's good to be able to mute the shutter sound. Finally, you can choose from three shutter sounds. If you want to silence all sounds quickly while also disabling the flash and the AF assist lamp, and turning off the ND Filter if it was set to Auto, use the Silent Mode option on screen 1 of the Custom menu.

Headphone Volume

This option lets you set the volume of the signal heard through a pair of headphones that you connect to the headphone jack on the left side of the camera to monitor the sound that is recorded or played back by the camera for movies. There are 16 levels, from zero through 15.

Live View Mode

This menu item, whose options screen is shown in Figure 7-56, lets you choose 30 fps (frames per second) or 60 fps for the refresh rate of the camera's LCD display screen. The setting of 30 frames per second emphasizes quality, but the display may not always refresh quickly enough to keep up with a fast-moving subject. In addition, with some settings, such as the Rough Monochrome or Silky Monochrome settings, the display slows down as the camera processes the effect. If you choose the 60 fps setting, the display will be better able to show any action smoothly, or to maintain a smooth appearance as you pan across the scene. The quality of the display may suffer slightly, but not badly.

So, if you find the display stuttering or smearing, you may want to try the 60 fps option.

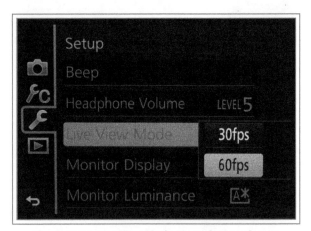

Figure 7-56. Live View Mode Menu Options Screen

This setting does not affect the recorded images, just the display on the LCD screen during recording.

MONITOR DISPLAY

As shown in Figure 7-57, this menu option provides five linear scales for making adjustments. Use the Up and Down buttons or the touch screen icons to select a scale, and then use the Left and Right buttons, the front or rear dial, or the touch screen to adjust the setting on the scale for each item. The normal settings are in the middle of the scale; move the yellow blocks to the left of the scale to decrease a setting, or to the right to increase the value.

Figure 7-57. Monitor Display Adjustments Screen

Starting from the top, the scales control brightness, contrast, saturation, red tint, and blue tint. When you have made your adjustments on all scales, you have to press the Menu/Set button to make them take effect.

I have never found a need to adjust the settings for the LCD display, but if you find the color, contrast, or brightness of the screen is not to your liking, you can use these adjustments as you wish.

MONITOR LUMINANCE

This setting affects the brightness of the LCD display. This setting is different from the brightness setting of the previous menu option in that it provides overall, on-or-off adjustments, rather than a sliding scale. As shown in Figure 7-58, this menu item has four settings, each accompanied by an asterisk: A*, 1*, 2*, and 3*.

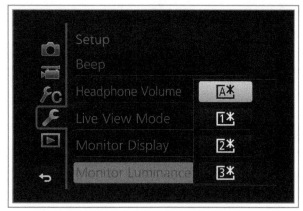

Figure 7-58. Monitor Luminance Menu Options Screen

With the A* (Auto) setting, the brightness will adjust according to ambient lighting conditions. With the 1* setting, the screen becomes extra-bright to compensate for sunlight or other conditions that make it hard to see the screen. It reverts to normal if no controls are used for 30 seconds, but you can press any control button to restore the brightness. The 2* setting provides standard illumination, and the 3* setting sets the display to a dimmer level than normal. The A* setting is not available in playback mode.

Using the A* or the 1* setting decreases battery life. If you find it hard to see the screen in bright sunlight, you might want to try the 1* setting to see if the added brightness gives you enough visibility to compose your shots or view your recorded images clearly.

I use the A* setting myself, and always keep an extra battery handy.

The items on screen 3 of the Setup menu are shown in Figure 7-59.

Figure 7-59. Screen 3 of Setup Menu

ECONOMY

The next option on the Setup menu, Economy, has three sub-options: Sleep Mode, Sleep Mode (Wi-Fi), and Auto Monitor Off.

Sleep Mode

The Sleep Mode option puts the camera into a dormant state after a specified period when you have not used any of the camera's controls. The period can be set to one, two, five, or ten minutes, or the option can be turned off, in which case the camera never turns off automatically (unless it runs out of battery power). To cancel Sleep Mode, press the shutter button halfway and the camera will come back to life. Sleep Mode does not turn off the camera during a slide show or when an AC adapter is connected, or during the recording or playback of a motion picture, along with a few other situations.

Sleep Mode (Wi-Fi)

With this setting, the camera goes dormant after 15 minutes, but only if there is no Wi-Fi connection active. This setting is useful if you are using the camera for transferring images or another activity using a wireless network connection, which may require the camera to sit for fairly long periods without any controls being activated. If there is no Wi-Fi connection active, there is no need to let the camera stay active, so it can be powered down.

Auto LVF/Monitor Off

The Auto LVF/Monitor Off setting controls how soon the viewfinder or monitor turns off when no controls have been used for a time. The possible choices are five minutes, two minutes, or one minute. After the display goes blank, you can press any control button or touch the screen to restore the display. As with the Sleep

Mode setting, this setting does not operate during slide shows, during a Time Lapse Shot session, and in a few other situations.

USB MODE

If you are going to connect the camera directly to a computer or printer, you need to go to this menu item and select the appropriate setting from the choices shown in Figure 7-60: Select on Connection, PictBridge (PTP) (for connecting to a printer), or PC (for connecting to a computer). PTP stands for Picture Transfer Protocol.

Figure 7-60. USB Mode Menu Options Screen

If you choose Select on Connection, you don't select the setting until after you have plugged the USB cable into the device to which you are connecting the camera. The FZ2500 connects to a computer using the USB 2.0 connection standard, assuming your computer has a USB port of that speed. (If not, the camera will still connect at the slower speed of the computer's older USB port.)

TV CONNECTION

This menu item has two sub-options: HDMI Mode (Play) and Viera Link. The first option sets the output resolution for the images that are sent to an HDTV when the camera is connected to the TV with a micro-HDMI cable in playback mode. The available choices are Auto, 4K, 1080p, 1080i, 720p, and 480p. Ordinarily, if you select Auto the images should appear properly on the HDTV. If they do not, you can try one of the other settings to see if the display improves.

The Viera Link option is for use when you are connecting the FZ2500 to a Panasonic Viera HDTV using a micro-HDMI cable. If you leave this option turned off, then the operations of the camera are controlled by the camera's own controls. If you turn it on, then the Viera TV's remote control can also control the operations of the camera, so you can play slide shows or review individual images and movies. As far as I could determine, Viera TVs are not widely available as current models in the United States, so this option may not be of great use in the future.

M/FT

This option lets you choose whether distance is displayed using meters or feet as the unit of measure on the zoom scale.

MENU RESUME

This menu item can be set either on or off. When it is turned on, whenever you enter the menu system, the camera displays the last menu item you had selected previously. When this option is turned off, the camera always starts back at the top of the first screen of the Recording menu. If there is a particular menu item you need to adjust often, this option can be of considerable use, because you can just press the Menu/Set button and the item will appear, ready for you to make your setting. For example, if you need to change the Metering Mode setting frequently, you can turn on Menu Resume. Then, whenever you need to get back to the Metering Mode setting, just press Menu/Set, and the item will be there at your fingertips. (Of course, you also could set a function button to bring up this option, or you could use the Quick Menu, but this is one other approach to consider.)

Screen 4 of the Setup menu is shown in Figure 7-61.

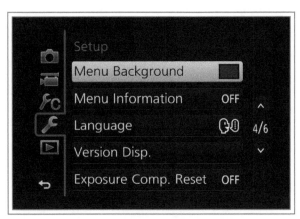

Figure 7-61. Screen 4 of Setup Menu

MENU BACKGROUND

This option lets you choose the background color for the menu screens. If you don't like the default option of dark gray, you can choose another selection. You might find menus are more readable with one of the lighter colors, but I have found no reason to change this setting.

MENU INFORMATION

This option lets you turn on or off the display of information at the top of each menu screen, which provides a line of informative text explaining the function of whichever menu item is currently highlighted. For example, Figure 7-62 shows this feature in use when Quality is highlighted on screen 1 of the Recording menu.

Most of the entries are too long to fit on one line, and they scroll across the display. There are entries for all of the main menu items and for many of the sub-options as well. I find this feature to be helpful and it is not obtrusive, so I always leave it turned on.

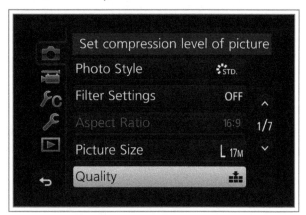

Figure 7-62. Menu Information Display for Quality Option

LANGUAGE

This option gives you the choice of language for display of commands and information on the LCD screen and in the viewfinder. The first screen of the language selection option for my U.S. version of the camera is shown in Figure 7-63. Presumably, models sold elsewhere offer different choices. If your camera happens to be set to a language that you don't read, you can find the language option by going into the Setup menu (look for the wrench icon), and then scrolling to this option, which is marked by an icon showing a person's head with a word balloon, as seen above in Figure 7-61.

Figure 7-63. Language Selection Screen

VERSION DISPLAY

This item has no settings; when you select it, it displays the version of the camera's firmware that is currently installed. As I write this, my FZ2500 has version 1.0 of the firmware installed, as shown in Figure 7-64.

Firmware is somewhat like both software and hardware; it is the programming electronically recorded into the camera, either at the factory or through your computer if you upgrade the firmware with an update provided by Panasonic. A new version of the firmware can fix bugs and can even provide new features, so it's well worthwhile checking the Panasonic website periodically for updates. Instructions for installing an update are provided on the website. The process usually involves downloading a file to your computer, saving that file to an SD card formatted for the camera, then placing that card in the camera so the firmware can be installed.

You can go to the following web address to check for updates: http://av.jpn.support.panasonic.com/support/global/cs/dsc/download/index.html.

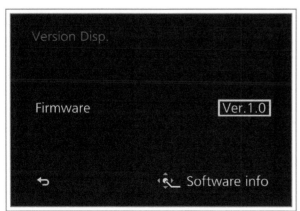

Figure 7-64. Version Display Screen

EXPOSURE COMPENSATION RESET

This option controls whether or not an exposure compensation value that has been set will be retained in memory when the camera is turned off or the shooting mode is changed. By default, this option is turned off, and any positive or negative brightness value is not reset to zero. In other words, the value is retained in memory for the next time the camera is turned on, or the current recording mode is selected again.

If you set this option to On, then the exposure compensation value is reset to zero when the camera is powered off or the shooting mode changes.

I generally leave this option set to On, because I am unlikely to want to use the same amount of exposure compensation the next time I use the camera, and I might forget to reset it to zero on my own. However, if you have a practice of usually shooting with a certain amount of exposure compensation, you might want to leave this option off, so the value will be retained in memory from one shooting session to the next.

Screen 5 of the Setup menu is shown in Figure 7-65.

Figure 7-65. Screen 5 of Setup Menu

NUMBER RESET

This function lets you reset the folder and image number for the next image to be recorded in the camera. If you don't use this option, the numbers of your images will keep increasing until they reach 999, even if you change to a different memory card. If you want each new card to start with images numbered from 1 up, use the Number Reset function each time you start a new card, or a new project for which you would like to have freshly numbered images. I prefer not to reset the numbers, because I find it easier to keep track of my images if the numbers keep getting larger; I would find it confusing to have images with duplicate numbers on my various SD cards.

RESET

This menu option resets menu settings to their original states. This is a convenient way to restore the camera to its default mode, so you can start with fresh settings before you experiment with new ones. The camera prompts you several times, asking if you want to reset all Recording menu settings other than Face Recognition and Profile Setup values, then all Face Recognition and Profile Setup settings, and then all Setup/Custom menu parameters. Folder numbers and date and time settings are not reset by this option.

RESET WI-FI SETTINGS

This option resets all Wi-Fi settings for the camera. You might want to use this option if you are selling your camera, to avoid giving away information about your wireless networks. You also might want to use this option if you are having trouble getting the Wi-Fi settings configured and you want to make a fresh start.

SYSTEM FREQUENCY

This menu option controls which video system the camera uses for recording movies—NTSC, PAL, or Cinema. The NTSC system records video at frequencies based on a speed of about 60 frames per second or 30 frames per second. (For technical reasons, the actual frame rate is 59.94 or 29.97 fps.) You also can record video at 24 fps using the NTSC system. The NTSC system is used in the United States and other parts of North America, as well as Japan, South Korea, and some other countries.

The PAL system is based on a standard rate of 50 fps. With that system, you can record at 50 fps or 25 fps. That system is used in many parts of Asia, Africa, and Europe.

The Cinema system records only at 24 fps, which is one of the frame rates that is also available with the NTSC system, and is very close to the 25 fps setting that is available with the PAL system. The reason to use the Cinema setting for System Frequency with the FZ2500 camera is that it provides the possibility of recording movies using the Cinema 4K (C4K) setting for Recording

Quality on the Motion Picture menu. As I will discuss later in this chapter, that setting provides the highest 4K resolution available with this camera. The C4K setting has a resolution of 4096 x 2160 pixels, whereas the normal 4K settings available with the NTSC and PAL systems provide a resolution of 3840 x 2160 pixels.

So, if you want to use the C4K setting, with the highest available resolution for 4K footage, you have to set System Frequency to the Cinema setting.

In general, unless you need to use the C4K setting, you should use the System Frequency setting that is standard for the area where you will be using the camera. I live in the United States, so I set the camera to NTSC, where the frame rates are in multiples of 30 (except for the few 24p options).

It is important to choose this setting before you start recording files on your memory card. If you change the System Frequency setting after recording some videos, those videos will not play back in the camera with a different setting in place unless you replace the memory card with one that is formatted with the new setting in place. In addition, some video formats will not record unless you change the card.

LEVEL GAUGE ADJUSTMENT

This option gives you a way to make sure that the level gauge display is properly aligned. To use it, select the menu option, which will then display the screen shown in Figure 7-66, with choices for Adjustment and Level Gauge Value Reset. To make an adjustment, select the first option, and the camera will prompt you to place the camera on a surface that is known to be horizontal. When you press OK, the camera will display a screen with three horizontal lines and a Start icon. When the camera is set on a horizontal surface, press the Start icon on the screen or press the Menu/Set button, and the camera will carry out the adjustment.

If you later change your mind about using the adjusted calibration, select the second option, Level Gauge Value Reset, and the camera will restore its original default setting for the level gauge.

The sixth and final screen of the Setup menu is shown in Figure 7-67.

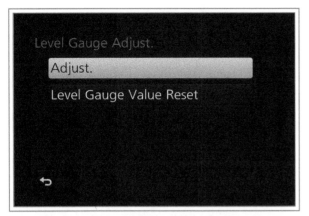

Figure 7-66. **Level Gauge Adjustment Screen**

Figure 7-67. **Screen 6 of Setup Menu**

ACTIVATE

This menu option is provided so you can activate an optional feature for the camera after purchasing an activation code from Panasonic or a dealer. The only such option that I am aware of for the FZ2500 is the V-Log L option, which lets you record video using a special gamma curve with wider dynamic range than usual, but which requires special post-processing. That option is sold as a Panasonic accessory, model number DMW-SFU1. After it is activated, the camera will have the V-Log L option added to the Photo Style item on the Motion Picture menu, when the camera is set to Creative Video mode.

If you purchase the V-Log L option (which cost $97.00 when I purchased it), you will receive a sealed envelope with a key code inside it, and a brief pamphlet with detailed instructions in several languages for activating the option. Essentially, you use the Activate menu option to export the camera's serial number to a memory card in the camera, using the Activate/Export Serial Code menu option. You then place that card in a card reader connected to a computer and go to the

website https://eww.pavc.panasonic.co.jp/enhance/, where you upload the serial code. You also need to enter the key code that you purchased, when prompted at the site. You will then receive an activation code, which you need to save to the memory card. You then place the card back in your camera and use the Activate menu option, this time choosing the Import Activation Code option. After you have seen a confirmation screen and powered the camera off and back on, the V-Log L option will be activated in the camera.

DEMO MODE

If you choose this option, the camera takes a fairly long time to carry out an internal process and then places a demonstration image on the screen, with several different areas of possible focus. You can then touch the screen to see how the Post Focus option works. You also can touch the Peak icon for a demonstration of focus peaking. To cancel this demonstration, press the shutter button halfway.

FORMAT

This last item on the Setup menu is one of the more important menu options. Choose this process only when you want or need to completely wipe all of the data from a memory card. When you select the Format option, the camera will ask you if you want to delete all of the data on the card, as shown in Figure 7-68.

Figure 7-68. **Format Confirmation Screen**

If you reply by selecting Yes, the camera will proceed to erase all images and videos, including any that have been locked using the Protect option on the Playback menu. It's a good idea to use this command with any new memory card you place in the camera for the first time, so the card will be properly formatted to store new images and videos.

Chapter 8: Motion Pictures

Panasonic is known for producing cameras, such as the Lumix DC-GH5, with sophisticated video features. The FZ2500 does not quite equal the GH5 in its video capabilities, but it is well above average when compared to many other cameras that are primarily designed for still photography. In this chapter, I will discuss the many video features of the FZ2500.

Basics of FZ2500 Videography

One aspect of motion picture recording with the FZ2500 that can be confusing is how to select the shooting mode. For still photography with this camera, when you choose a shooting mode by turning the mode dial on top of the camera, that is the mode that you will shoot your pictures in. That is not quite how it works with movie recording. In the motion picture arena, the position of the mode dial has some effect on your shooting, but not as direct an effect as for still photos.

Figure 8-1. **Mode Dial at Creative Video**

If you look at the mode dial, as shown in Figure 8-1, you will see icons for the various shooting modes for still photography: Intelligent Auto, Program, Aperture Priority, Shutter Priority, Manual, Custom, Panorama, Scene, and Creative Control. There is also one entry on the dial for movies, represented by the letter M with a movie camera icon: Creative Video mode, which is selected in this illustration. However, because of the red motion picture button, you do not have to set the mode dial to Creative Video mode to record a movie (though you certainly can, as I'll discuss shortly). In fact, you can set the mode dial to any of its settings except Panorama

and still record a movie. (For the C setting, it depends on what shooting mode was saved to the Custom mode slot.) But the results may not be what you would expect based on the name of the shooting mode.

For example, when the mode dial is set to M for Manual exposure mode, if you press the red button you will not be shooting a movie in Manual exposure mode. In fact, you'll be shooting a movie with the camera adjusting exposure automatically by setting aperture and shutter speed. This is the same result you'll get with any of the four PASM shooting modes on the mode dial (Program, Aperture Priority, Shutter Priority, and Manual).

Here is where the situation gets slightly complicated. As I just noted, when you set the mode dial to some of the major still-shooting modes, such as A, S, or M, the camera does not follow that mode's behavior for setting exposure when you press the red motion picture button. But the camera does use some (but not all) of the other settings that have been made in that shooting mode.

For example, if the camera is set to Aperture Priority mode on the mode dial, when you press the red button to make a movie, the camera does not let you set the aperture; instead, it chooses both aperture and shutter speed. However, the camera does use some of the settings that have been chosen through the Recording menu while the camera was in Aperture Priority mode, such as Photo Style, Metering Mode, and Highlight Shadow. Of course, several options on the Recording menu make no sense when recording movies, and therefore have no effect when you press the red button, including Flash Mode, Bracket, and Burst Rate.

You also can set the mode dial to Intelligent Auto mode, and the camera will take over even more of the settings for your movies, or you can set it to Scene mode and for movies it will use the basic settings for the type of scene you select, in many cases. For certain settings, though, the camera will use different scene types, as follows: For the Clear in Backlight scene type, the camera will use the Portrait type. For Clear Nightscape, Artistic Nightscape, Handheld Night Shot, and Clear Night Portrait, the camera will use what Panasonic calls the "Low Light mode."

If you want to have more control over the camera's exposure settings while shooting a movie, that's the role of the movie-oriented setting on the mode dial, Creative Video, which is selected in Figure 8-1.

After you turn the mode dial to that position, go into the menu system and select the top icon in the column at the left, which looks like a movie camera and represents the Motion Picture menu.

Then navigate to the Exposure Mode item on screen 2 of the Motion Picture menu and select it. The screen will display a menu of four exposure modes: P, A, S, and M, for Program, Aperture Priority, Shutter Priority, and Manual Exposure, as shown in Figure 8-2. (You also can get to a smaller menu for selecting an exposure mode by touching the icon in the upper left corner of the display that represents the currently selected mode.)

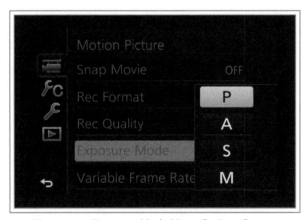

Figure 8-2. Exposure Mode Menu Options Screen

You have to select one of those modes, which will then be in effect when you press the red button to record a movie. These modes work in ways similar to their still-photography counterparts, but they are distinctly separate, video-oriented shooting modes.

If you select Program, the camera chooses shutter speed and aperture, just as it does when the camera is set to one of the basic still-shooting modes on the mode dial (P, A, S, or M).

If you choose Aperture Priority, you use the front or rear dial to select the aperture, and the camera will adjust its shutter speed for the correct exposure, if

possible. The FZ2500 has the same range of apertures available for setting in Creative Video mode as in Aperture Priority and Manual exposure mode: f/2.8 to f/11.0 when the lens is zoomed back to its full wide-angle position, and f/4.5 to f/11.0 when the lens is zoomed in to focal lengths approaching full telephoto.

If you choose Shutter Priority, you set the shutter speed and the camera sets the aperture. Because of the nature of video footage, which is normally recorded (in the United States) at 24 or 30 frames per second, the slowest shutter speed you can normally choose is 1/25 second (but see the note below under Manual mode, for an exception). You can choose from a wide range of faster shutter speeds, though. In fact, for motion pictures in Creative Video mode, the camera has a special range of shutter speeds for video recording: 1/25 second to 1/16000 second when recording with a 24 fps, 25 fps, or 50 fps format, and 1/30 second to 1/16000 second when recording with a 30 fps or 60 fps format.

If you choose Manual Exposure, you set both shutter speed and aperture, in the same way as for still photography. As with shooting stills, the camera will not make any changes until you change one or both of the values, so, if the lighting changes, the exposure may be incorrect.

There is one more benefit in terms of creative options if you shoot your video in this Manual mode: If you also have the focus mode set to manual focus, you can set the shutter speed as slow as 1/2 second. This shutter speed setting results in an effective video frame rate of two frames per second, considerably slower than the normal (U.S.) frame rate of 30 frames per second. It lets you record movies in conditions of very low light and can result in interesting effects, such as ghost-like streaks on the video frames if you move the camera. You would not want to use this slow shutter speed for taking video of a sporting event, but if you're making a science-fiction or horror movie, this feature could present some promising possibilities. Audio is recorded normally when using slow shutter speeds.

Note that you can change either shutter speed or aperture, or both, during your shot. So, for example, if you're shooting a movie in Creative Video mode using the Shutter Priority or Manual Exposure setting, you can gradually increase the shutter speed to faster and faster values to make the picture fade gradually to black. One problem is that the motions of the front or rear dial may be heard on the audio track. But you can correct that problem in post-production by replacing or editing the audio track using video editing software such as Adobe Premiere Elements, if you are so inclined.

With the Manual Exposure mode for video recording, you can adjust the ISO setting, as with the other advanced modes. However, you cannot set ISO to Auto ISO when recording movies with Manual Exposure mode; ISO must be set to a numerical value from 125 to 6400. (The Extended ISO settings and settings above 6400 are not available for video recording.)

With the Program, Aperture Priority, and Shutter Priority settings for Exposure Mode in Creative Video mode, you can adjust exposure compensation during the recording, just as with still photography, by pressing the Fn4 button and then adjusting the on-screen scale. However, you can only adjust it up to 3.0 EV positive or negative, as opposed to the 5.0 EV adjustments available for still photography. Also, when the camera is set to Creative Video mode, you can use the shutter button to start and stop video recording. In all other modes, pressing the shutter button will take a still picture, but in this one situation, you can use either the red motion picture button or the shutter button to control movie-making. This means, of course, that you cannot take still pictures with the camera in this mode. However, it also means that you can use a wired remote control to start and stop movie recording; see Appendix A for compatible devices.

Making Other Settings When Recording Movies

You likely will get excellent results if you use the camera's default settings and shoot your video using Intelligent Auto mode. But there are numerous other settings you can make using the camera's physical controls and the menu system. I will discuss those settings next, so you can take advantage of the flexibility they provide for motion picture recording with the FZ2500.

THE MOTION PICTURE MENU

First, I will discuss the one menu system I have not discussed in detail—the Motion Picture menu, designated by the movie camera icon, as shown earlier in Figure 8-2. Before I discuss the individual items on the

menu, there are a couple of general points to mention. First, the menu has eight screens in most recording modes, but only one screen with five items when the camera is in the basic Intelligent Auto mode. In that mode, the only Motion Picture menu settings you can adjust are Snap Movie, Recording Format, Recording Quality, and AFS/AFF, and Sound Output. In Scene mode, all eight screens are available with several scene type settings, but with others, including Glistening Water, Glittering Illuminations, and Soft Image of a Flower, you cannot record movies at all, and the Motion Picture menu is not available when one of those settings is selected. The same is true of several settings for Creative Control mode: Rough Monochrome, Silky Monochrome, Soft Focus, Star Filter, and Sunshine.

Second, when the full Motion Picture menu is available, 11 of the items on that menu also appear as items on the Recording menu: Photo Style, Filter Settings, AFS/AFF, Metering Mode, Highlight Shadow, i.Dynamic, i.Resolution, Diffraction Compensation, i.Zoom, Digital Zoom, and Stabilizer. These settings are included on the Motion Picture menu for convenience in setting them. You can adjust any of these 11 settings using either menu system, and the adjustment will take effect for both menus at the same time. For example, if you set Photo Style to Monochrome on the Recording menu, you will see that the Photo Style setting on the Motion Picture menu has also changed to Monochrome. Or, if you turn on Digital Zoom on the Motion Picture menu, you will see that Digital Zoom has been activated on the Recording menu as well.

Following is the list of all items that can appear on the Motion Picture menu. I will not include detailed information here for the settings that also appear on the Recording menu; for more information about them, see Chapter 4.

Screen 1 of the Motion Picture menu is shown in Figure 8-3.

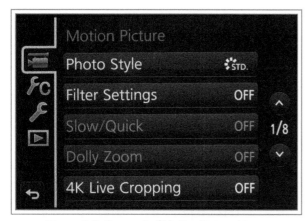

Figure 8-3. Screen 1 of Motion Picture Menu

Photo Style

This setting lets you choose the "look" of your footage. In most respects, it works the same as it does for still photos. The basic choices are Standard, Vivid, Natural, Monochrome, Scenery, Portrait, and Custom. For more details about those settings, see Chapter 4. However, there are two settings for Photo Style that appear on the menu only in Creative Video mode: Cinelike D and Cinelike V. In addition, if you purchase the V-Log L option for the FZ2500 camera, the Photo Style menu will include V-Log L as the final option. Figure 8-4 is a chart showing the three movie-oriented settings along with Standard for comparison.

Motion Picture Photo Style Chart for FZ2500

Standard   Cinelike D

Cinelike V   V-Log L

Figure 8-4. Motion Picture Photo Style Comparison Chart

Cinelike D: This setting, which is available only in Creative Video mode, is intended to produce images with a "film-like" look. It uses a gamma curve that is designed to use a broad dynamic range. It is a good setting to use if you are going to use software to edit your video and apply post-processing corrections to optimize its appearance.

Cinelike V: This setting, also available only in Creative Video mode, uses a gamma curve that places emphasis on contrast.

V-Log L: This setting, which is sold as an optional extra for about $99.00 and is available only in Creative Video mode, uses a "log" gamma curve, which produces footage that looks quite flat and dull, but that can be processed with software to produce a broader dynamic range than other settings. One good option is to use DaVinci Resolve software; see Appendix C for information on where to find it.

Filter Settings

This second menu item lets you select one of the numerous filter effects for your video. Several of the settings are not available with video recording: Rough Monochrome, Silky Monochrome, Soft Focus, Star Filter, and Sunshine. None of the settings are available when 4K Live Cropping is active, and Miniature Effect is not available when 4K recording is active.

Slow/Quick

This option sets up the camera to let you change the frame rate while you are recording, to speed up or slow down action temporarily. For example, if you are capturing video of children at play and you want to record with a slow-motion effect for a short time, with this feature you can press and hold a button and record footage that will be slowed down in playback. Conversely, you can record action that will appear speeded up when played back.

To use this option, set the mode dial to Creative Video. Then set Recording Format on screen 2 of the Motion Picture menu to a value other than MP4, and set Recording Quality to a setting that permits the use of the Variable Frame Rate option, such as FHD/100M/30p, FHD/100M/24p, FHD/24M/30p, or FHD/24M/24p. (When Variable Frame Rate is available for a Recording Quality setting, the large black area on the menu screen will display the caption, "VFR Available.") However, you have to leave the Variable Frame Rate menu option turned off. Finally go to the Slow/Quick menu option and turn it on.

Once all those settings are made, start recording a video. When you want to record a portion of the video that will be speeded up when played back, press and hold down the Fn1 button for as long as you want that sequence to last. When you want to record a portion that will be played back in slow motion, press and hold down the Fn2 button for as long as you want. The speeded-up and slowed-down sequences will be recorded with no sound. The Quick sequences will be recorded at half the normal speed so they will play back at twice the normal speed, and the Slow ones will be recorded at twice the normal speed, so they will play back at half the normal speed.

Naturally, when Slow/Quick is activated, the Fn1 and Fn2 buttons will not be available for other functions, such as the Slow Zoom function, that are assigned to those buttons by default or through the menu system.

Dolly Zoom

This feature is somewhat similar to the Slow/Quick feature discussed above, because it gives you a way to accomplish a cinematic special effect with a minimum of effort. In this case, the effect is a special kind of zoom, sometimes called "dolly zoom," "reverse tracking," or the "Vertigo effect," among other names. According to some accounts, it was first notably used by Alfred Hitchcock in his 1958 movie, *Vertigo*. In a typical use of this effect, the camera focuses on a person's face, which remains centered in the frame at the same size while the background zooms behind the person, either approaching the camera or receding from it. The result can be a disorienting distortion of the background, meant to convey a feeling of strangeness or danger.

I have found this effect tricky to carry out using the FZ2500, but it can be worthwhile. First, as with the Slow/Quick feature, you have to put the camera into Creative Video mode and choose Recording Format and Recording Quality settings that allow the use of Variable Frame Rate, such as MP4 (LPCM) and FHD/100M/30p. Do not turn on Variable Frame Rate, though. Set the focus mode lever to use autofocus (AFS/AFF or AFC). Set the Dolly Zoom menu option to On.

Then, aim the camera at a person's face, zooming in to a fairly close view. The camera will place a red frame in the center of the display, near the autofocus frame, which will be automatically set to use face detection. Zoom the lens in or out until the red frame is located over the autofocus frame and is the same size as that frame. At that point, the red frame will turn green.

Position yourself with the camera, with enough space to move backward or forward as needed. Press the red movie button, and then press and hold down the Fn1 button while moving back, away from the subject, trying to keep the subject's face the same size on the camera's display as you move, or press and hold the Fn2 button while moving toward the subject, keeping the face the same size as you move. When you have finished moving, release the button.

I have it found it easier to use this feature when pressing the Fn2 button and moving toward the subject, just because it is easier to move smoothly forward than backward. Also, if you can place the camera on a tripod with wheels, or an actual dolly, that can help. One user of the FZ2500 has posted some examples on YouTube at https://youtu.be/St5CZSqh4XE.

4K Live Cropping

This feature uses the FZ2500's 4K video capability to create full HD video footage that is smoother and quieter than might otherwise be possible. It is designed to address two problems with normal video shooting. First, if you pan the camera (move it from side to side) across a scene, unless you have a tripod with a fluid pan head or some sort of mechanical or electronic stabilizing system, the footage is likely to be somewhat jerky, moving unevenly from side to side and possibly jerking up and down as well. Second, if you zoom the lens in on a subject, there may be some jerkiness and some sound from the zoom mechanism.

With the 4K Live Cropping feature, you shoot such scenes in the ultra-HD 4K format, and, because of the extra resolution in 4K footage, the camera is able to crop the full video frames down to create an in-camera panning or zooming effect. For example, if you shoot a 4K scene showing a garden wall that is fairly distant, the camera can crop the video frames down to show the same wall closer up, in full HD instead of 4K, and artificially create a panning effect across that wall. Similarly, if you shoot a building in the distance, the camera can crop the 4K footage to a closer, HD view of the building and create a zooming effect in the camera.

Figure 8-5 shows how a scene showing a shelf loaded with various items looked when shot in 4K, and Figure

8-6 shows how that scene looked after it was cropped using Live Cropping, so the camera could pan across it.

Figure 8-5. 4K Live Cropping Turned Off

Figure 8-6. 4K Live Cropping in Use

These are the steps to take to use this feature.

1. Turn on the camera and set the mode dial to the Creative Video position.

2. Select 4K Live Cropping from screen 1 of the Motion Picture menu.

3. On the next menu screen, choose 20 seconds or 40 seconds. That is the duration the camera will use for the panning or zooming motion it creates.

4. The camera will display a screen with a yellow frame with arrows at the sides.

5. Using the touch screen or the direction buttons, move the frame where you want the pan or zoom to start and resize it as you wish using the touch screen or the rear dial. If there is a feature you want the camera to pan across, for example, set the frame over the starting area for the panning motion. Press the Menu/Set button or touch the Set icon to lock the frame in place. This is the starting frame.

6. The camera will then display the ending frame. Use the same process to size and locate the frame over the ending area for the panning or zooming action. If you want the camera to create a panning

action, keep both frames the same size. If you want a zooming-in effect, make the ending frame smaller than the starting frame; for a zooming-out effect, make the ending frame larger than the starting frame. Figure 8-7 shows the Start and End frames ready to be locked in place. Use Menu/Set or the Set icon to lock the two frames in place.

7. If you need to go back and change the locations of the frames, press the Fn6 button to make the adjustment screen active again.

8. When the start and end frames are set as you want them, press the motion picture button and release it, to start the recording. Hold the camera as steady as possible, or have it on a tripod. After the set time period (20 or 40 seconds), the recording will end.

Figure 8-7. Start and End Frames for 4K Live Cropping

The result should be a smooth, professional-looking zoom or pan sequence for which you never had to move the camera or zoom the lens, and which therefore has no jerky motions and no sounds from the zooming mechanism. This feature is worth experimenting with.

Screen 2 of the Motion Picture menu is in Figure 8-8.

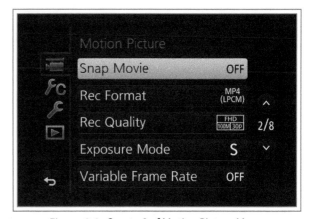

Figure 8-8. Screen 2 of Motion Picture Menu

Snap Movie

This feature lets you set up the camera to take a "snap movie," which is Panasonic's term for a video version of a snapshot. The resulting video is very short—just two, four, six, or eight seconds in duration, recorded using the FHD/20M/30p setting for MP4. (The setting will be FHD/20M/25p if System Frequency is set to 50Hz, in areas using the PAL video system.) You can specify whether to add a pull-focus effect (dramatic changing of focus from one object to another) or a fade-in and/or fade-out effect, to add extra visual interest. Here are the steps to follow.

1. Turn on the camera in any recording mode other than Panorama. (Make sure 4K Live Cropping, Slow/Quick, Dolly Zoom, and Variable Frame Rate are turned off.)

2. Select Snap Movie from the first screen of the Motion Picture menu. Press the Menu/Set or Right button to get to the screen with options of On, Off, and Set. Select Set to move to the next screen with setup options, as seen in Figure 8-9.

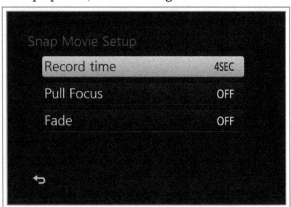

Figure 8-9. Snap Movie Setup Options Screen

3. On the Snap Movie setup screen, set the recording time to two, four, six, or eight seconds, turn Pull Focus on or off, and leave Fade turned off, or select from white-in, white-out, black-in, black-out, color-in, or color-out. You have to scroll through two screens to see all of the Fade options. The white and black options fade to or from a white or black screen. The color Fade options involve transitions between color and monochrome.

4. Go back to the main options screen and select On for Snap Movie, then press the Fn6 button to go to the shooting screen.

5. If you turned on Pull Focus, touch your finger on the screen over the object that should start out in focus, then drag your finger to the second object, which should have the focus "pulled" to it. (To use physical buttons for this setting, press the AF Mode button at each position for the Pull Focus frames.) For the best Pull Focus effect, choose objects that are at dramatically different distances from the camera, such as an item in the far background and one in the close foreground.

6. Press and release the motion picture button and hold the camera as still as possible, keeping the Pull Focus objects in their proper locations, if Pull Focus is turned on.

The result should be a brief video snapshot, optionally including a fade-in or fade-out effect, and possibly a Pull Focus action as well. The camera records sound, though the audio fades in or out if a fade option is selected. You might find it worthwhile to use this option with no effects as a way to record a brief view of a scenic vista or an historic site, for example. If you record multiple snap movies, you can send them to your smartphone via Wi-Fi, as discussed in Chapter 9, and then combine them using the Panasonic Image App.

Recording Format

With this setting, you choose the video format for any movies you make—AVCHD, MP4, MP4 (LPCM), or MOV. Following are details about each of these options.

AVCHD

AVCHD stands for Advanced Video Coding High Definition. This format, developed jointly by Sony and Panasonic, provides excellent quality for movies you will display on an HDTV set. However, AVCHD files can be complicated to edit on a computer. In fact, just finding the AVCHD video files on a memory card can be a challenge. When you insert a memory card from the FZ2500 camera into a card reader for viewing on a computer, you can find the still-image files and .mp4 video files within the folder labeled DCIM and then within sub-folders with names such as 100MSDCF.

The AVCHD files, however, are inside a different folder named PRIVATE. Inside that folder you will find another one called AVCHD, and within that one another one called BDMV. Open that folder and you will see more files or folders, including a folder called STREAM, which contains files with the extension .mts. The

.mts files are the AVCHD files that can be edited with programs such as Adobe Premiere Pro. (You don't have to worry about finding the file names if you connect your camera to the computer using the USB cable, only if you use a memory card reader, as I do.)

With the AVCHD format, you can use the Variable Frame Rate option, discussed later in this chapter, but you cannot record 4K video footage.

MP4

MP4 is another standard video format, which provides excellent quality and can be readily edited with any modern computer and video editing software. The first MP4 option on the Recording Format menu, labeled simply "MP4," uses the Advanced Audio Coding (AAC) format for its audio component, as opposed to the Linear Pulse Code Modulation (LPCM) format used by the next MP4 option on the menu. The AAC format is an excellent one, which was developed as an improvement over the widely used MP3 format. However, it uses compression to reduce the file size, whereas the LPCM format is an uncompressed one, which can provide higher quality for audio tracks.

If you choose MP4 for Recording Format, you will have somewhat limited choices for the next menu option, Recording Quality. MP4 can provide excellent quality for videos to be viewed on an HDTV, shared through the Internet, or viewed on a computer. However, if you want the highest quality for video files to be edited on a computer, you should choose MP4 (LPCM) or MOV.

MP4 (LPCM)

As discussed above, this option uses the superior LPCM format for encoding audio, and it also provides more options for selecting the Recording Quality option, discussed below. This option is probably the best one to select for the highest video image quality for footage to be edited on a Windows-based computer.

MOV

The MOV video format is another high-quality format, which is especially compatible with Macintosh computers. It provides image and audio quality equal to that of the MP4 format. (It uses the LPCM format for its audio tracks.) If you are using a Macintosh computer to edit videos and want the highest quality, you may want to choose this format.

Recording Quality

The choices for this next menu option depend on what you select for Recording Format, above. The FZ2500 camera offers a broad variety of Recording Quality settings and other options, including Variable Frame Rate and related options that let you record footage that is speeded-up or slowed-down in the camera, as I discuss elsewhere in this chapter. These options are available only with certain Recording Quality settings. In addition, some of the Recording Quality settings cause the camera to generate video files of large sizes that can be burdensome to edit with a computer. Following are the factors to consider for making this selection, based on your choice for Recording Format.

The following discussion of options assumes that System Frequency on screen 5 of the Setup menu is set to 59.94 Hz (NTSC). If it is set to 50.00 Hz (PAL), the options will be different, with frame rates that are multiples of 25, rather than 30, and no options with frame rates of 24. If System Frequency is set to 24.00 Hz (Cinema), all frame rates will be 24.

AVCHD

If you choose AVCHD for Recording Format, the choices for Recording Quality are FHD/28M/60p, FHD/17M/60i, FHD/24M/30p, and FHD/24M/24p. All of these provide Full HD (FHD) video with a resolution of 1920 x 1080 pixels. The 28M, 17M, and 24M figures state the maximum bit rate for each format, meaning the maximum number of megabits of information recorded per second. For example, the highest-quality AVCHD format records up to about 28 million bits of information per second. The higher the bit rate, the more information is available to provide a clear image.

The last three characters of each format state the frames or fields per second that are recorded, along with the letter "p" or "i" standing for progressive or interlaced. With progressive formats, the camera records full frames of information; with interlaced formats, the camera records fields, or half-frames, and then interlaces them to form full video frames. In the United States the normal rate for recording and playing back video is 30 frames per second (fps). So, the FHD/24M/30p format yields full HD video with the normal frame rate, recording 30 full frames each second. The FHD/17M/60i option yields the same frame rate by recording 60 fields and interlacing them to form 30 full frames.

The FHD/24M/24p option is provided for those users who like to use a 24 fps video format. That frame rate is the one traditionally used by film-based movie cameras, and some people believe that using this standard provides a more "cinematic" appearance than the 30 fps option.

Finally, with the FHD/28M/60p setting, the FZ2500 records 60 full frames per second, which yields higher quality than the alternative, which is "interlaced" video. The 60 frames are later translated into 30 frames for playback at the standard rate of 30 fps. However, if you want to, and your video editing software has this capability, you can play 60p footage in slow motion at one-half the normal speed and still maintain full HD quality.

This possibility exists because, as noted above, the 60p footage is recorded with twice the number of full frames as 30p or 60i footage, so the quality of the video does not suffer if it is played back at one-half speed. (With other video formats, playback at half speed will appear choppy or jerky, because not enough frames were recorded to play smoothly at that speed.) So, if you think you may want to slow down your footage significantly with a computer for playback, you should choose the 60p setting. Of course, the sounds would also be slowed to half speed, so you need to consider whether that factor would make this setting impractical for a particular situation.

MP4

If you choose MP4 for the Recording Format, the Recording Quality choices are the following, in descending order of quality: 4K/100M/30p; 4K/100M/24p; FHD/28M/60p; FHD/20M/30p; and HD/10M/30p.

The two available 4K options are special cases. The ability to shoot 4K video is one of the distinguishing features of the FZ2500 camera. The standard known as 4K, sometimes known as UHD for ultra-HD, is a relatively recent option for HDTVs. The 4K stands for 4,000, meaning each frame has a horizontal resolution of about 4,000 pixels. A standard HDTV has a horizontal resolution of 1920 pixels and a vertical resolution of 1080 pixels. The 4K format of the FZ2500

has a horizontal resolution of 3840 and a vertical resolution of 2160. The overall resolution of this 4K image is about eight megapixels, while the resolution of full HDTV is about two megapixels, so a 4K picture has four times the resolution of full HDTV.

To get the full benefit of 4K video footage, you should view it on a 4K-capable TV set or monitor. However, if your editing software permits, you can shoot using the 4K format and then convert it to the more standard 1080 format for ordinary HDTV sets. With that approach, your video footage will contain considerably more detail than if you just recorded it using one of the 1080 formats.

There is one caveat about recording with the 4K quality setting: As noted earlier in this chapter, to record with this setting (or with any other setting that includes a bit rate of 100M or more) you have to use a memory card of the fastest speed class, which is UHS Speed Class 3.

If you are not planning to record using the 4K setting, the other MP4 formats give you excellent options. You can record in full HD with a 28 megabit-per-second bit rate, giving you excellent quality. You can choose 60p for highest quality and the ability to produce slow-motion footage at one-half speed, or the more standard 30p option. If you would like to work with smaller files that still produce excellent quality, you can choose to record with the HD/10M/30p option, which records using HD rather than FHD, meaning the image size is 1280 x 720 pixels, rather than 1920 x 1080.

MP4 (LPCM)

If you choose MP4 (LPCM) for the Recording Format, the choices for Recording Quality are the following: 4K/100M/30p; 4K/100M/24p/; FHD/ALL-I/200M/60p; FHD/100M/60p; FHD/50M/60p; FHD/ALL-I/200M/30p; FHD/100M/30p; FHD/50M/30p; FHD/ALL-I/200M/24p; FHD/100M/24p; and FHD/50M/24p.

These options include some high-bit-rate settings beyond the 4K settings, such as FHD/100M/60p. In addition, they include three settings that use the All-Intra method for compression of the files. That option, shown as ALL-I in the list of settings above, uses a compression method that preserves image quality better than other methods, but produces larger files. It is a good option if you need to maximize image quality at all costs. However, if your footage does not include a lot of motion and is shot on a tripod (such as an interview or landscape scene), standard compression should not affect image quality noticeably, and it may not be worthwhile to use a format that will generate such large files.

MOV

If you choose MOV for the Recording Format, the choices for Recording Quality are: 4K/100M/30p; 4K/100M/24p; FHD/ALL-I/200M/60p; FHD/100M/60p; FHD/50M/60p; FHD/ALL-I/200M/30p; FHD/100M/30p; FHD/50M/30p; FHD/ALL-I/200M/24p; FHD/100M/24p; and FHD/50M/24p. These choices are the same as for the MP4 (LPCM) option.

Using the Cinema 4K (C4K) Setting for Recording Quality

As you may notice, none of the Recording Quality settings listed above include the Cinema 4K (C4K) option. That is because, as stated earlier, this discussion assumed that System Frequency on screen 5 of the Setup menu is set to 59.94 Hz (NTSC). If, instead, that menu item is set to 24.00 Hz (Cinema), the options for Recording Quality change accordingly. With that setting in place, the only options available for Recording Format are MP4 (LPCM) and MOV. The only options for Recording Quality are those in the lists above with 24p for the frame rate, and one additional value is added in place of the 4K/100M/30p option. That new setting is C4K/100M/24p.

The C4K, or Cinema 4K setting, provides a higher-resolution 4K format. The standard 4K format used by the FZ2500 is sometimes called UHD, for ultra-high definition. That format has a resolution of 3840 x 2160 pixels. The C4K format has a resolution of 4096 x 2160 pixels, which gives it an aspect ratio of 256:135 or 1.90:1, whereas the normal 4K format has an aspect ratio of 16:9 or 1.78:1. The 16:9 aspect ratio is the common ratio used by most HDTVs, so the added width of the C4K format may not be of much use, unless the video frame is reduced in size so the entire width will fit on a TV screen, with black bars at the top and bottom of the frame. However, if you want to use the highest possible resolution for your 4K footage, the C4K option is available, if you set System Frequency on screen 5 of the Setup menu to 24.00 Hz (Cinema).

Exposure Mode

I discussed this option earlier. It is available for selection only when the mode dial is at the Creative Video position. It provides choices of Program, Aperture Priority, Shutter Priority, or Manual Exposure for the mode for recording motion pictures. With the Aperture Priority, Shutter Priority, and Manual Exposure modes, you can control aperture and/or shutter speed. With the Manual and Shutter Priority settings, you can select a shutter speed as fast as 1/16000 second and as slow as 1/25 second, depending on the recording format. With the Manual Exposure setting, you can select a shutter speed as slow as 1/2 second when manual focus is in effect.

Variable Frame Rate

This option, abbreviated as VFR, lets you choose a non-standard frame rate for recording your video, in order to produce an in-camera slow-motion or fast-motion effect. You can set the frame rate to a value from 2 to 120 frames per second. The effect of this setting will vary according to the current setting for Recording Quality. For example, if Recording Quality is set to FHD/100M/30p, the frame rate for a normal recording is 30 fps. If you then set VFR to 2 fps, the camera will record only two frames each second, but they will be played back at the standard speed of 30 fps, resulting in action that is speeded up 15 times, looking almost like time lapse footage or a wild comedy sequence.

If, on the other hand, you set VFR to 120 fps, the resulting footage will be slowed down to one-fourth the normal speed, having a definite slow-motion appearance. Note, though, that using a frame rate above 60 fps is likely to result in reduced image quality.

This setting is available only with certain settings for Recording Format and Recording Quality. It is not available at all when Recording Format is set to MP4. When Recording Format is set to MP4 (LPCM) or MOV, VFR is available when Recording Quality is set to FHD/100M/30p or FHD/100M/24p. When Recording Format is set to AVCHD, VFR is available when Recording Quality is set to FHD/24M/30p or FHD/24M/24p. If System Frequency is set to 24.00 Hz (Cinema), VFR is available only when Recording Quality is set to FHD/100M/24p.

When you scroll through the settings for Recording Quality, the camera displays the message, "VFR Available" whenever you have highlighted a setting for which VFR can be selected, as shown in Figure 8-10.

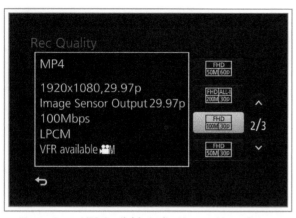

Figure 8-10. VFR Available Indication on Menu Screen

When VFR is in use, the camera will not use autofocus and will not record audio. This setting cannot be used when 4K Live Cropping is turned on through screen 1 of the Motion Picture menu.

Screen 3 of the Motion Picture menu is in Figure 8-11.

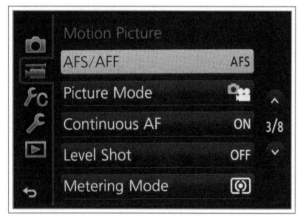

Figure 8-11. Screen 3 of Motion Picture Menu

AFS/AFF

This next menu option, as discussed earlier, mirrors the same setting on the Recording menu. It does not matter whether you choose AFS or AFF for purposes of autofocus for video recording, so you should select the option that you will want to use for recording still images. The camera's autofocus behavior for video recording is controlled by the Continuous AF menu option, discussed below. If you have Continuous AF turned off, the camera will not focus on its own during video recording; you have to press the shutter button halfway to cause the camera to use its autofocus mechanism. If you have Continuous AF turned on, the camera focuses continuously during video recording. (Of course, the focus mode lever has to be set to AFS/AFF or AFC for the camera to use autofocus at all.)

Picture Mode

When you are recording video footage with the FZ2500, you can press the shutter button during the recording to take a still picture with an aspect ratio of 16:9, with certain limitations. The Picture Mode option controls the settings the camera uses for those still pictures. There are two options, as shown in Figure 8-12: Video Priority (top icon) and Photo Priority (bottom icon).

If you choose the first option, the still pictures will be captured as JPEG (not Raw), no matter what menu settings are in effect for still image recording. With this setting, the camera can record up to 40 still images while recording the video, without disrupting the video recording, unless the camera is set for 4K video recording. In that case, the limit is 10 images.

With the second option, the camera will take still pictures using the settings made through the Recording menu for Picture Size and Quality, but you can take only 10 images during the video recording, and each time you do there will be a brief interruption in the audio of the video recording. Also, the camera's display will black out briefly while the still image is being recorded. (If the camera is recording 4K video, the limit is five images.) With this option in effect, you cannot capture still images if Recording Quality on the Motion Picture menu is set to a 24p setting, or if drive mode is set to 4K Photo.

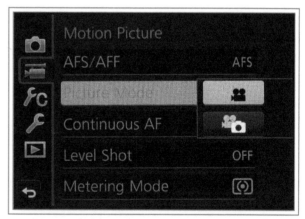

Figure 8-12. Picture Mode Menu Options Screen

The Picture Mode feature is not available when the camera is set to Intelligent Auto, Creative Video, or Panorama mode, when Recording Quality is set to C4K, or when Snap Movie is turned on.

Continuous AF

As discussed above, this setting controls how the FZ2500 uses its autofocus during video recording, assuming you have the focus mode set to an autofocus setting. If the Continuous AF option is turned on, the camera will adjust its focus continuously as the distance to the subject changes. If it is turned off, the camera will use its autofocus only when you press the shutter button halfway.

Level Shot

This option is designed to correct a tilt away from the horizontal in a video sequence. When this function is turned on, if the camera detects that the camera is tilted to one side or the other, it will correct the tilt to make the video frame appear horizontal, to the extent possible. The camera uses electronic processing to crop the frame slightly to accomplish this leveling, so some pixels are lost at the edges of the frame.

I have found this function to be quite capable of straightening a video frame, within some limits. Figures 8-13 and 8-14 illustrate how well the camera leveled a scene that was shot with a noticeable tilt.

Figure 8-13. Level Shot Turned Off

Figure 8-14. Level Shot Turned On

For these images, I recorded two brief videos of the same scene with the FZ2500 on a tripod, in both cases with the camera tilted to one side, but with Level Shot turned on for one version.

Figure 8-13 is a still frame saved from the video with Level Shot turned off, showing the degree of tilt. Figure 8-14 is a frame from the video with Level Shot turned on, in which the camera electronically corrected the tilt so the scene looks level. Of course, there may be times when it is appropriate for the scene to be tilted. In that case, be sure to leave this option turned off. This feature does not affect still images, only video. It also cannot be used with 4K or C4K video, when Variable Frame Rate is in use, or when Stabilizer is set to Off in the Recording menu/Motion Picture menu.

Metering Mode

This menu option gives you access to the same three metering methods found on the Recording menu: Multiple, Center-weighted, and Spot. As with several other Motion Picture menu options, this one mirrors the item on the Recording menu; if either one is changed, the corresponding entry on the other menu is changed to the same setting. If AF Mode is set to an option with a movable focus frame, such as Face/Eye Detection or 1-Area, and Spot metering is also active, you can move the focus frame and Spot metering cross around the frame during video recording, just as with still shooting.

Screen 4 of the Motion Picture menu is in Figure 8-15.

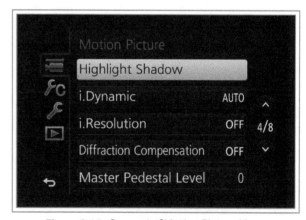

Figure 8-15. Screen 4 of Motion Picture Menu

Highlight Shadow

This option, also, is identical to the corresponding one on the Recording menu.

Intelligent Dynamic

This setting works the same as the similar setting on the Recording menu and mirrors its setting.

Intelligent Resolution

This setting also works the same as its still-photo counterpart, except that the Extended setting will be changed to Low when recording movies.

Diffraction Compensation

This setting operates the same way as the option on the Recording menu.

Master Pedestal Level

With this setting, you can adjust the black level used by the FZ2500, to alter the way the camera processes dark and light tones in video footage. This setting is available for adjustment only when the mode dial is set to Creative Video.

When you select this menu item, you will see the adjustment screen shown in Figure 8-16. Using the front or rear dial, the Left and Right buttons, or the touch screen, you can adjust the setting to any value up to plus or minus 15 units from the default level of zero. If you adjust it to a positive value, the camera will lighten the darkest parts of the image, potentially pulling additional details out of areas that would otherwise be black. If you adjust it to a negative value, the darkest areas may remain black, while the camera will darken the highlights, potentially pulling more details out of areas that otherwise might be too bright.

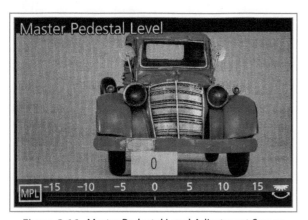

Figure 8-16. Master Pedestal Level Adjustment Screen

For example, Figure 8-17 is a frame from a video taken with Master Pedestal Level set to zero; Figure 8-18 is from a video with the value set to -15, and Figure 8-19 is from a video with the value set to +15.

Figure 8-17. Master Pedestal Set to Zero

Figure 8-18. Master Pedestal Level Set to -15

Figure 8-19. Master Pedestal Level Set to +15

Screen 5 of the Motion Picture menu is shown in Figure 8-20.

Figure 8-20. Screen 5 of Motion Picture Menu

Luminance Level

This menu item is available for adjustment in all shooting modes other than the basic Intelligent Auto mode and Panorama mode, but it actually operates only during movie recording.

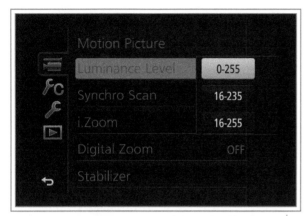

Figure 8-21. Luminance Level Menu Options Screen

As you can see in Figure 8-21, it has three options: 0-255, 16-235, and 16-255. Those numbers represent the luminance range for motion pictures captured with the camera. The default value is 0-255, which means that all possible brightness values are being captured. The other two options let you adjust the luminance range to a limited subset of the overall range of 0-255. The only reason to select one of those ranges is if you will be using video editing software that uses one of those limited ranges. If you are not certain that you need one of the limited ranges, I suggest you use the 0-255 setting for all purposes.

Synchro Scan

This option is provided for use when you are capturing video of a television or computer screen, or some other device that emits a flickering signal. This menu item is available for adjustment only in Creative Video mode, when Exposure Mode is set to Shutter Priority or Manual Exposure on screen 2 of the Motion Picture menu. In that case, after you turn this option on, the shooting screen will appear like that in Figure 8-22, with a special display of the current shutter speed near the bottom of the frame.

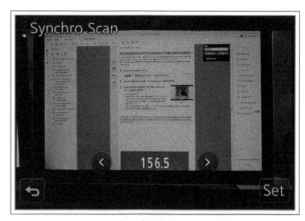

Figure 8-22. Synchro Scan Setting Screen

You can use the front or rear dial, the Left and Right buttons, or the touch arrow icons on the screen, to adjust the shutter speed with considerable precision, including tenths of a second. You can press and hold down the Left or Right button to change the value more rapidly. You can view the camera's display as you gradually adjust the shutter speed, to reduce the flickering produced by the television screen or other device you will be filming.

Intelligent Zoom

This setting is another one that is no different from the version on the Recording menu.

Digital Zoom

This is another setting that's the same as that on the Recording menu.

Stabilizer

The Stabilizer setting is another one that mirrors the same setting on the Recording menu. You can set this option to Normal to provide general stabilization, or Off. The Panning setting, which counteracts motion only in the vertical direction, is available for selection on this menu in still-shooting modes, but it cannot be selected in Creative Video mode and it does not operate when recording motion pictures in any shooting mode.

When recording movies, the camera can use its 5-Axis Hybrid Image Stabilizing Function, which electronically corrects image jitter in five directions. It is selected through the E-Stabilization sub-option of the Stabilizer item. As a side-effect of this internal processing, motion picture frames may become cropped to a narrower angle of view than normal. The 5-Axis system does not operate when recording 4K movies, using Variable Frame Rate, or using Digital Zoom.

Screen 6 of the Motion Picture menu is shown in Figure 8-23.

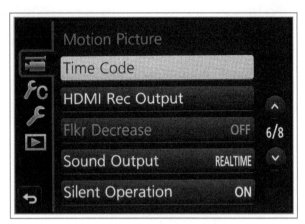

Figure 8-23. Screen 6 of Motion Picture Menu

Time Code

This menu item provides several sub-options that are helpful if you use the FZ2500 for advanced video production. For example, because of its ability to shoot 4K video, the FZ2500 camera can be used as part of a multi-camera setup for a professional production. In such a setup, it can be useful to control whether and how the camera outputs time code, a type of metadata used when editing video sequences.

This menu option is available for selection only when Recording Format on screen 2 of the Motion Picture menu is set to AVCHD, MP4 (LPCM), or MOV. It is not available with the MP4 setting.

I won't discuss the use of time code in detail in this book, but I will give a brief overview. Time code for video files includes numbers in a format like the following: 02:12:23:19, which stands for hours, minutes, seconds, and frames. In this example, the time code shown would mark the point in the video clip at 2 hours, 12 minutes, 23 seconds, and 19 frames into the next second.

Because video (in the NTSC system) is played back at 30 fps or 24 fps, the number in the final position is based on those values. With a Recording Quality value of 60p, 60i, or 30p, the number of frames can be set from 00 to 29. When Recording Quality is set to 24p, the number of frames can be set only to a value from 00 to 23. For PAL areas, the number of frames can go from 00 to 24, because the video is played back at 25 fps.

When you see a time code like the one in the above example, you know what frame of the video is being identified, so you can make an edit at that point or synchronize this video clip with another video clip, as long as both clips are using the same time code format and had the time code recorded in synchronization.

If you are not going to use your camera for that sort of video production, you can largely ignore this menu option, though it is helpful to know what settings you can control. The sub-options are discussed below.

Time Code Display

This first sub-option turns the time code display on or off. If it is turned on, the time code numbers display on the recording screen when a video is being recorded and when the camera is in standby mode. You also can turn the time code display on or off for playback mode using this option.

Count Up

This option lets you choose either Rec Run or Free Run for the time code. With Rec Run, the time code increases only while the camera is actually recording. With Free Run, the time code continues to run all the time. Which system to choose is a matter of preference, depending on how you will use the time code for editing. With Rec Run, there should be no gaps in the time code, which can be an advantage. With Free Run, you can set up the time code to match the time of day, which can be useful if you need to find a clip that corresponds to a particular time during the day's video recording. (You can do that using the Time Code Value option, discussed below.)

Free Run time code continues to run even when the camera is powered off. When you turn the camera on again and set it to Movie mode, the current time should be displaying in the lower left corner of the display, assuming you set the initial value for the time code to the current time.

Time Code Value

With this option, you can set the initial value for the time code to be used when the next video recording starts. With Reset, the value is reset to all zeroes. With Manual Input, you can input any allowable values for hours, minutes, seconds, and frames. As noted earlier, the highest value for frames will be 29, 23, or 24, depending on the settings for Recording Quality and System Frequency. With Current Time, the camera will use the time from its internal clock for hours, minutes, and seconds, and set the frames to zero.

Time Code Mode

This option lets you select either DF (drop-frame) or NDF (non-drop-frame) format for the time code, assuming you are using time code and are using the NTSC video system with a Record Setting option other than 24p. Drop-frame time code is not used for PAL video, and this menu option is dimmed and unavailable if System Frequency is set to 50.00 Hz (PAL) in the Setup menu.

This is a technical setting that you can adjust to make sure the time code you use is compatible with that of other cameras and with your editing facilities. Drop-frame time code is used because the NTSC standard of 30 frames per second does not record exactly 30 frames every second. For technical reasons, the actual rate is 29.97 frames per second (or 59.94 fps for the 60p settings). To count the frames accurately, video editors use the drop-frame system, which drops a few frames from the counting process at specified intervals, so the actual number of frames is counted accurately.

You can leave this option set to DF if you are using the NTSC system, unless you know of a specific reason to use NDF.

HDMI Time Code Output

This last sub-option for the Time Code menu option, located on the second screen of the sub-options, is available for selection only in Creative Video mode. When it is turned on, the camera outputs time code through its HDMI port. This option is needed if you record video to an external video recorder, as discussed later in this chapter. In order to use the HDMI Recording Control sub-option of the HDMI Recording Output menu item, discussed below, the HDMI Time Code Output must be turned on.

HDMI Recording Output

This next option on the Motion Picture menu has several sub-options for use when you connect the FZ2500 camera to an external monitor or video recorder through the HDMI port.

Bit Mode

This first sub-option for HDMI Recording Output is available for selection only in Creative Video mode. The

choices for this setting are 4:2:2 8-bit or 4:2:2 10-bit, as shown in Figure 8-24.

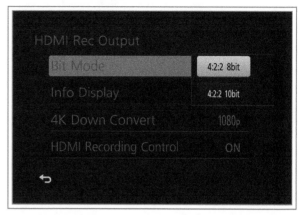

Figure 8-24. HDMI Recording Output/Bit Mode Options Screen

These numbers concern the amount of data that is available for reproducing ranges of colors. The 4:2:2 standard provides excellent color, and a system with 8 bits of color information is sufficient to produce about 16 million different colors. However, a system with 10 bits can produce about a billion colors. For most purposes, the 8-bit option is sufficient, but, if you want to produce the highest-quality video footage possible, the 10-bit option is worth having available.

If you use the 4:2:2 8-bit setting, you can record video to the camera's memory card while the video signal is being sent through the HDMI port to an external monitor or recorder. However, if you use the 4:2:2 10-bit setting, the video cannot be recorded to the memory card in the camera; it can only be output to the external device.

Info Display

This setting, which can be turned either on or off, controls whether or not the video signal that is output through the camera's HDMI port includes the icons, labels, and other information overlays that appear on the shooting screen, or just the video signal itself. If you turn this option off, the camera sends only the video signal, which is then called a "clean" HDMI output. That is the option to use when you are recording video using an external recorder. It also can be of use if you want to use a camera to display video on a large monitor for a purpose such as entertainment at a party or other event, when you would not want the information overlays to be included.

If you are outputting video through the HDMI port and have Bit Mode set to 4:2:2 10-bit, as discussed above, the Info Display option is automatically forced off, because there is a presumption in that situation that you are recording video using an external recorder.

4K Down Convert

This option controls what happens when Recording Quality is set to 4K or C4K in the Motion Picture menu and the video signal is being output through the HDMI port to an external device. The choices are Auto, 1080p, or Off. If you choose Auto, the camera will output 4K video unless the external device is not compatible with 4K video. In that case, if the external device does not respond in a way that indicates it is compatible, the FZ2500 will automatically down-convert the video signal from 4K to 1080p, or regular high-definition (HD) video.

If you choose 1080p, the camera will output 4K video in the 1080p format, even if the external device is capable of receiving 4K video. If you choose Off, the camera will not attempt to down-convert the video. If the external device is not capable of receiving 4K video, the image may not be visible, or may not be processed by the external device.

HDMI Recording Control

This final sub-option for HDMI Recording Output lets you determine whether or not the controls on the FZ2500 camera can control the operation of an external video recorder when you are outputting a video signal through the HDMI port. This option is available for selection only in Creative Video mode, when HDMI Time Code Output is turned on. (The Recording Quality item on screen 2 of the Motion Picture menu must be set to AVCHD, MP4 (LPCM), or MOV for the Time Code options to be available.)

The choices for this option are On or Off. If it is turned on, then, when the FZ2500 is outputting video through the HDMI port with Time Code Output turned on, pressing the red movie button or the shutter button to start or stop a video recording can control the operation of the connected external recorder, assuming that device is compatible with this operation.

Flicker Decrease

This next Motion Picture menu option is not available when the mode dial is set to the Creative Video position; it is available only in the PASM shooting modes, when you have no other way to control the shutter speed used for video recording. It provides a way to set the shutter speed so as to reduce the flickering effect that can occur in some cases. You can leave the option turned off, or select 1/50, 1/60, 1/100, or 1/120 second.

Sound Output

This option is available in all shooting modes other than Panorama. It lets you choose Real Time or Recorded Sound for the sound that is monitored by headphones when you are recording video. If you choose Real Time, the sound you hear is not delayed; it is the same sound being directed to the camera's recording. If you choose Recorded Sound, you will hear the sound after it has been processed for recording by the camera, so there will be a slight delay between the actual sound and the sound you hear through the headphones.

To hear sound with no delay, choose Real Time. To make sure sound is properly processed and recorded, with a brief delay, choose Recorded Sound. If you record to an external device through the HDMI port, this setting is forced to Recorded Sound.

Silent Operation

This menu option is available for selection only when the mode dial is at the Creative Video position. When it is turned on, the camera displays a special set of touch screen icons that you can use to control settings during motion picture recording, to avoid using physical controls that might make sounds that are recorded with the video.

To use this feature after the menu item has been turned on, touch the movie camera icon at the top of the line of touch icons on the right side of the screen, as shown in Figure 8-25. The camera will open up a tab with a set of video-related icons, as shown in Figure 8-26.

Figure 8-25. Movie Camera Icon for Silent Operation

Figure 8-26. Touch Icons for Silent Operation

Touch one of those icons to control the setting it represents. From the top, they stand for zoom, aperture (F-stop), shutter speed, exposure compensation, ISO, and microphone level adjustment. Of course, aperture and shutter speed are adjustable for video recording only if the Exposure Mode menu option is set to a mode that permits that adjustment, namely, Aperture Priority, Shutter Priority, or Manual Exposure. To control any setting, use the touch slider control that appears beneath the active tab, as shown in Figure 8-27, where the exposure compensation control has been activated. Touch the single triangle icons for normal adjustments, or the double triangle icons for larger adjustments.

Figure 8-27. Exposure Compensation Control for Silent Operation

If you want to change to another setting, touch the top icon to open up the line of control icons again, and touch another one. One point worth noting about this feature is that it is available for use even if the Touch Screen item is turned off through the Touch Settings item on screen 10 of the Custom menu. So, you can use silent operation for video recording even if all other touch screen features have been disabled. In that case, the Silent Operation icon will be the only touch icon on

the screen in recording mode, until you touch that icon to call up the other icons.

Screen 7 of the Motion Picture menu is in Figure 8-28.

Figure 8-28. Screen 7 of Motion Picture Menu

Microphone Level Display

This first option on screen 7 of the Motion Picture menu can be turned either on or off. If you turn it on, the camera puts two small graphic audio meters in the lower left corner of the display, as shown in Figure 8-29. Those meters react to changes in the audio levels being recorded by the left and right sides of the stereo microphone built into the camera, or by an external microphone.

Figure 8-29. Microphone Level Display in Use on Shooting Screen

You can use those meters to decide whether you need to adjust the audio recording level using the next menu option. When the Microphone Level Limiter option, discussed below, is turned off, this option is forced on.

Microphone Level Adjustment

This option displays a pair of graphic audio meters in the middle of the screen, as shown in Figure 8-30, so you can test the audio input level and adjust it. (These meters are temporary, for the purpose of level adjustment, unlike the meters set by the previous menu option, which remain in place on the display screen during video recording.)

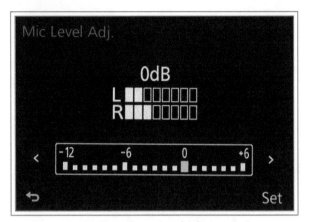

Figure 8-30. Microphone Level Adjustment Screen

With this display on the screen, aim the camera at your subject and adjust the audio level using the Left and Right buttons, the front or rear dial, or the touch screen. More of the empty blocks on the display will turn white as the volume of the test sound increases. If they turn red, that indicates excessive volume, leading to distortion. There are 19 levels of adjustment available, with the default value set at 0 dB (decibels).

Special Microphone

This option is available for selection only when a particular Panasonic microphone is attached to the camera. As far as I know, the only model that qualifies is a shotgun microphone, model number DMW-MS2, which is discussed in Appendix A. When that microphone is plugged in to the camera, the menu provides a range of options for the pattern the microphone uses in picking up sounds. This menu item includes two screens of options. For each option, the camera displays a pattern on the left that illustrates the way that pattern picks up sounds, as shown in Figure 8-31.

The following patterns are available:

Stereo

With the first option, the microphone uses a standard stereo pattern, picking up sounds in a wide range to the left and right.

Figure 8-31. Special Microphone Menu Options Screen

Lens Auto

With this option, the microphone's directional pattern changes according to the focal length of the zoom lens. That is, when the lens is zoomed in to a longer focal length, the microphone's pickup pattern is narrowed to pick up sounds in a range directly in front of it, rather than from the sides. As the lens is zoomed farther back to a wide-angle setting, the pickup pattern widens out to the sides.

Shotgun

With this setting, the shotgun microphone acts in a standard shotgun manner, reducing its range of pickup to a narrow area directly in front of the microphone.

S. Shotgun

With this "super shotgun" setting, the range of pickup is narrowed even more, to a very thin slice of area in front of the microphone.

Manual

If you select Manual, the camera displays the screen shown in Figure 8-32. On that screen, you can use the Left and Right buttons, the front or rear dial, or the touch screen to adjust the directivity of the shotgun microphone from a wide pickup pattern at the left to a narrow pickup pattern at the right. The camera also displays level adjustment meters, so you can test the sound as you make adjustments to the pattern. Note that you can display this screen quickly by assigning the Microphone Directivity Adjustment option to a function button using the Function Button Set item on screen 7 of the Custom menu.

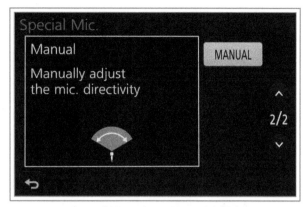

Figure 8-32. Special Microphone Manual Adjustment Screen

Noise Reduction for External Microphone

This next menu option is explained quite well by its title. It can be turned either on or off, and is effective only when an external microphone is connected to the camera. When this option is turned on, the camera processes recorded sounds to reduce noises ordinarily made by the camera, such as the sound of the lens being zoomed in and out.

Microphone Level Limiter

This option can be turned either on or off. If it is turned on, the camera automatically limits the volume of recorded sound, within a range that is designed to avoid distortion from excessively loud sounds. If you are recording casual footage for a family gathering, you may want to turn this option on. However, if you are using an external microphone and adjusting sound levels yourself, you may want to turn this option off so you will maintain greater control of the sound levels. When this option is turned off, the Microphone Level Display option, discussed earlier, is forced on.

Screen 8 of the Motion Picture menu is in Figure 8-33.

Figure 8-33. Screen 8 of Motion Picture Menu

Wind Noise Canceller/Wind Cut

This setting on the Motion Picture menu changes its name according to whether an external microphone is attached to the camera or not. If only the built-in microphone is being used, this menu option is called Wind Noise Canceller, and it has only three settings: Off, Standard, or High. If an external microphone is attached, this option is called Wind Cut and can be left turned off or set to Low, Standard or High.

With either version of this option, when it is turned on, the camera attempts to reduce the noise from wind while recording a video sequence. With the higher settings, the reduction of noise is stronger, and is more likely to remove some sounds other than wind noise. Either level of this processing may have an adverse effect on the quality of the audio. If you are recording casual scenes from a vacation, I recommend turning this option on when recording in a windy area. If you will be using video-editing software, though, you may want to turn this setting off, because, at either level, it can reduce some wanted sounds, and you can adjust the sound track later with your software to minimize the unwanted sounds.

Zoom Microphone

This next option on the Motion Picture menu, which works only with the camera's built-in microphone, can be turned either on or off. If it is turned on, the camera's built-in microphone concentrates on recording more distant sounds as the lens zooms in. I have not found this option to make much difference, and I generally leave it turned off.

SS/Gain Operation

This menu item gives you the option of choosing a different system for displaying the shutter speed and gain settings on the shooting screen in Creative Video mode. The three options are SEC/ISO, Angle/ISO, and SEC/dB. The standard setting, and the one I always use, is the first, SEC/ISO, which stands for seconds and ISO. With this system, the shutter speed is shown as a fraction of a second and the gain, or sensitivity to light, is shown by the ISO value.

With the second system, sometimes used by professional cinematographers, the shutter speed is displayed as an angle, such as 360d, for 360 degrees, and the gain is shown as ISO.

With the third system, the shutter speed is shown as a fraction of a second and the gain is shown as dB, for decibels.

If you are more comfortable with either of the two alternative systems, they are available for your use.

Color Bars

This last option on the Motion Picture menu gives you three options for displaying a test pattern of color bars on the camera's screen, as shown in Figure 8-34.

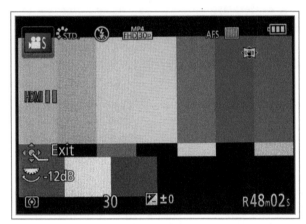

Figure 8-34. SMPTE Color Bars in Use

The three options are SMPTE, ABU, and ARIB, which are three organizations that develop and publish broadcasting standards. SMPTE (Society of Motion Picture and Television Engineers) is based in the United States; ABU (Asia-Pacific Broadcasting Union) has its headquarters in Malaysia; and ARIB (Association of Radio Industries and Businesses) is based in Japan.

To display any of these sets of color bars, select the option on the menu and press the Menu/Set button. The bars will display on the camera's screen and a high-pitched tone will be generated. You can adjust the sound level of the tone by turning the rear dial. You can stop the bars and tone by pressing Menu/Set again. If you press the red movie button while the bars are displayed, you can record the pattern in a video.

If you want to record a brief sequence of the bars and tone at the beginning of a video, use this menu option to generate the bars and tone, and start the recording to capture a few seconds of the pattern. Then, while continuing the recording, press the Menu/Set button. The bars and tone will stop, and you can proceed with the recording of your subject.

Recording Still Images During Video Recording

When the FZ2500 is recording a video sequence, you can press the shutter button to capture a still image. This function is available in all shooting modes in which movies can be recorded, except for Creative Video mode. (Movies cannot be recorded in Panorama mode.) In Creative Video mode, pressing the shutter button starts or stops a video recording. You can capture up to 40 still images during a video sequence. You can use the touch shutter function to take the pictures, if that option is turned on. A red camera icon appears in the upper left corner of the display as each picture is taken.

There are some limitations on recording still images during video recording, as was discussed earlier in connection with the Picture Mode option on screen 3 of the Motion Picture menu.

Recording to an External Video Recorder

The Panasonic FZ2500 camera has excellent features for advanced video production, and you can record movies to the camera's memory card with no problems. However, Panasonic also has equipped this camera with options for sending video and audio signals to an external video recorder. I will not discuss all possible scenarios for using the FZ2500 with a recorder, but I will describe the steps I took to record video with the camera connected to an Atomos Shogun 4K recorder, discussed in Appendix A. There undoubtedly are many other approaches that will work; this happens to be one that worked for me.

First, make sure the Shogun is powered by a battery or power supply and has a formatted storage disk installed. I used a SanDisk Extreme Pro 480 GB solid state drive (SSD). Connect headphones to monitor sound. On the Input menu, enable HDMI input and HDMI Trigger. I selected Apple ProRes HQ as the recording format.

Connect the HDMI input port of the Shogun to the HDMI output port of the FZ2500 using a micro-HDMI cable. If you use the settings in the table, below, you do not have to have a memory card in the camera. If you want to record to a memory card, change the setting for HDMI Rec Output/Bit Mode to 4:2:2 8-bit and insert a card rated in Speed Class UHS-3 into the camera.

Turn on the camera and recorder. Set the camera's mode dial to the Creative Video position. Set the focus mode lever to the AFS/AFF or AFC position so the camera will use autofocus, unless you prefer to use manual focus. Set System Frequency on screen 5 of the Setup menu to the appropriate video standard for your area, or use the Cinema standard if you want to use C4K for the recording format. Then make the settings on the Motion Picture menu as shown in Table 8-1.

Table 8-1.   **Suggested Settings on FZ2500 Camera for Recording 4K Video to an Atomos Shogun Recorder**

MOTION PICTURE MENU	
Photo Style	Cinelike D
Filter Settings	Off
Slow/Quick	Off
Dolly Zoom	Off
4K Live Cropping	Off
Snap Movie	Off
Recording Format	MP4 (LPCM)
Recording Quality	4K/100M/30p
Exposure Mode	P
Variable Frame Rate	Off (Not Available)
AFS/AFF	AFS
Picture Mode	(Not Available)
Continuous AF	On
Level Shot	Off (Not Available)
Metering Mode	Multi
Highlight Shadow	Use as needed
i.Dynamic	Off
i.Resolution	Off
Diffraction Compensation	Off
Master Pedestal Level	0
Luminance Level	0-255
Synchro Scan	Off (Not Available)
i.Zoom	On
Digital Zoom	Off
Stabilizer/Operation Mode	Normal/Off if use tripod
Time Code/Time Code Display	On
Time Code/Count Up	Rec Run
Time Code/Time Code Value	All zeroes, or as needed
Time Code/Time Code Mode	DF, unless NDF needed
Time Code/HDMI Time Code Output	On
HDMI Rec Output/Bit Mode	4:2:2 10-bit
HDMI Rec Output/ Info Display	Off
HDMI Rec Output/4K Down Convert	Auto
HDMI Rec Output/HDMI Rec Control	On

Flicker Decrease	Off (Not Available)
Sound Output	Rec Sound
Silent Operation	On
Microphone Level Display	As Needed
Microphone Level Adjustment	As Needed
Special Microphone	As Needed
Noise Reduction for Ext. Mic	As Needed
Microphone Level Limiter	Off
Wind Cut/ Wind Noise Canceller	Off
Zoom Microphone	Off
SS/Gain Operation	SEC/ISO
Color Bars	As Needed

Some of the above settings are optional or unnecessary and some, such as Exposure Mode and metering mode, can be changed according to your preferences. The important ones are Recording Format, Recording Quality, and the HDMI Recording Output settings.

Once the connections and settings are made, press the movie button on the FZ2500. The screen on the Shogun recorder should indicate that the recording has begun. Use the controls on the camera to zoom or adjust settings as needed. When you are ready to stop the recording, press the movie button again, and the recorder should stop.

I used the above settings with no memory card in the FZ2500 with no problems. The Shogun recorded the video as expected and the resulting file imported readily into Adobe Premiere Pro CC for viewing and editing.

Physical Controls

Next, I will discuss options for using the camera's physical control buttons, switches and dials in connection with video recording. The situation is complicated because each of the seven physical function buttons can be assigned to any one of about 80 options. Table 8-2, below, lists all of the physical controls and shows whether their settings will have an effect during video recording, as well as whether the control can be activated during video recording. For the function buttons, the table lists all of the possible assignments.

Table 8-2.   Use of Camera Controls Before and During Motion Picture Recording

Control or Function	Effective if Used Before Video Recording	Effective if Used During Video Recording
Physical Controls		
Focus Ring	Yes	Yes
Zoom Ring	Yes	Yes
Focus Mode Lever	Yes	Yes
Zoom Lever	Yes	Yes
Front Dial	Yes	Yes
Rear Dial	Yes	Yes
Display Button	Yes	Yes
ISO Button	Yes	Yes (only in Creative Video mode)
WB Button	Yes	Yes
Macro Mode Button	Yes	Yes
AF Mode Button	Yes	Yes
Menu/Set Button (access to menus)	Yes	No
Drive Mode Dial	No	No
AF/AE Lock Button	Yes	Yes
ND Filter Switch	Yes	Yes
Shutter Button	Yes	Yes
Functions Assigned to Function Buttons		
Exposure Compensation	Yes	Yes
Wi-Fi	Yes	No
Q. Menu	Yes	No
LVF/Monitor Switch	Yes	Yes
LVF/Monitor Display Style	Yes	Yes
AF/AE Lock	Yes	Yes
AF-On	Yes	Yes
Preview	No	No
One Push AE	No	No
Touch AE	Yes	Yes
Level Gauge	Yes	Yes
Focus Area Set	Yes	Yes
Slow Zoom T/W	Yes	Yes
1 Shot Raw + JPG	No	No
1 Shot Spot Metering	No	No
Cursor Button Lock	Yes	No
Dial Operation Switch	Yes	Yes
Photo Style	Yes	Yes
Filter Effect	Yes	No
Aspect Ratio	No	No
Picture Size	No	No
Quality	No	No
AFS/AFF	Yes	Yes
Metering Mode	Yes	Yes
Burst Rate	No	No
4K Photo	No	No

Control or Function	Effective if Used Before Video Recording	Effective if Used During Video Recording
Self Timer	No	No
Bracket	No	No
Highlight Shadow	Yes	Yes
i.Dynamic	Yes	Yes
i.Resolution	Yes	Yes
HDR	No	No
Shutter Type	No	No
Flash Mode	No	No
Flash Adjustment	No	No
Wireless Flash Setup	No	No
i.Zoom	Yes	No
Digital Zoom	Yes	No
Stabilizer	Yes	No
4K Live Cropping	Yes	No
Snap Movie	Yes	No
Motion Picture Recording Format	Yes	No
Motion Picture Recording Quality	Yes	No
Variable Frame Rate	Yes	No
Picture Mode	Yes	No
Synchro Scan	Yes	No
Time Code Display	Yes	Yes
Microphone Directivity Adjustment	Yes	Yes
Color Bars	Yes	Yes
Silent Mode	No	No
Peaking	Yes	Yes
Histogram	Yes	Yes
Guide Line	Yes	No
Zebra Pattern	Yes	Yes
Monochrome Live View	Yes	Yes
Recording Area	No	No
Video-Priority Display	Yes	No
Zoom Lever	No	No
Zoom Ring	No	No
Touch Screen	Yes	No
Headphone Volume	Yes (only when headphones connected)	Yes (only when headphones connected)
Sensitivity	Yes	Yes (only in Creative Video mode)
White Balance	Yes	Yes
WB-Auto White Balance	Yes	Yes
WB-Daylight (etc.)	Yes	Yes
WB-White Set 1-4	Yes	Yes
WB-Color Temperature 1-4	Yes	Yes
AF Mode/MF	Yes	Yes
Macro Mode	Yes	Yes

As you can see from the above table, there are many options for using the physical controls before and during video recording. For example, you can switch focus mode between autofocus and manual focus, and you can move the autofocus area around the display during recording. You can turn on or off the Zebra patterns, the histogram, or the peaking feature for manual focus while recording a video sequence.

However, there are some limitations. For example you can adjust Sensitivity (ISO) during video recording using a function button assigned to that setting, but you can only set it to Auto ISO or a value from 125 through 6400, and only in Creative Video mode. You cannot use the lowest or highest settings or the Intelligent ISO feature. The ISO Limit setting on the Recording menu does not apply for video recording.

You can select a filter effect that will work during recording, but you cannot select an effect during the recording. You cannot record a motion picture using the Rough Monochrome, Silky Monochrome, Soft Focus, Star Filter, or Sunshine effect. You cannot record a video at 4K quality using the Miniature setting. When you use the Miniature effect for a motion picture, the camera does not record sound, and the footage is recorded at about one-tenth the normal speed, resulting in playback that is speeded up ten times faster than normal to help simulate the appearance of a tabletop model layout.

Using the Touch Screen During Video Recording

The touch screen is available for use during motion picture recording, provided the appropriate options are turned on through the Touch Settings option on screen 10 of the Custom menu. If Touch Screen, Touch Tab, Touch AF, and Touch Pad AF are turned on through that menu option, you can use all of those functions while the camera is recording a motion picture. However, these actions are limited by the same restrictions set out above in Table 8-2. For example, although you can use the Touch Tab to get access to various settings, you cannot turn on or off a filter effect during motion picture recording, because that function cannot be controlled during recording.

You can, however, use the Touch Tab to adjust zoom, autoexposure, and function button actions, provided

the functions in question are available for use. If AF Mode is set to an option with a movable frame, such as 1-Area, you can use the Touch AF function to move the frame around the screen and resize it during a video recording. When the mode dial is set to a still-shooting mode, you can use the Touch Shutter function to take still pictures while recording a video.

Also, as discussed earlier in this chapter, if you turn on the Silent Operation item on Screen 6 of the Motion Picture menu (available only in Creative Video mode), you can use touch screen controls for zoom, aperture, shutter speed, exposure compensation, ISO, and microphone level adjustment. As noted earlier, you can use this option even if all other touch screen operations have been turned off through the Touch Settings item on the Custom menu.

Recommendations for Recording Video

Now that I have covered the essentials of recording video footage with the FZ2500, here are some recommendations for that process. For everyday use, such as for video clips of a vacation trip or a birthday party, it's probably a good idea to stick with the Intelligent Auto setting and, on the Motion Picture menu, set Recording Format to MP4 and Recording Quality to FHD/20M/30p. The result should be excellent-quality video, well exposed, and ready to show on an HDTV or to edit with video-editing software.

If you aren't ready to deal with a whole host of manual settings, but would like to add some flashy coloring to your movie scenes, consider shooting in Program mode (mode dial at P), and use the Filter Settings menu option to add an effect such as Impressive Art. If you would like to produce slow-motion footage, use a 60p setting for Recording Quality and slow the footage to one-half speed using your editing software. For even slower motion, but with no sounds, turn the mode dial to the Creative Video position and use the Variable Frame Rate setting on screen 2 of the Motion Picture menu.

The FZ2500's movie-making features provide a framework for a great array of experimentation. So consider the options, and don't hesitate to press the red motion picture button when inspiration strikes.

Motion Picture Playback and Editing

To locate movie files, scroll through images and videos in the camera until you find those with a movie camera icon in the upper left corner. To narrow down the search, you can use the Playback Mode option on screen 1 of the Playback menu and choose Video Only.

To play a motion picture in the camera, display the file you want and press the Up button to start playback, as indicated by the movie camera icon and up arrow, shown in Figure 8-35.

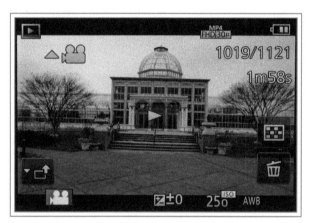

Figure 8-35. Movie Ready to Play in Camera

(If the icons have disappeared, press the Display button to bring them back on the display.) You also can touch the playback triangle icon in the center of the screen, provided the Touch Settings option on screen 10 of the Custom menu has the Touch Screen item turned on. The motion picture will start to play, and the camera will briefly display at the bottom of the screen a line of icons for the playback controls, as shown in Figure 8-36: Up button for play/pause; Right button for fast forward; Down button for stop; and Left button for fast backward.

Either during playback or when playback is paused, you can adjust the volume using the rear dial. When playback is paused, the camera displays more icons, as shown in Figure 8-37: Left button for frame backward; Down button for stop; Up button for play/pause; Right button for frame forward; and Menu/Set button to save a still frame from the video.

Figure 8-36. Initial Movie Playback Controls

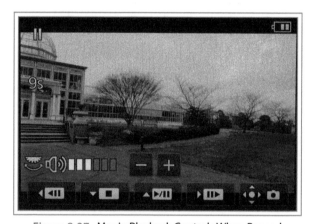

Figure 8-37. Movie Playback Controls When Paused

You cannot do much editing of a video in the camera, but you can trim its length or split it into two segments. To do that, follow the steps below.

1. Find the movie to divide and display its first frame in playback mode. Don't start it playing yet.

2. Press the Menu/Set button and select Video Divide from screen 2 of the Playback menu.

3. Press the Menu/Set button or touch the Set icon to start playing the video in the camera.

4. Press the Up button to pause the video at the approximate place where you want to divide it.

5. Use the Right and Left buttons to locate the splitting point more precisely.

6. When you are satisfied with the position, press the Down button to divide the video into two sections, as indicated by the scissors icon in the group of icons at the bottom of the display, as shown in Figure 8-38.

Figure 8-38. Scissors Icon for Video Divide Option

7. The camera will display a message asking you to confirm the operation. If you confirm it, the camera will divide the video into two parts. You will then have two separate video files; the original will no longer exist. You can delete either segment if you want, or keep them both.

You also can save a still image from a video file. To do that, follow the steps below.

1. Find the video that contains the image you want and start playing it in the camera.

2. At the approximate place where the image is located, press the Up button to pause the video.

3. Use the Right and Left buttons to find the location of the desired image.

4. Press the Menu/Set button or the corresponding touch screen icon, and the camera will display a message asking if you want to save this image, as shown in Figure 8-39.

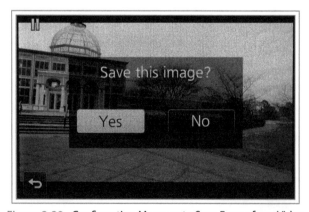

Figure 8-39. Confirmation Message to Save Frame from Video

5. If you confirm the operation, the camera will save the image in Standard quality with an aspect ratio of 16:9. The image's size will be 9 MP if the video was recorded with C4K quality, 8 MP if it was recorded with 4K quality, or 2 MP for other quality settings.

EDITING WITH A COMPUTER

You can edit video files from the FZ2500 camera using most standard editing software that has been updated to handle recent video formats. For example, I have found it easy to import all formats of video from the FZ2500 into the iMovie software on my Macintosh. One way to do that is to copy the video files from your camera's memory card to your computer. The .mp4 files are easy to find on the card; they are in the same folders as the still images. For example, an SD card I am using now has .rw2 (Raw), .jpg (JPEG), and .mp4 files in a folder whose path is LUMIX:DCIM:101_PANA.

The AVCHD video files are harder to locate. The actual video files you can import into editing software have the extension .mts. They are located in a folder with the path LUMIX:PRIVATE: AVCHD:BDMV:STREAM. On my Macintosh, you cannot see the contents of the AVCHD and BDMV folders directly; you have to right-click on those folder names in the Finder and select the menu command, Show Package Contents. Once you do that, you can find all of the .mts files and import them into iMovie or any other modern video editing software, which can edit them readily.

On a computer running Microsoft Windows 10, I was able to import all formats of movies from the FZ2500 into the Easy Movie Maker software that came pre-installed on the computer, and the .mp4 and .mov files played with no problems. I had to use the program's included transcoding tools to convert an AVCHD video to the .mp4 format, and then it played well.

CHAPTER 9: WI-FI AND OTHER TOPICS

Using Wi-Fi Features

The Panasonic FZ2500 camera has a good set of features for using Wi-Fi (wireless) networks to transfer images and videos to smartphones and other devices or to control the camera remotely from a smartphone or tablet. You also can upload images directly from the camera, smartphone, or tablet to social networks. There are several approaches to making wireless connections, and I will not discuss all of the possibilities in this book. The Panasonic user's guide provides general guidance for making the connections. I will discuss the steps that worked for me to accomplish various Wi-Fi-related activities.

CONNECT TO A SMARTPHONE OR TABLET

To connect the camera wirelessly with a smartphone or tablet, you can either use the Wi-Fi menu item on screen 1 of the Setup menu or you can press a function button that is assigned the Wi-Fi function. By default, the virtual Fn8 button (touch screen icon) is assigned to Wi-Fi in recording mode, and the Fn4 button in playback mode, but you can assign other buttons if you want.

I will discuss here the steps for using the Fn8 button to make this connection with an iPhone. For later connections, you will not need to follow all of these steps, as noted in Step 5, below. The steps are similar for an Android device, except that the screen may appear different, and, for example, you use Google Play instead of the App Store to download the Image App.

The steps included here assume that you have set the Wi-Fi Password menu option to Off, under the Wi-Fi Setup option under the Wi-Fi item on screen 1 of the Setup menu. If you turn the Wi-Fi Password option on, you will have to enter a password or read a QR code on the camera's screen in order to establish a Wi-Fi connection. In most situations, I find it much easier to leave the password option turned off.

1. Go to the App Store for iOS devices, and install the Panasonic Image App, whose icon is indicated by the arrow in Figure 9-1.

Figure 9-1. Panasonic Image App Icon on iPhone

2. Touch the Fn icon at the bottom of the line of icons at the right side of the camera's display screen. Then touch the Fn8 icon, with a Wi-Fi icon beneath it, at the top of the line of icons, as shown in Figure 9-2.

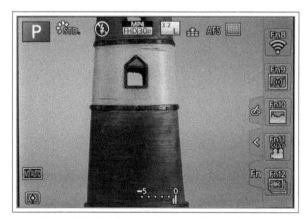

Figure 9-2. Fn8 Icon on Camera's Display Screen

3. The Wi-Fi connection lamp on top of the camera (in the same position as the power-on lamp) should turn solid blue.

4. The camera will display the screen shown in Figure 9-3 giving the SSID (identification data) of the camera's Wi-Fi network, and telling you to use the Wi-Fi settings on your phone to connect to that network. You can follow that prompt and connect immediately by selecting the camera's Wi-Fi network ID in your phone's Settings app.

Figure 9-3. Camera's Display of its Network ID

-or-

5. As noted on the camera's screen, you can press the Display button (or touch the on-screen icon) to go to the screen shown in Figure 9-4, which gives you the option of starting a new connection or choosing one from history or favorites. If you just want to connect to your phone, it may be simplest just to go ahead and use the Wi-Fi Settings app on your phone to connect to the camera's Wi-Fi network. The steps below assume you pressed the Display button to go to the camera's screen for New Connection and other options.

Figure 9-4. Camera's Screen for New Connection or History

6. Choose New Connection, and the camera will display a screen like that in Figure 9-5 with several options. For now, select Remote Shooting & View.

Figure 9-5. Camera's Options for New Connection

7. The camera will display a screen like that in Figure 9-6, advising you to connect your smartphone to the Wi-Fi network listed on the screen. (This screen is slightly different from the one in Figure 9-3.)

Figure 9-6. Camera's Screen with Network for New Connection

8. On the iPhone, select the Settings app, then Wi-Fi, and select the SSID (network ID) sent by the camera. That ID should be FZ2500, followed by several other characters, such as FZ2500-330C3F, as shown in Figure 9-7.

9. Once you do this, the camera will display a screen advising you to launch the Image App on the phone. Touch the app's icon on the phone to launch it. The camera will briefly display a message saying Under Remote Control and then its screen will go black until you take further action with the Image App, which will display a warning about extending the camera's lens.

Figure 9-7. Camera's Network ID on iPhone Screen

10. When the Image App starts with a Wi-Fi connection established, you should see on the phone a screen like that in Figure 9-8 with various options for remote operation, image transfer, geotagging, and others. (If you see a different screen, press the Home icon at the bottom left of the screen.)

Figure 9-8. Main Screen of Panasonic Image App

CONTROLLING THE CAMERA WITH A SMARTPHONE OR TABLET

Once you have established a connection between the camera and the phone using the steps above, you are ready to control the camera using the Image App. Select the Remote Operation icon at the upper left of the app's Home screen, as shown in Figure 9-8, and you will see a display on the phone like that in Figure 9-9.

Figure 9-9. Image App Remote Operation Screen

You can touch the icons on this screen to zoom the lens in and out; change the mix of icons on the display with the DISP. icon; and get access to various other settings, including Photo Style, Filter Settings, Aspect Ratio, Picture Size, Quality, Macro Mode, Metering Mode, and others by pressing the Q. Menu icon.

Figure 9-10. Additional Settings for Remote Operation

To take a picture, press the camera icon at the center bottom. To record a video, press the red button in the lower right corner. If you press the down-pointing arrow below the battery status icon, as seen in Figure

9-9, you will get access to additional settings, as shown in Figure 9-10, including white balance, ISO, AF mode, and exposure compensation. If the camera is in a recording mode that lets you change the shutter speed or aperture, there will be an SS icon (for shutter speed) or an F icon (for f-stop, or aperture), for making that setting. In Program mode, there will be a Program Shift icon. To change the recording mode, you have to turn the mode dial on the camera.

The touch shutter icon, which looks like a hand with a pointing finger and an X, causes the camera to focus and take a picture where you touch the phone's screen; the touch exposure icon, located below the touch shutter icon, does the same for exposure.

If the AF+MF option is turned on through screen 3 of the Custom menu, or if the camera is set to manual focus mode, you will see additional icons and controls for adjusting the focus point manually.

You also can use a feature called Jump Snap, represented by the icon at the bottom of the app's screen that looks like a jumping person, as seen to the left of the red video recording icon in Figures 9-9 and 9-10. If you select that icon, you will see the screen in Figure 9-11 with settings for this option.

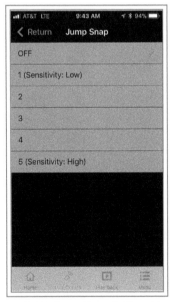

Figure 9-11. Jump Snap Settings Screen

You can leave it turned off, or set the sensitivity to low, high, or a medium value. Once Jump Snap is turned on, you use it by aiming the camera at a person who is holding the phone while the app is active. The camera will sense when the person jumps, and will snap a still

picture at the highest point of the jump. The result should be an image like that in Figure 9-12, catching the subject in an awkward and candid position.

Figure 9-12. Jump Snap Sample Image

SENDING IMAGES AND VIDEOS TO A SMARTPHONE OR TABLET

Once the FZ2500 is connected to your smartphone or tablet, instead of controlling the camera from your device, you can choose the option at the upper right of the Image App's home screen, Transfer Image. When you select that option, the phone will display a screen with choices of Transfer Selection or Batch Transfer. If you choose Transfer Selection, the app will display a screen like Figure 9-13, with thumbnail images for the items on the camera's memory card.

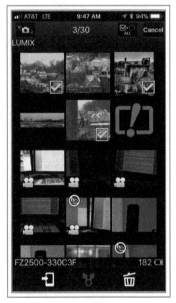

Figure 9-13. Transfer Selection Screen in Image App

If you press the camera icon in the upper left corner of this screen, the app will display the screen shown in

Figure 9-14 so you can choose to see images currently on the phone, in the camera, or in a Lumix Club folder.

Figure 9-14. Image App Screen with Choices for Images to View

You can scroll through the images stored in the camera, as shown in Figure 9-13, by flicking up and down the screen. It may take quite a while for all of the images and videos to load.

The thumbnails that have a movie camera icon in the lower left corner represent motion picture files. Other thumbnails may have an icon showing a camera and a phone with a line through the circle around them; that icon means that image or video cannot be transferred to the phone. In Figure 9-13, there are two thumbnails with that icon; those thumbnails represent Raw images or AVCHD or 4K videos, which cannot be transferred to a phone or tablet.

If you want to transfer one of the images or videos to your phone, first, tap on it to enlarge it on the display, as shown in Figure 9-15. If it is a video that can be played on the phone, you can press the Play icon on the phone's display to play it.

If you select the icon at the lower left, showing an arrow going to a phone, the phone will display a message saying it is copying the file. You will then have a copy of that image or video in the standard area for photos or videos on the phone.

On the main playback screen in the Image App, shown in Figure 9-13, if you press the Select icon in the upper right corner, you can mark images and videos

with green check marks by tapping them; once you have selected them, you can select the download icon (arrow going to phone) at the bottom of the screen to download them to the phone or tablet.

From any screen that displays the sharing icon (two arrows going up out of a circle, as seen in Figure 9-15), you can tap that icon to bring up a menu that will let you upload an image or a group of selected images or videos to a social media site, including Facebook, Twitter, and others, as shown in Figure 9-16. In order to complete that upload, you need to sign up for an account with Panasonic's Lumix Club. I will discuss that process in the next section of this chapter.

Figure 9-15. Image Selected for Transfer to Phone

Figure 9-16. List of Sites Available for Sharing

Back on the home screen of the Image App, you also can select Geotagging, Snap Movie, or Photo Collage. I discussed Geotagging in Chapter 6. Basically, that function lets you transmit geolocation data from your smartphone to the camera by creating a synchronized log on the phone and later uploading the data from that log to the camera.

If you choose the Snap Movie option, the app will ask if you want to copy any videos on the camera that were shot using Snap Movie mode. As I discussed in Chapter 8, Snap Movie is a function that lets you record very brief movies, lasting no more than eight seconds each, that may have fade-in, fade-out, and pull focus effects added. If you select this option, the app will import those videos and combine them into a single movie that you can save to the phone. You also can share the imported snap movies on social networks using the sharing icon.

The Photo Collage function lets you choose several images to be combined on the phone or tablet in a collage within a frame. You can choose the shape of the frame and then select images from the phone's display to be arranged within that frame. Figure 9-17 is an example of the result of this operation.

Figure 9-17. Photo Collage Example

If you select Menu, the final icon at the bottom right of the Image App's screens, you will see the screen shown in Figure 9-18, with options for the connection destination, Live Control settings, and other items. With the Playback Settings option, you can set the

size for images copied from the camera or uploaded to websites.

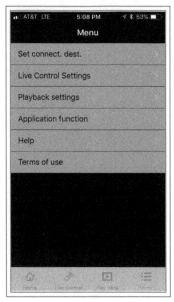

Figure 9-18. Menu Options in Image App

UPLOADING IMAGES BY WI-FI TO SOCIAL NETWORKS

As I mentioned briefly in the previous section, when your smartphone or tablet is connected to the FZ2500 over a Wi-Fi network, you can tap on the Share icon to upload an image directly from the phone or tablet to a social network such as Facebook. You also can upload images in this way directly from the camera. There are some preliminary steps you have to take to make these uploads. Following are the basic steps to get this done.

1. On the camera, go to screen 1 of the Setup menu, choose Wi-Fi, then, on the next screen, Wi-Fi Setup, then Lumix Club, then Set/Add Account, then New Account.

2. If you have not previously set up an account, the camera will prompt you to connect to a Wi-Fi network using WPS Push or by entering the network ID and password. If you can use WPS push, do so; you just need to select WPS Push on the camera, then press the WPS button on the Wi-Fi router within two minutes, and the connection will be established.

3. The camera will ask you to agree to the terms for the Lumix Club account and will display a login ID assigned to your camera, consisting of 12 numerical digits. The camera also will display a screen where

you create and enter a password for the account. It must have from 8 to 16 characters and contain both letters and numbers.

4. Once the camera has accepted the login ID and password, use a computer or other device to go to the following web address: http://lumixclub. panasonic.net/eng/c/, and log in using the 12-digit user ID and password from Step 3. You will then be prompted to enter your e-mail address and a security question, so you can reset your password later if necessary.

5. After you have logged in at the Lumix Club website, you will receive an e-mail message from Panasonic to confirm the registration. After you confirm it, you will be able to log in to the page where you can link your Lumix Club account to any or all of the following social networks (as of this writing): Facebook, Twitter, YouTube, Picasa, Flickr, and VKontakte. You also can link your account to Google Drive for storage of images in the cloud.

6. Once you have linked your Lumix Club account to one or more social networks, you can upload to those networks at any time. To do that on the camera, from playback mode, press the Down button and the camera will ask if you want to upload the current image by Wi-Fi. If you say yes, the camera will establish a Wi-Fi connection if possible, or prompt you to establish one. It will then display a screen like that in Figure 9-19, where you can highlight the service to send the image to.

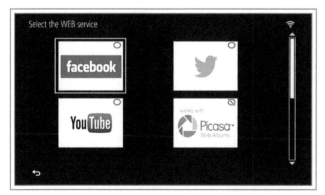

Figure 9-19. Camera Display of Sites for Uploading

7. Select the icon you want and press Menu/Set; the camera will display a screen with the estimated time to upload the image; with my tests, it took anywhere from about 20 seconds to two minutes, depending on the image. The image will then

appear on the appropriate web page for Facebook or another service.

8. You also can upload an image from your smartphone or tablet, when you see the Share icon, as shown earlier in Figure 9-15, using a similar procedure. (If this function does not work on the phone, go to the Menu icon in the lower right corner of the Image App home screen, and select Playback Settings, then Lumix Club Settings, and, on the next screen, activate the button for Start Lumix Club Function Use, as shown in Figure 9-20.)

Figure 9-20. Lumix Club Settings Menu Option in Image App

For more information about Image App features, see http://av.jpn.support.panasonic.com/support/global/cs/soft/image_app/.

CONNECTING TO A COMPUTER TO TRANSFER IMAGES WIRELESSLY

The FZ2500 camera also has the ability to transmit images wirelessly from the camera to a computer on a local network. This feature is intended to work with Panasonic's PHOTOfunSTUDIO software on a Windows-based PC, or with file sharing turned on on a Macintosh. Following are the steps to use with a PC:

1. Install and run the PHOTOfunSTUDIO software on a Windows PC, as discussed in Chapter 1. (The program is not compatible with Macintosh.) Make sure the PC is connected to your local network via Wi-Fi.

2.	The program should prompt you to create a folder for receiving images from the camera. If it does not, go to Tools-Settings-General-Registration Folder and create the folder, using the Auto-create option, or create it manually. When I used Auto-create, the program created the folder C:\Users\Public\Pictures\LumixShare.

3.	On the FZ2500, go to screen 1 of the Setup Menu, choose Wi-Fi, then Wi-Fi Function, then New Connection, then Send Images While Recording.

4.	Follow the prompts on the camera's display to select the network, then the PC on the network, as shown in Figure 9-21. If prompted for a user name and password, enter the user name and password for logging onto the PC you are sending images to. Then select the folder, such as LumixShare, and follow the prompts.

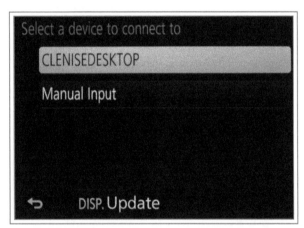

Figure 9-21. Camera Display of Computer ID on Network

5.	When you take pictures with the camera, the new images will soon appear in the LumixShare folder, or other folder you have designated.

6.	If you want to transfer existing images or videos from the camera to the PC instead of new ones as they are taken, in Step 3 select that option from the menu. Then, when you establish the connection, the camera will give the option of sending a single image or selecting multiple images to send. Make your choice, and the camera will start sending one or more images to the designated folder on the PC.

7.	Once you have established a connection as described above, you can choose Select a Destination from History, and go immediately to one of the connections listed by the camera. As you can see in Figure 9-22, each previous destination

has an icon and a name to indicate whether that connection is for sending images to a PC or for connecting to a phone or other device. Select a destination to a PC, and the camera will be set up for the transfer of new or old images and videos.

Figure 9-22. Screen with Destinations from History

Sending Images to Other Devices

You also can send images directly from the camera to other devices using the Wi-Fi menu. To do this, go to screen 1 of the Setup menu, select Wi-Fi, then Wi-Fi Function, then New Connection, then Send Images Stored in the Camera. On the next screen, you can select from Smartphone, PC, Cloud Sync. Service, Web Service, AV Device, or Printer. Follow the prompts in the menu system to connect to the device you select. You also can send images from the camera to other devices while recording, though not to a printer. To do that, choose Send Images While Recording instead of Send Images Stored in the Camera.

Viewing Images Wirelessly on TV

Another option for using the Wi-Fi features of the FZ2500 is to view your still images on a TV set that is compatible with the DLNA standard for sharing media files. (DLNA stands for Digital Living Network Alliance; see dlna.org for more information.) I will describe the setup I used to get my FZ2500 to display images wirelessly on a TV set. This sort of setup can be complicated, and you have to use devices that work together with your network. I don't recommend trying this option unless you have some experience using a DLNA server or don't mind digging into technical details with media devices and computers.

In my case, I used a device called WD TV Live, made by Western Digital, and connected it by HDMI cable to an HDTV. Then, on the camera, I went to screen 1 of the Setup menu and selected Wi-Fi, then Wi-Fi Function, then New Connection, then Playback on TV, then Direct, then Wi-Fi Direct. The camera then found the WD TV Live device.

I pressed the Menu/Set button, and the camera announced that it was connected. I could then play back images stored on the camera's memory card, and they appeared on the TV screen. Also, when I took a new picture with the camera, it almost immediately appeared on the TV screen. When I turned off the Auto Review option on screen 7 of the Custom menu, though, a new image would not appear on the TV screen. You have to have Auto Review turned on, though not for a long time period; as long as it is turned on, a new image will remain on the TV screen.

When I tried to play back a video through the TV, the TV displayed only the first frame of the video and did not produce the sound.

Macro (Closeup) Shooting

Macro photography is the art or science of taking photographs when the subject is shown at actual size (1:1 ratio between size of subject and size of image) or slightly magnified (greater than 1:1 ratio). So if you photograph a flower using macro techniques, the image of the flower on the camera's sensor will be about the same size as the actual flower. You can get wonderful detail in your images using macro photography, and you may discover things about the subject that you had not noticed before taking the photograph.

Figure 9-23. Macro Example

For example, I used the FZ2500 to take a photograph of a flower. I handheld the camera and turned on Focus Bracket to increase the chances of getting a sharp image. The result, shown in Figure 9-23, provides a detailed view of the subject.

To shoot macro images with the FZ2500, you have only one basic setting to change: With the focus mode lever at the AFS/AFF position, press the Down button, marked with a flower and MF, to bring up the Macro Mode menu, and select AF Macro, as shown in Figure 9-24.

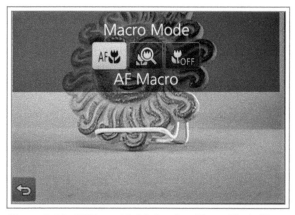

Figure 9-24. AF Macro Highlighted on Macro Mode Menu

Using AF Macro, the camera can focus as close as 1.2 inch (3 cm) from the subject, when the zoom lever is pushed all the way to the wide-angle setting. With the lens zoomed in for its full optical zoom, the camera can focus as close as about 3.3 feet (1 meter) in Macro mode or regular autofocus mode.

You don't have to use the AF Macro setting to take macro shots; if you use manual focus by selecting MF on the focus mode menu, you can also focus on objects very close to the lens. You do, however, lose the benefit of automatic focus, and it can be tricky finding the correct focus manually.

When using the AF Macro setting, you should use a tripod if possible, because depth of field is very shallow at close distances and you need to keep the camera steady to avoid motion blur. It's also a good idea to use the self-timer. If you do, you will not be touching the camera when the shutter is activated, so the chance of camera shake is minimized. If you need extra light, you could consider using a special unit designed for closeup photography, such as a ring light that is designed to provide even lighting surrounding the lens. You also could use the camera's built-in flash, and place a small piece of translucent plastic or a light-colored cloth in front of the flash to diffuse it.

When doing macro photography with the FZ2500, you can take advantage of the Post Focus feature to increase the likelihood of getting a sharp image. See Chapter 5 for details about that feature, with which the camera records a 4K video sequence and extracts a sharp image with focus centered on an area you choose after the fact. In the most challenging focus situations, you can use the Focus Stacking feature, by which the camera combines several images from a Post Focus series to create a single image with focus as sharp as possible in all areas.

One question you may have is: If the camera can focus down to 3 centimeters and out to infinity in AF Macro mode, why not just leave it set in AF Macro mode? The answer is that in AF Macro mode, the focusing system is set to favor short distances, and it is not as responsive in focusing on farther objects. So in AF Macro mode you may notice that it takes more time than usual to focus on subjects at greater distances. If you don't need the fastest possible focusing, you can just leave the camera set to AF Macro at all times, if you want the whole range of focusing distances to be available.

Using the Zoom Lens

One of the distinctive features of the Panasonic FZ2500 camera is the long telephoto range of its built-in lens. This camera has a relatively large image sensor for a compact model, and most cameras with such a large sensor do not have a lens with such a long maximum focal length. In this section, I will provide some advice about taking advantage of the reach of the lens.

One of the most useful steps you can take is to use a solid tripod or other support when shooting at long focal lengths such as 480mm. If you can't use a tripod, use a monopod, fence post, or other steady support. You might be able to sit on a bench with the camera in your lap and tilt up the LCD monitor so the camera can sit firmly against your legs. Also, when using a tripod, it is a good idea to use the self-timer so the camera will not be moved when you press the shutter button to capture an image. You also can use a smartphone to trigger the camera remotely, as discussed earlier in this chapter, or you can use a wired remote control device to trigger it, as discussed in Appendix A.

If you cannot put the camera on a solid support, you can place the neck strap around your neck and hold the camera tightly against the strap to anchor it. Turn on the Stabilizer option on screen 7 of the Recording menu. Follow this rule of thumb for shutter speed when using a long zoom lens: Use a shutter speed whose denominator is greater than the current focal length. For example, if you are shooting with the lens zoomed in to 480mm, use a shutter speed faster than 1/480 second, which would mean 1/500 second or faster. To do this, you would need to use Shutter Priority or Manual exposure mode, or, with Program mode, you could try to set a fast shutter speed using Program Shift.

Note that the depth of field can be very shallow when using a long focal length, especially for objects relatively close to the lens. Therefore, you can use a long focal length to blur the background and isolate the subject, as seen in Figure 9-25.

Figure 9-25. Example of Zoom Used to Isolate Subject

You also can use the compressing or flattening effect of a long focal length to achieve a certain look, as in Figure 9-26, which makes the houses in the distance appear to be almost all flattened into the same plane.

Figure 9-26. Example of Flattening Effect with Long Zoom

Also, remember the features discussed earlier in this book that can help you use the FZ2500's lens to its full advantage. For example, you can assign the Slow Zoom feature to two buttons (for wide-angle and telephoto zooms); by default these functions are assigned to the Fn1 and Fn2 buttons. Then you can use those buttons to carry out a smooth, slow zooming action. Also, you can use the step zoom feature, with which the lens zooms only to specific focal lengths, such as 100mm, 200mm, and others. To do that, use the Zoom Lever item on screen 7 of the Custom menu and select Step. You can make a similar setting for the zoom ring using the Zoom Ring option on screen 8 of that menu.

You can further control the functioning of the Slow Zoom option using the Slow Zoom Button Setting, Slow Zoom Speed, and Soft Zoom options on screen 8 of the Custom menu.

Finally, be aware of the advantages of using continuous shooting to increase the chances of getting one or more usable images when shooting under challenging conditions, such as using a long focal length.

Street Photography

The FZ2500 is well suited for street photography—shooting candid pictures in public settings, often without being noticed by the subjects. Its 24mm wide-angle lens takes in a broad field of view, so you can shoot from the hip without framing the image carefully on the screen. You can tilt up the LCD screen and look down at it to frame your shot, which lets you take photographs without attracting attention to yourself. The f/2.8 lens lets in plenty of light, and it performs well at high ISO settings, so you can use a fast shutter speed to avoid motion blur. You can make the camera completely silent by turning off the beeps and shutter sounds, and by using the electronic shutter. It has superior options for shooting bursts of images, so you can capture a large group of shots to choose from.

Here are some settings to start with and modify as you see fit. To get the gritty "street" look, set Photo Style to Monochrome, but dial in -2 Noise Reduction and -1 Sharpening. Set Quality to Raw & Fine to give you a good image straight out of the camera, while preserving your post-processing options. Set aspect ratio to 3:2. Set ISO to 800 for good image quality while boosting sensitivity enough to stop action with a fast shutter

speed. Turn on burst mode at the High setting so you'll get several images to choose from for each shutter press.

When you're ready to start shooting, select manual focus mode and set the focus to approximately the distance you expect to shoot at, such as 6 feet (2 meters). Assign a physical function button, such as Fn4, to the AF-On function. When you're ready to snap a picture, press the Fn4 button to make a quick fine-tuning of the focus. For exposure, set the camera to Aperture Priority mode, with the aperture set to about f/4.5. When shooting at night, you may want to open the aperture a bit wider, and possibly boost the ISO to 1600. You will probably want to leave the lens zoomed back to its full wide-angle position, both to increase the depth of field and to take in a wide angle of view.

Figure 9-27. Street Photography Example

In Figure 9-27, I used Intelligent Auto Plus mode to catch a quick shot when I saw a couple of people heading toward me on a pedestrian bridge over the river.

APPENDIX A: ACCESSORIES

There are several optional items that can be useful for getting the most out of your FZ2500.

Cases

I like to carry my camera in a case or bag that has room for extra batteries, battery charger, USB cable, and other items. I sometimes use the VanGoddy Laurel case, shown closed in Figure A-1 and open in Figure A-2. This case can just fit the camera if the lens hood is reversed, and the case is convenient to carry by its handle.

Figure A-1. VanGoddy Laurel Case Closed

Figure A-2. VanGoddy Laurel Case Open

The Crumpler 6 Million Dollar Home Bag, model number MD6002-X01P60, shown closed in Figure A-3 and open in Figure A-4, with its large flap in front, has more than enough room for the camera and items such as external flash units, batteries, filters, and other items for a day trip.

Figure A-3. Crumpler Bag Closed

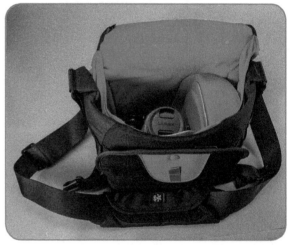

Figure A-4. Crumpler Bag Open

Finally, a case that I use often is the Lowepro Inverse 100 AW, shown in Figures A-5 and A-6. This case easily holds the FZ2500 camera, and has additional storage space for batteries, chargers, filters and other items.

Figure A-5. Lowepro Inverse 100 AW Case Closed

Figure A-6. Lowepro Inverse 100 AW Case Open

It also has straps on the bottom for carrying a tripod, and it has two expandable mesh pockets on the sides that can hold small water bottles.

Batteries and Chargers

I use the camera pretty heavily, and I run through batteries quickly. You can't use disposable batteries, so if you're out taking pictures and the battery dies, you're out of luck unless you have a spare battery (or a power adapter with a power source; see below). The Panasonic battery, model number DMW-BLC12PP (in the United States), sells for about $46.00 as I write this, but you can find generic replacement batteries for considerably less. These batteries are available alone or with included chargers, as shown in Figure A-7.

Figure A-7. Generic Charger and Batteries for FZ2500

I have used generic batteries extensively in my FZ2500 with no problems, though some people have reported that some generic batteries do not hold a charge as well as the genuine ones. You may note that the battery shown in Figure A-7 has a slightly different model number than the Panasonic battery, but that is not a problem; this battery has worked well for me as a replacement for the Panasonic battery.

AC Adapter

Another alternative for powering the FZ2500 is the Panasonic AC adapter, although it is hard to find and inconvenient to use. You need to obtain not only the AC adapter, model no. DMW-AC10, but also the DC Coupler, model number DMW-DCC8. That device looks like the battery, but has a connecting port in its side. At the time this book is being written, the genuine Panasonic coupler has proved to be impossible to find. I found a non-Panasonic version through an online seller, but it did not fit with the connecting cord of the Panasonic AC adapter.

The non-Panasonic coupler did work properly with a matching non-Panasonic AC adapter, which is shown connected to the camera with the coupler in Figure A-8.

Figure A-8. Generic AC Adapter and DC Coupler Connected to FZ2500

You have to insert the coupler into the battery compartment of the camera, then close the battery door, open up a small flap in that door, and connect the cord from the AC adapter to the port in the coupler, as shown in Figure A-8.

Providing power to the camera is all this adapter does. It does not act as a battery charger, either for batteries outside of the camera or for batteries while they are installed in the camera. It is strictly a power source for the camera. It may be useful if you are doing extensive indoor work in a studio or laboratory setting, to eliminate the trouble of constantly charging batteries. It also could be useful for a lengthy series of time lapse or stop motion shots. This is not a very efficient setup because of the multiple devices and cords needed. But, if you need constant power for a long period of time, this system works well.

I also found another type of power adapter from a manufacturer of generic replacements. As shown in Figure A-9, that device does not plug into AC power, but, rather, into one or two USB power ports. The other end uses a generic DC coupler, similar to the one shown above. In this illustration, the adapter is plugged into a Mophie PowerStation XL USB power supply, which holds a considerable charge. So, you can use this setup to provide portable power to the FZ2500 for long periods of time.

Figure A-9. Generic USB-Powered AC Adapter with USB Battery

External Flash Units

Whether to buy an external flash unit depends on how you will use the FZ2500. For everyday snapshots not taken at long distances, the built-in flash unit should suffice. It works automatically with the camera's exposure controls to expose images well. It is limited by its low power, though.

If you need more flash power to take photos of groups of people in large spaces, or if you want to take advantage of the benefits of using off-camera flash, such as using multiple units and better angles for less harsh lighting, you can use one of several compatible units from Panasonic, some of which also provide wireless capability for controlling remote flash units.

The smallest Panasonic unit available for the FZ2500 is model number DMW-FL200L, shown in Figure A-10. As discussed in Chapter 4, that flash is compatible with Panasonic's wireless flash protocol, and it can act as the controller or a remote unit using that system.

Figure A-10. Panasonic DMW-FL200L Flash

The next larger unit, model number DMW-FL360L, is shown in Figure A-11. It, too, can act as either a controller or remote unit for the Panasonic wireless flash system. The largest of these units, DMW-FL580L, is not shown here.

Figure A-11. Panasonic DMW-FL360L Flash

If you want to supplement the light from the camera's built-in flash unit, you can use an optical slave, which detects the light from the camera's small flash and fires its own flash when the camera's flash is fired. One excellent unit with optical slave capability is the LumoPro LP180, shown in Figure A-12. This unit has settings that let it ignore the pre-flash fired by the camera's built-in flash unit, which can confuse the optical slave and cause it to fire prematurely. When I used the LumoPro flash with the Panasonic FZ2500, I set the flash to its S2-1 mode, which caused it to fire the flash at the proper time for a good exposure.

Figure A-12. LumoPro LP180 Flash

When using a flash like this, you need to set the camera to Manual exposure mode and experiment or use an external light meter in order to arrive at a proper exposure. There are other flash units with similar capability, such as the Yongnuo YN560-IV, shown in Figure A-13. That unit needs to be set to its S2 slave mode, and its sensor on the front needs to be in line of sight from the flash emitted by the camera's built-in unit. There also are separate optical slave units, to which you can attach any compatible flash unit.

Figure A-13. Yongnuo YN560-IV Flash

External Microphones

One useful feature of the FZ2500 is its jack for an external microphone, located on the left side of the camera. As I discussed in Chapter 8, Panasonic sells a special shotgun microphone, model number DMW-MS2, that plugs into that jack and whose pickup pattern can be adjusted using the Special Microphone option on

screen 7 of the Motion Picture menu. That microphone, shown in Figure A-14, can provide excellent audio-recording capability for the camera.

Figure A-14. Panasonic DMW-MS2 Microphone

You also can use microphones that are not made by Panasonic, such as the Rode Videomic Pro, shown in Figure A-15. Such microphones plug into the camera's microphone jack, but they do not have the special plug that activates the Special Microphone menu option. However, they still can provide excellent sound-recording capability.

Figure A-15. Rode Videomic Pro Microphone

Wired Remote Control

As I discussed in Chapter 9, you can control the FZ2500 remotely from a smartphone or tablet using the Panasonic Image App with the camera's Wi-Fi capability. That system works quite well, but there is a simpler system available as an alternative. Figure A-16 shows the camera connected to a wired remote control sold by Panasonic, model number DMW-RSL1. This remote, which plugs into the Remote port on the right side of the camera, is very simple. It has only one large button, which you can press to operate the camera's shutter. You can hold the button down to fire a burst of shots in burst mode or to hold the shutter open in BULB mode. You can press the button forward into the locking position to leave it locked for a BULB exposure until you release the lock. When the camera is in Creative Video mode, you can press the button on the remote to start or stop a video recording.

Figure A-16. Panasonic DMW-RSL1 Remote Control

You also can find a generic substitute for considerably less expense, such as the Pholsy-branded remote shown in Figure A-17. That device works the same as the Panasonic model, but costs about $12.00 as opposed to $58.00 for the Panasonic version.

Figure A-17. Pholsy Remote Control

Tripods

For time exposures, multiple exposures, HDR shots, and many other types of photography, it is virtually essential to use a tripod. In addition, for macro photography and any other shots for which focus is critical, it is desirable to have a solid support when

using the camera. I have not attempted to survey multiple tripods; I will just mention two models that I have found to be especially useful because of their excellent features and light weight.

Figure A-18. Manfrotto BeFree Carbon Fiber Tripod

These models both are versions of the BeFree tripod by Manfrotto. The version shown in Figure A-18, model number MKBFRC4-BH, is especially light in weight because of its carbon fiber construction. Model number MKBFRA4-BH, shown in Figure A-19, is somewhat heavier because of its aluminum construction, but is considerably less expensive. Either one works very well with the FZ2500 camera.

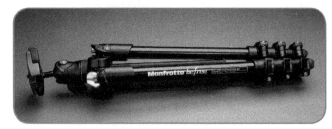

Figure A-19. Manfrotto BeFree Aluminum Tripod

External Video Recorder

In Chapter 8, I discussed how to take advantage of the FZ2500's video features to output its 4K video signal via the HDMI port to an external video recorder. Using this system, you can record 4K video without having to obtain an especially fast memory card for the camera; you can record with no memory card in the camera at all.

The recorder I used for this process is the Atomos Shogun, a capable device though expensive, at about $1,500 as of the time of this writing. The Shogun can be mounted on top of the camera as shown in Figure A-20, where I used a Vello Multi-Function Ball Head; the Shogun has tripod sockets on its top and bottom edges.

Figure A-20. Atomos Shogun Video Recorder with FZ2500

The combination of FZ2500 and Shogun performed well. The recorder's menu system is easy to work with and the device produces high-quality video files. At the highest quality, the files can be extremely large, so be prepared with a strong computer capability for editing. There are other 4K video recorders that might work as well, such as the Odyssey7 series of recorders from Convergent Design or devices from Blackmagic Design, as well as less expensive models from Atomos, though I have not tested any of those.

Filters

The lens of the FZ2500 is threaded to accept standard photographic filters with a diameter of 67mm. You can use polarizing filters, UV filters, neutral density filters (though the camera has a built-in ND filter that should be sufficient for most purposes), and others.

Some people may wish to attach a teleconverter or other auxiliary lens to the FZ2500, to increase the optical zoom power. I have not tried this myself, because the camera's natural optical zoom range of 480mm is sufficient for my purposes, and I don't want to take the risk of adding a heavy item at the end of the lens. However, there are options that can be considered, as discussed in the following thread at dpreview.com: https://www.dpreview.com/forums/thread/4111404.

APPENDIX B: QUICK TIPS

This appendix includes tips and hints for using the FZ2500 that might be useful as reminders. These are small bits of information that might help you in certain situations, or that might not be obvious to everyone.

Check physical controls before shooting. Each time you start a shooting session, check the main physical controls to make sure they are set properly: the mode dial, the focus mode lever, and the drive mode dial. You also should check the ND Filter switch.

Use the movable autofocus area in conjunction with Spot metering. When you do this, using an AF Mode setting such as 1-Area or Pinpoint, you can move the focus and metering area together around the screen with the direction buttons or the touch screen, so you can focus and meter a small, specific area of your scene. This procedure can add precision to your metering and focusing, and give you more control over your results.

Use Manual exposure mode with Auto ISO. Not all cameras let you use Auto ISO with Manual mode. This feature lets you keep aperture and shutter speed at fixed values, while the camera adjusts ISO to obtain a normal exposure if possible. This is useful, for example, when you need to stop action with a fast shutter speed and also control depth of field with a narrow aperture. (This feature does not work when recording videos with the Creative Video version of Manual Exposure mode.)

Be aware of extending lens. Be careful when turning on the camera or when switching to recording mode from playback mode, because the lens will quickly extend fairly far out and could strike an object if you're not careful.

Be careful of touching touch screen by accident. When you're using the viewfinder, your nose can touch the LCD monitor and change the position of the focus frame, if a movable focus frame is in use. To deal with this problem, you might want to assign the Touch Screen option to a function button, so you can temporarily turn off the touch screen settings with the press of a button. Or, you can go to the Touch Settings option on screen 10 of the Custom menu and set Touch Pad AF to Off, which will disable the ability to move the focus frame by touching the LCD when the viewfinder is in use.

Diffuse the flash. If you find the built-in flash produces light that's too harsh for macro or other shots, try using a piece of translucent plastic as a flash diffuser. Hold the plastic up between the flash and the subject. An approach you can try when using fill-flash outdoors is to use the Flash Adjustment menu setting to reduce the intensity of the flash by -2/3 EV.

Use the self-timer to avoid camera shake. Use the Self-timer option on screen 3 of the Recording menu to select a setting for the self-timer. When you're ready to use it, turn the drive mode dial to its next-to-last position. This feature is not just for group portraits; you can use it whenever you need to avoid camera shake. It can be especially useful when you're doing macro photography.

Use the 4K Photo option for burst shooting. With this option, found at the third position on the drive mode dial (or assigned to a function button), you can set the camera to capture 4K-quality video that can generate a high-quality still image from each frame. This option gives you a burst shooting mode with Large-sized images and continuous focusing, at a rate of 30 frames per second (in the United States and other areas that use the NTSC video standard; 25 fps elsewhere). You have to use a memory card with a speed in UHS Class 3, but this is an excellent capability for action shots, shots of wildlife, and street photography.

Create a custom autofocus zone that uses the entire focusing area. Although the FZ2500 has an AF Mode setting called 49-Area, that setting actually uses no more than nine of the 49 possible focus zones. If you want to have a setting that uses the full extent of the display area, you have to create it yourself. To do that, use the Custom Multi option of AF Mode to create a focus setting with all 49 zones. Chapter 5 explains how to do this.

Use the zoom lever and the Display button to speed through menu screens. These options can save time when you need to scroll through menus with as many as 10 screens (or even more for some sub-menus, such as Function Button Set). When a menu screen is displayed, press the zoom lever in either direction to move forward or backward a full screen at a time. You also can press the Display button to move a screen at a time, in the forward direction only.

Use the front dial to move among menu systems, as opposed to screens. Whenever a menu screen is displayed, you can turn the front dial to move to a different menu, even if the highlight is on an item on the menu screen, rather than on the menu icon in the far left column. For example, if the highlight is on an item on a screen of the Recording menu, you can turn the front dial to move directly to any other menu system, such as Custom, Playback, or Setup.

Be careful of using Raw for Quality when shooting with filter effects using the Filter Settings option or Creative Control mode. The FZ2500 will let you set Quality to Raw when shooting with picture effects that are accessed through the Filter Settings menu option or Creative Control mode, such as Silky Monochrome, Impressive Art, Star Filter, and others. The recorded images will appear to have the effects added when viewed in the camera, but that is only because a small JPEG file is embedded in the Raw file. When you open the Raw file on a computer, the picture effect will not be there. You can try to recreate it using software settings, but it is difficult to recover the full effect as recorded by the camera. (The only way I know is to use the Irfanview program to extract the preview JPEG file from the Raw file.) So, you might think you have taken some great shots using creative effects, but when you view them on your computer the effects will have disappeared. To avoid this problem, shoot using Fine, or, probably the best option, Raw & Fine for Quality.

Use the in-camera processing features before uploading images. The FZ2500 has a good set of options for transferring images using Wi-Fi to a smartphone, tablet, or computer, and for uploading

directly to social networks. Before you do that, you may want to use options on the Playback menu such as Raw Processing, Cropping, and Resize in order to send images at the optimal size and with the appearance you want. You also can use the remarkably effective Clear Retouch menu option to remove an unwanted person or object from an image.

Use the remote control capability of the Panasonic Image App. With this app, you can take self-portraits and capture images and videos of birds and other subjects while controlling the camera from a distance through a wireless network. Set the camera on a good tripod near a bird feeder to catch shots of birds, or set the camera in a good location to record video of a school play while you sit nearby and control the camera from your smartphone. You can change settings on the camera while it is under remote control, and use functions such as burst shooting and stop motion animation.

Take advantage of the many shortcuts available with use of the touch screen. For example, when the camera is in Intelligent Auto mode, touch the iA icon in the upper left corner of the display to switch between Intelligent Auto and Intelligent Auto Plus modes. In Scene Mode or Creative Control mode, touch the icon in the upper left corner to select a different scene type or filter effect setting.

Reassign a function button quickly. You can change the assignment of a function button to a menu option or other operation using the Function Button Set option on screen 7 of the Custom menu. To make that setting much more rapidly, press and hold a function button for several seconds, and the camera will display a menu that lets you change the button's assignment. (This system will not work if the function button is currently assigned to a setting that interferes with the reassignment operation, such as AF-On. It also does not work for the Fn1 or Fn2 button, which are designed by default to zoom the lens in and out when held down. (It will work if those buttons are assigned to different settings that do not interfere with the reassignment.)

Use the Post Focus feature in tricky focusing situations. When you are shooting extreme closeups or other shots for which focus is critical, take advantage of the Post Focus capability, as discussed in Chapter 5. The camera will shoot a 4K video sequence using multiple focus points, and you can choose the most sharply focused shot after the fact. You also can use the Focus Bracket option on screen 2 of the Recording menu for this purpose.

Be aware of the function button settings. On several occasions, I have been surprised to see the blue lamp on top of the camera light up and a Wi-Fi connection start to be initiated, when I had not wanted to do that. I eventually realized that the Fn4 button is assigned by default to the Wi-Fi function, for playback mode only. So, when the camera is in playback mode, if you accidentally press the Fn4 button, a Wi-Fi connection will be triggered. If you don't want that to happen, either reassign the button to another option or be careful not to press it in playback mode.

Check for conflicting settings. There are many settings that cause other settings to be unavailable—too many to try to list in one place. For example, when Quality is set to Raw in the Recording menu, you cannot use the HDR or Digital Zoom menu options. Also, when the Wireless option is turned on for Flash on screen 5 of the Recording menu, you cannot use the Flash Synchro or Flash Adjustment menu options. So, when you are not using a wireless flash setup, be sure to turn off the Wireless menu option.

Use the Display button to switch dial functions. When using exposure compensation, you can press the Display button to switch the functions of the front and rear dials between adjusting exposure compensation and adjusting flash compensation.

Use the C4K setting if it suits your needs. It is not immediately obvious how to take advantage of the C4K (Cinema 4K) setting for Recording Quality for movies, because it does not ordinarily show up on the Motion Picture menu. In order to make the C4K option available, you have to go to the System Frequency item on screen 5 of the Setup menu and set it to 24.00 Hz (Cinema). Once that setting is made, you can get access to the C4K option under Recording Quality on screen 2 of the Motion Picture menu.

Upload images directly to Google Drive. I have found it quite convenient to use the FZ2500's Wi-Fi features to upload files to the cloud, so they will be available on any computer or other device I use for photo editing. To do this, go to the Wi-Fi option on screen 1 of the Setup menu, and choose Wi-Fi Function - New Connection - Send Images Stored in the Camera - Web Service. Then select an available Wi-Fi network, followed by Google Drive, or any other service you have enabled through the Lumix Club setup procedure, as discussed in Chapter 9.

Appendix C: Resources for Further Information

Photography Books

A visit to any large general bookstore or library, or a search on Amazon.com or other sites, will reveal the vast assortment of currently available books about digital photography. Rather than trying to compile a long bibliography, I will list a few books I have found especially helpful.

C. George, *Mastering Digital Flash Photography* (Lark Books, 2008)

C. Harnischmacher, *Closeup Shooting* (Rocky Nook, 2007)

H. Horenstein, *Digital Photography: A Basic Manual* (Little, Brown, 2011)

Websites

Following are several sites that are useful for finding further information about the FZ2500 or about digital photography in general:

Digital Photography Review

http://forums.dpreview.com/forums/forum.asp?forum=1033

This is the current web address for the "Panasonic Compact Camera Talk" forum within the dpreview.com site. Dpreview.com is one of the most established and authoritative sites for reviews, discussion forums, technical information, and other resources concerning digital cameras. If you have a question about a feature of the FZ2500, there is a good chance you can find an answer through this forum.

Official Panasonic and Related Sites

http://shop.panasonic.com/cameras-and-camcorders/cameras/lumix-point-and-shoot-cameras/DMC-FZ2500.html

The Panasonic company provides resources for the FZ2500 at the above web address, including the downloadable version of the user's manual for the FZ2500, full specifications, and other technical information.

http://panasonic.jp/support/global/cs/dsc/

The above web address is one where Panasonic provides support information for the FZ2500, the Panasonic Image App, and other devices and software.

http://lumixclub.panasonic.net/eng/c/

At the above address, you can get information about the Lumix Club, which you need to join in order to upload images from the FZ2500 to social network sites.

http://panasonic.net/avc/sdcard/information/sdxc.html

The above site provides information about the compatibility of SDXC cards with the FZ2500.

http://www.isl.co.jp/SILKYPIX/english/p/support/

At the above site, you can download the manual for the Silkypix software included with the FZ2500.

http://loilo.tv/product/20

The above site is where you can download a trial version of LoiLoScope2 software for editing videos.

http://www.cambridgeincolour.com

The above site is an excellent resource for general information about a wide range of photographic topics.

VIDEOS

https://youtu.be/U5XBGf6ts5o

The video in the above link includes several hands-on reviews of the FZ2500 camera.

https://youtu.be/IL5loVIxF_c

The link above also leads to an excellent and detailed review of the FZ2500 in the field.

https://youtu.be/nv_KRegF-Z0

The link above is to another YouTube video review of the FZ2500.

https://youtu.be/0w0PdbAjXmU

The link above is to a video that explains how to shoot slow-motion video with the FZ2500.

https://youtu.be/St5CZSqh4XE

The link above is to a group of examples of the Dolly Zoom feature, taken with the FZ2500.

WRITTEN REVIEWS OF THE FZ2500

Following are links to written reviews of the FZ2500:

https://www.dpreview.com/reviews/panasonic-lumix-dmc-fz2500-fz2000

https://www.cameralabs.com/panasonic-lumix-fz2000-fz2500-review/

http://www.imaging-resource.com/PRODS/panasonic-fz2500/panasonic-fz2500A.HTM

https://www.pocket-lint.com/cameras/reviews/panasonic/138720-panasonic-lumix-fz2000-review-premium-superzoom-premier-league

http://www.photographyblog.com/reviews/panasonic_lumix_dmc_fz2000_review

https://www.cnet.com/products/panasonic-lumix-fz2500/preview/

http://www.techradar.com/reviews/panasonic-lumix-fz2500-fz2000

https://www.pcmag.com/review/351014/panasonic-lumix-dmc-fz2500

https://www.digitaltrends.com/digital-camera-reviews/panasonic-lumix-fz2500-review/

https://www.ephotozine.com/article/panasonic-lumix-fz2000--fz2500--expert-review-29912

OTHER INFORMATION

If you are going to use the V-Log L option for Photo Style when recording movies, as discussed in Chapter 8, you need to use post-processing software to make the footage look good. One excellent option is DaVinci Resolve. A free version is available at the link below:

https://www.blackmagicdesign.com/products/davinciresolve/.

https://youtu.be/SfdQH8on9Os

The link above is to a YouTube video that compares the Cine D and V-Log L Photo Style settings, as recorded with the Panasonic DC-GH5 camera.

https://youtu.be/EouWmmsJuT8

The link above is to a video tutorial on how to process ("grade") V-Log L footage using Adobe Premiere Pro software.

https://youtu.be/rsOLAdVccEk

The above link is to a video on how to expose V-Log L footage using the Panasonic GH5 camera.

https://youtu.be/ydgarm_kQeM

The above link is to a follow-up video by the author of the previous one, on how to color-grade V-Log L footage from the GH5 camera.

http://photojoseph.com/gh5/

The above link is to a site that includes links to training information for the Panasonic GH5 camera, much of which is of interest to users of the FZ2500, including information about using the V-Log L Photo Style setting.

Index

CPSIA information can be obtained
at www.ICGtesting.com
Printed in the USA
LVHW070621200723
752767LV00016B/291